Personal Reality

Personal Reality
Volume I

*The Emergentist Concept of Science,
Evolution, and Culture*

Daniel Paksi

James Clarke & Co

James Clarke & Co
P.O. Box 60
Cambridge
CB1 2NT
United Kingdom

www.jamesclarke.co
publishing@jamesclarke.co

Paperback ISBN: 978 0 227 17716 7
PDF ISBN: 978 0 227 90717 7

British Library Cataloguing in Publication Data
A record is available from the British Library

First published by James Clarke & Co, 2020

Copyright © Daniel Paksi, 2019

Published by arrangement
with Pickwick Publications

All rights reserved. No part of this edition may be reproduced, stored electronically or in any retrieval system, or transmitted in any form or by any means, electronic, mechanical, photocopying, recording, or otherwise, without prior written permission from the Publisher (permissions@jamesclarke.co).

For the Memory of Michael Polanyi

Contents

Volume 1

List of Figures and Tables | xi
Acknowledgments | xiii

Part One: Personal Knowledge

Chapter 1: The Origin of Personal Reality | 3
    1.1 Preface · 3
    1.2 The Meaning of Evolution and the Theory of Natural Selection · 4
    1.3 Personal Reality from Personal Knowledge · 14
    1.4 Conclusion · 19

Chapter 2: The Laplacian Ideal of Knowledge | 20
    2.1 Preface · 20
    2.2 The Knowledge of the Demon according to Laplace · 21
    2.3 The Knowledge of the Demon according to Polanyi · 24
    2.4 The Physics of the Demon · 30
    2.5 Laplacian Faults or Deceptive Substitutions · 37
    2.6 Conclusion · 43

Chapter 3: Personal Knowledge | 45
    3.1 Preface · 45
    3.2 The Tacit Roots of Scientific Discovery · 46
    3.3 The Tacit Roots of Personal Knowledge · 54
    3.4 The Tacit Roots of Explicit Sentences · 63
    3.5 The Tacit Roots of the Critical Method of Doubt · 73
    3.6 The Tacit Fundament of Personal Beliefs: Commitment · 83
    3.7 Conclusion · 91

Chapter 4: The Meaning of Randomness | 93
    4.1 Preface · 93
    4.2 The Concept of Order · 95
    4.3 The Recognition of Order · 98
    4.4 The Appraisal of the Deepness of an Order · 109
    4.5 Randomness as Emergence · 113
    4.6 Absolute Randomness · 118
    4.7 Emergence and Evolution: The Origin of Personal Knowledge · 123
    4.8 Conclusion · 133

Part Two: Emergence

Chapter 5: Emergence | 137
    5.1 Preface · 137
    5.2 The Concept and Original Meaning of Emergence · 138
    5.3 Reduction and Materialism · 147
    5.4 Reduction as Emergence · 151
    5.5 The Two Janus Faces of Emergence · 161
    5.6 Polanyi's Understanding of Emergence · 166
    5.7 A Short Reductionist Argument against Materialism · 174
    5.8 The Main Contra-Arguments of Materialism · 178
    5.9 Conclusion · 184

Chapter 6: Space, Time, and Matter | 187
    6.1 Preface · 187
    6.2 Alexander's Concept of Space-Time · 188
    6.3 Einstein's Theory of Special Relativity · 198
    6.4 Understanding Special Relativity · 204
    6.5 Einstein's Theory of General Relativity · 212
    6.6 Understanding General Relativity · 222
    6.7 Conclusion · 233

Chapter 7: The Theory of Boundary Conditions | 236
    7.1 Preface · 236
    7.2 The Concept of Boundary Conditions · 237
    7.3 Boundary Conditions from Physics · 241
    7.4 Boundary Conditions in Physical Sciences · 246

7.5 Boundary Conditions in Life Sciences and Engineering · 249
7.6 Boundary Conditions in the Light of Philosophy · 258
7.7 The Reality of Time · 264
7.8 Conclusion · 267

Bibliography | 271

Volume 2

List of Figures and Tables | ix

Part Three: Evolution

Chapter 8: The Logic of Achievement | 3
    8.1 Preface · 3
    8.2 Machines and the Rules of Rightness · 5
    8.3 Living Beings and the Rules of Rightness · 10
    8.4 The Knowledge of Machines · 16
    8.5 The Knowledge of Computers · 23
    8.6 Conclusion · 29

Chapter 9: Evolution | 31
    9.1 Preface · 31
    9.2 The Concept of Evolution · 32
    9.3 The Ordering Principles of Life and Evolution · 41
    9.4 The General Theory of Evolution · 46
    9.5 The General Theory of Organization · 59
    9.6 Knowledge and Biology: Acknowledging the Emergent Reality of Life · 74
    9.7 Personal Knowledge and Natural Selection · 87
    9.8 Conclusion · 96

Chapter 10: Cultural Evolution | 98
    10.1 Preface · 98
    10.2 The Concept of Cultural Evolution · 100
    10.3 The Theory of Memes · 107
    10.4 The Concept of Cultural Transmission · 115

10.5 The Origin of Cultural Organization · 120
10.6 Individuals, Groups, and Persons · 133
10.7 The Emergence of Cultural Organization · 151
10.8 Writing as an Information Recording and Transmitting System · 160
10.9 Conclusion · 178

Part Four: Personal Reality

Chapter 11: Scientific and Cultural Reality | 183
    11.1 Preface · 183
    11.2 The Concept of Scientific Revolutions · 185
    11.3 Thomas S. Kuhn and the Evolutionary View of Science · 193
    11.4 Relativism and Absolutism: David Bloor vs. Pope Benedict XVI · 214
    11.5 Scientific Revolutions, Personal Knowledge, and Truth · 233
    11.6 Personal Reality and Demolished Idols · 250
    11.7 Conclusion · 266

Chapter 12: Moral and Intellectual Reality | 269
    12.1 Preface · 269
    12.2 Modern Dynamic Societies and their Embedded Menace · 270
    12.3 Moral Inversion and Marxism · 276
    12.4 The Intellectual (Spurious) Forms of Moral Inversion · 286
    12.5 The New Forms of Moral Inversion · 297
    12.6 Conclusion · 303

Chapter 13: The Future of Personal Reality | 305
    13.1 Preface · 305
    13.2 Truth and Morality · 305
    13.3 God and Matter · 307
    13.4 Evolution and Emergence · 311
    13.5 Science and Wisdom · 312
    13.6 Conclusion · 314

Bibliography | 315

Figures and Tables

Figure 1. The logical structure of the Darwinian notion of natural selection. | 6

Figure 2. The structure of human skills. | 62

Figure 3. The two poles of commitment. | 80

Figure 4. The Wales lettering. | 95

Figure 5. Random pebbles. | 95

Figure 6. Multiple realizability. | 96

Figure 7. Case 1. | 99

Figure 8. Case 2. | 99

Figure 9. Case 3. | 99

Figure 10. Changing pebbles. | 119

Figure 11. The logical structure of natural selection. | 126

Figure 12. The structure of reduction. | 152

Figure 13. The structure of reduction in the case of parts-whole relationships. | 153

Figure 14. The structure of reduction in the case of the so-called "relational base." | 153

Figure 15. The structure of the successful reduction. | 154

Figure 16. The structure of the unsuccessful reduction. | 156

Figure 17. The structure of the successful reduction. | 156

Figure 18. The structure of the unsuccessful reduction. | 161

Figure 19. The structure of ontological reduction. | 163

Figure 20. The structure of epistemological emergence. | 167

Figure 21. Polanyi's understanding of the structure of "conceptual"/epistemological emergence. | 173

Figure 22. The structure of the (synchronic/epistemological) reduction of reduction. | 176

Figure 23. The consequence of the (synchronic/epistemological) reduction of reduction. | 177

Figure 24: The structure of the materialist understanding of the causal closure of the physical world and downward causation. | 183

Table 1: Tangible and intellectual tools. | 60

Table 2: The relation of random and ordered systems to lower-level, random systems. | 107

Table 3: The relationship between reduction and ontological positions. | 162

Table 4: The three ontological positions concerning the relationship between different kinds of realities. | 166

Table 5: The relationship between reduction and ontological positions. | 175

Table 6: The main types of boundary conditions, following Pattee and Polanyi. | 240

Acknowledgments

I would like to thank my grant, the Bolyai János Postdoctoral Scholarship of the Hungarian Academy of Sciences. Without the support, this book could never have been born. I would also like to thank my colleague, Mihály Héder, and *Appraisal*, the journal of The British Personalist Forum, for the countless opportunities for publication.

Part One

Personal Knowledge

1

The Origin of Personal Reality

1.1 Preface

Personal reality is who we are, and we are what we want to become, can become, and have to become over time as well as a result of where we have come from. Are we the creations of a Higher Intelligence or the achievement of evolution? Or are we just piles of quarks and electrons as materialism claims? There are few answers offered to this fundamental question about the origin of man in Western civilization—in fact, only these three—and we have to choose. Our choice will determine both our personal lives and the future of our civilization, but we are not even aware of the fact that we have a third option, that there is an essential difference between being the achievement of evolution and being material complexes of quarks and electrons. Our thinking is paralyzed with the false conceptual dichotomies of modernity between God and matter, knowledge and belief, reason and passion, truth and morality, objectivity and subjectivity, etc. Still, in spite of all these harsh difficulties, we are not given the option to delay this fundamental choice or to pretend that these answers can be compatible with each other in any way.

To answer the question about the origin of our reality, everybody should ask themselves what he/she thinks about the existence of his/her soul. Take a minute and ponder. Do you believe in the reality of your soul? Perhaps the answer seems obvious to you, but everyone should be well aware that materialism—which has become the most influential ideology of twentieth and twenty-first century science and society—excludes even the possibility of the existence of human souls. The term soul or mind has no real existential meaning; humans are nothing more than a pile of quarks and electrons, as any rock in a random mountain.

As a philosopher, I am only committed to truth and to speak the truth, and I believe with all my heart that the right answer for the question of our origin is that we are the children of evolution. Contrary to the materialist concept, *we have souls*—it is a major part of our personal reality—*but there is nothing divine in them*. Contrary to traditional Christian thought, *they are the achievement of evolution*. So, to understand what personal reality is, what is hiding in the deepness of our souls, we have to understand the real meaning of our evolutionary origin—and this will lay out a third option for us to choose.

The road to answering this question is, however, far more difficult than one might guess because it concerns and affects our most fundamental scientific, religious, and political concepts, beliefs, and values. Therefore, everyone who ignores this fact and tries to answer this question on the basis of his particular political, religious, or even scientific beliefs has failed and will fail. Merely our commitment to truth can show us the path to the true meaning of our evolutionary origin. We start with our actual beliefs—for example, with our belief in the existence of our soul. It is not possible to start with a clean sheet or to pretend that our belief in the reality of our soul does not matter in scientific discourse. Evolution is an organic, developmental process that begins at birth and leads us to develop our actual concepts and beliefs; it is not a distinct, objective process. Therefore, to be able to reach our goal, we have to face our starting point and be ready to give up even our most precious scientific beliefs on the altar of truth. To be honest with you, it will be a hard road since *most of our concepts and beliefs, both religious and scientific, are grounded in the explicit negation of the notion of evolution*. Actually, no matter how shocking it sounds, even our ruling scientific theory of "evolution" denies the possibility and real meaning of evolution.

1.2 The Meaning of Evolution and the Theory of Natural Selection

Since Charles Darwin, the notions of evolution and natural selection have become widespread, but the real meanings of them are not well-known at all. Philosophers usually think that evolution is not part of their field or they simply accept the ruling neo-Darwinian view without even considering its philosophical consequences. On the other hand, biologists do not care about general philosophical questions and problems—of course, it is not their job. Generally speaking, we have no idea how many different theories of evolution were proposed or even exist today: for example, classical neo-Darwinism, represented by Ernst Mayr, which emphasizes the natural selection of individual beings; the radical gene-centric understanding of Richard Dawkins; James Lovelock's holistic Gaia-theory; or Vilmos Csányi's general theory of evolution, which emphasizes different evolutionary levels. The most notable theories of the past include J.-B. Lamarck's vitalistic view, Henri Bergson's notion of evolution by time, and the concept of emergent evolution from the British Emergentists. Naturally, one of the latter theories is Michel Polanyi's concept of emergent evolution, which, according to him, is the origin and source of human personal knowledge and reality.

Evolution is a Latin term meaning a kind of development between at least two different things or states. It is, of course, a truism; everybody knows it. Nevertheless, we do not really understand the true meaning of the notion of evolutionary development. Imagine, for example, one of our progenitors, a prokaryote that lived, even without a nucleus, over three billion years ago. Ponder for a moment. What kind of knowledge did our progenitor possess? Compare that level with ourselves. What kind of knowledge do we possess? We should then ask, what is the relationship between the knowledge our brave prokaryote progenitor possessed and our own knowledge? Whether the prokaryote had more advanced knowledge or not? Are we equally developed? If we have the more advanced knowledge, there is an evolutionary relationship between the prokaryote and us. What do you believe?

If one accepts the ruling neo-Darwinian theory, perhaps they do not know it but, in fact, they *deny* that we are more developed than our prokaryote progenitors. According to the neo-Darwinian theory, there is not any single *objective, explicit* criteria on the basis of which such a statement could be formulated. Other criteria cannot be acknowledged because they are "subjective" and "anti-scientific." For example, the fact that humans can ride a bicycle and speak, while our prokaryote progenitor cannot, means nothing in neo-Darwinian terms. Both our prokaryote progenitors and ourselves successfully adapted to our respective environments and possessed the skills necessary and sufficient to survive. These respective environments differ from each other so completely and randomly that the skills of our prokaryote progenitor and our knowledge are not commensurable by objective, explicit, and independent standards.

According to the neo-Darwinian theory, there is only one fundamental mechanism of evolution: the Darwinian notion of *natural selection*. It is the driving force behind the environmental adaptation of living beings. On the one hand, during inheritance, *new variants* are created by mutation and, at the same time, there are generally (but not necessarily) *limited environmental resources*. When they exist, these two factors generate a selection race among the different variants. The consequence of this process is that whichever variants can utilize the limited environmental resources more successfully will survive and reproduce (see figure 1).

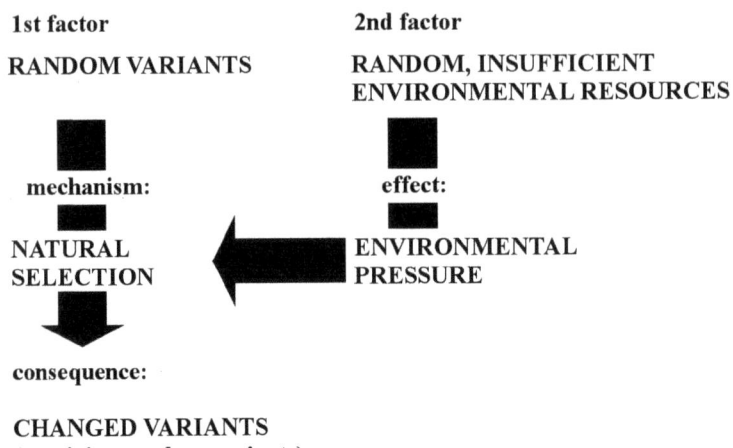

Figure 1. The logical structure of the Darwinian notion of natural selection.

With this mechanism, Darwin successfully explained how new life forms are created from old ones; however, he did not explain why living beings come to be more and more developed. The selective pressure on living beings is determined by the environmental resources that, in turn, ultimately depend on such contingent (random) material processes as the thermal radiation of the Sun, the inclination of the Earth's axis, or the drifting of the continents, etc. Although, these variables can be described very objectively and precisely (that is, scientifically), they do not and *cannot* configure any developmental processes because they are entirely random. The other factor, mutation, is also random. In most cases, mutation does not lead to more developed variants but rather to especially weak or even unviable individuals. This means that over time, an adaptation process governed by natural selection can be reversed and a species might, for example, lose the ability to see or to fly—abilities that most biologists regard as the greatest achievements of evolution. Darwin himself was precisely aware of this problem and did not even use the term evolution for his theory of natural selection.[1]

A process by Darwinian natural selection can be *just as likely to cause regression* as it is to cause development; therefore, "evolution," according to the neo-Darwinian theory, is not only the developmental process anybody would at once imagine (e.g., from primitive prokaryotes to highly developed primates) but also could be the complete opposite (the total

---

1. Sanderson, *Social Evolutionism*, 35.

regression of higher life forms to primitive bacteria). This is the reason Polanyi wrote the following:

> If we are to identify ... the presence of significant order with the operation of an ordering principle, no highly significant order can ever be said to be solely due to an accidental collocation of atoms, and we must conclude therefore that the assumption of an accidental formation of the living species is a logical muddle. It appears to be a piece of equivocation, unconsciously prompted by the urge to avoid facing the problem set to us by the fact that the universe has given birth to these curious beings, including people like ourselves. To say that this result was achieved by natural selection is entirely beside the point. Natural selection tells us only why the unfit failed to survive and not why any living beings, either fit or unfit, ever came into existence. As a solution for our problem, it is logically on a par with the method of catching a lion by catching two and letting one escape.[2]

Polanyi formulates three essential claims in this quotation. Firstly, any significant comprehensive order—including, of course, highly orderly living beings—is the consequence of an *ordering principle*. Therefore, evolution and the emergence of life have their own ordering principles. Secondly, since natural selection is not an ordering principle but rather a *mechanism*, it cannot explain the process of evolution, only its mechanical conditions (for example, how environmental resources affect the composition of a population). Thirdly, natural selection in itself *cannot* explain how living beings came into existence from inanimate primordial matter. At first sight, this third claim can again be surprising because neo-Darwinians tend to pretend that the clue to explaining the origin of life lies in Darwinian natural selection alone. Contrary to them, however, Darwin himself explicates the following claim in the last sentence of *The Origin of Species*, concluding the main point of his theory of natural selection:

> There is grandeur in this view of life, with its several powers, having been originally breathed by the Creator into a few forms or into one; and that, whilst this planet has gone cycling on according to the fixed law of gravity, from so simple a beginning, endless forms, most beautiful and most wonderful, have been and are being evolved.[3]

---

2. Polanyi, *Personal Knowledge*, 35.
3. Darwin, *Origin of Species*, 429.

Darwin's claim is not necessarily that God created life, but he clearly states that his theory of natural selection *does not explain the first formation of life* nor does it explain the evolution of more advanced, higher-level living beings, only the formation of new species. The Darwinian mechanism of natural selection, as we have seen, works by two factors, and one of these factors is the existence of new variants (using Darwin's word forms) that can transmit their typical features to the next generation. Since variants are naturally living beings, this means that the Darwinian theory of natural selection *presupposes life*: without any initial life forms, the first factor of natural selection—and, thus, natural selection itself—cannot be realized. Therefore, if we accept that that fundamental mechanism of evolution is natural selection, then it will be *logically impossible*—even a logical muddle, to use Polanyi's words—to explain the formation of life (and the real process of evolution) with the Darwinian theory of natural selection alone. This is one of the most ignored facts of modern science. Oddly enough, neo-Darwinians go against Darwin himself by not acknowledging that other fundamental principles besides natural selection are needed to explain the emergence of life and evolution.

The neo-Darwinian theory of "evolution" is not the theory of evolution. From this fact, we can draw two different conclusions. First, if we accept the scientific dogma that the neo-Darwinian theory is complete in its fundaments, then we will be forced to say that, on the one hand, *life just happened randomly* and, on the other, *there is no evolution*: you are not more developed than your prokaryote progenitors; therefore, there is no need to identify fundamental principles that can further explain the wonderful development of life. Second, if we insist that, based on our natural experience and personal evidence, we know more and are more developed than our prokaryote progenitors—that is to say, evolution does exist—it will mean that first, the neo-Darwinian theory is incomplete, and second, beyond the mechanism of natural selection, at least one other fundamental scientific principle is needed to explain the developmental process in life (and perhaps yet another to explain the first formation of life).

Persons who accept the notion of evolution generally believe in evolutionary development and honestly think that they are more developed than their prokaryote progenitors. Perhaps the reason the neo-Darwinian theory seems so attractive in their eyes is that it is highly explicit, exact, uses mathematics, is as mechanical as Newton's theory, and most of all, uses such *deceptive substitutions* that it misleads them about what it means. The most typical example is that neo-Darwinian theory is usually presented as the theory of evolution, explaining our evolutionary origin and development from our primitive prokaryote progenitors, when in fact it is only the *theory of change*, which, moreover, rejects any personal criteria by which any real evolutionary development could be determined. Yet, the scientists and biologists who explicitly acknowledge the neo-Darwinian theory believe in evolution very much; *tacitly, they understand from the neo-Darwinian "theory of evolution" what evolution really means.* The fact that the neo-Darwinian theory itself does not explain any evolution at all will be clear only through a detailed and explicit analysis of it and the tacit motivation of the neo-Darwinians. It is not random that perhaps the most influential neo-Darwinist, Richard Dawkins, is more of an apologist for *atheist materialism* than a real biologist.

So what does the notion of evolution really mean? What kind of criteria does a process need to correspond to in order to be considered a process of evolution? For now, let's think this over: is it possible to find a living being more developed than another using only the objective, entirely explicit, and exact criteria employed by the neo-Darwinians? This is a philosophical question, and my answer is no. *There are no such perfectly objective, explicit, and exact criteria by which we can consider our own knowledge more developed than that of our prokaryote progenitors.*

The other, ontological side of the problem is that on the material level, there are no essential differences between the material structure of a prokaryote and a man: both of them have their own DNA, which determines the other material structures they are comprised of, and the actual structure of that DNA resulted from the process of natural selection. We can precisely specify the base sequences of DNA and therefore assign them perfectly exact numerical parameters, but by what criteria is it possible to decide which sequence of numerical parameters is more developed than the other? There are no such criteria. The array of "13012321322231...," where each explicit number represents a nucleotide base, is not more advanced than the array of "23123011212313..." This is the reason that, according to the neo-Darwinian theory, it cannot be stated that we are more developed than our prokaryote progenitors; that would be an ungrounded, "unscientific," and anthropomorphic statement.

We see ourselves as being more developed, however, not because of any explicit numerical parameter or as a result of our specific material structure but because *we possess such personal knowledge—both biological and cultural—which essentially transcends the poor knowledge of our prokaryote progenitors.* We see ourselves more developed because we can ride a bicycle, we can speak, we have culture, and we practice science. This is the reason that our personal reality is much deeper than that of a prokaryote. We know this. But this knowledge cannot be defined by perfectly exact, objective parameters in the same way that we can represent the base sequence of DNA, so the neo-Darwinian theory, following the objectivist ideal of modern science—I call it the Laplacian ideal of objective knowledge—simply *ignores* these facts.

We can find the criteria and the additional principles of evolutionary development not in the material structures of living beings and the exact parameters of those structures but rather in the *biological* reality of living beings and *cultural* reality of man—that is, in our personal knowledge and in our personal reality. Evolution is not only successful adaptation by natural selection to the environment to survive and reproduce but *the emergence of life from inanimate matter to gradually possess more and more advanced knowledge*. The most primitive ancient prokaryote can sustain its metabolism and reproduce. Development does not stop at this ancient, tacit level but rather goes on to reach the specified skills of multicellular beings, the amazing abilities of primates, and eventually, the articulated knowledge of man encompassing, for example, man's cultivation of the science of evolution as a theoretical framework in which we may understand both our past and our future opportunities. Every major transition is unprecedented, creating new levels of knowledge comprised of their own principles and actions that are essentially different from the previous ones. This is the reason that there are no equally valid and applicable laws and methods for every level; biology is not physics.

It means that there is *emergent evolution* or there is *no evolution at all*. Natural selection is only the fundamental mechanism and condition of the emergence of more and more developed living beings that possess more and more knowledge to survive and reproduce:

> Darwinism has diverted attention for a century from the descent of man by investigating the conditions of evolution and overlooking its *action*. Evolution can be understood only as a feat of emergence.[4]

Polanyi's statement is a clear philosophical principle. Natural scientists are reluctant to face it, however, claiming it is "frivolous" and "non-scientific," but the real reason they try to reject it is that it contradicts their *materialist philosophical commitment* (whether it be pronounced explicitly or just believed tacitly and concealed). In consequence, although their theory explicitly excludes even the possibility of evolution and enables only a theory of change, they are still speaking about evolution and, in explicit contradiction with their materialist conviction, they often tacitly mean what they say. This contradiction, deeply rooted in today's science, is one of the cases of the

---

4. Polanyi, *Personal Knowledge*, 390.

intellectual forms of moral inversion.[5] I will explore this in greater detail in Part Four of this book—"Personal Reality"—to better understand the current problems of science and our intellectual life.

Nevertheless, concerning the concept of evolution, the philosophical situation is clear. If materialism is true, then a person who believes in it can consistently speak solely about change by natural selection at the material level exactly in the same way as a physicist discusses how the movements of the molecules change in a gas due to rising temperature and not as we speak about the development of living beings. If emergentism is true, however, there is a possibility that life emerges from primordial inanimate matter and the evolutionary development of knowledge starts culminating later, in the emergence of human culture and human souls. This is the real meaning of the notion of evolution, and those who truly believe in evolution understand it, at least tacitly, in this way.

Now, the question validly arises: if, according to the logic of emergence, natural selection is only the fundamental mechanism and condition of evolution, what are the ordering principles of the formation of life and evolution? Unfortunately, at this point, I am unable to answer this fundamental and challenging question. First, we have to tear down the false conceptual dichotomies of our thinking and establish the concept and logic of emergence in detail. I can shed some light on these principles of life and evolution with an example, but I will not present them in greater detail until Part Three, "Evolution." For this example, we have to double back to a problem we explored earlier. For neo-Darwinians, the first formation of life was a random, instantaneous event. Moreover, it has often been emphasized that even "evolutionary development" itself is a random process, driven by random mutations and natural selection. With this example, I would also like to shed light on why they believe in this falsity.

In his book, *The God Delusion*, Richard Dawkins, perhaps the most well-known, neo-Darwinian biologist, depicts a telling metaphor of how life started according to neo-Darwinism.[6] He uses the legendary aphorism of Fred Hoyle, who argued against the neo-Darwinist concept of the origin of life. Imagine a junkyard where every part necessary to building an operable Boeing 747 can be found. Then, imagine a hurricane that sweeps through that junkyard and leaves behind an airplane, ready to fly. According to Fred Hoyle, the likelihood that life could emerge through a random lightning strike into the so-called primordial soup—where, of course, every necessary ingredient for life (water, sunlight, favorable temperatures and pH balances,

---

5. Polanyi, *Personal Knowledge*, 233.
6. Dawkins, *God Delusion*, 137.

amino acids, etc.) could also be found—was *even smaller* than the likelihood for an operable Boeing to be assembled out of some leftover junk during a hurricane. Dawkins still claims that as unlikely as it may be, this is precisely what happened and how life originated. The argument stands that there was so much time and the never-ending primordial soup was so vast that it still just happened without any divine intervention.

Now it seems that this problem is all about chance: what is the probability for the creation of life by a random event? Was there enough time to realize such a small probability or not? And if this is true, then the secret of the origin of life can be solved by very exact probability calculations. All we need is "highly advanced" and explicit mathematics, such as the Drake-equation (used to calculate the probability of life on other planets). My claim is that this problem is not about chance at all. A real scientific answer *has to be based on empirical evidence and scientific principles*, not on chances. The only result of these exact and scientific probability calculations is the concealing of the real nature of the problem, just as the use of the term "evolution" conceals the fact that the neo-Darwinian theory is not about evolution at all.

The real nature of the problem is: do we really think that it is possible for an operable Boeing 747 to be created from junk instantaneously by a random hurricane? Similarly, do we really believe that it is possible that a viable living being can be created instantaneously by a random material event? If this is the case, then you can start calculating the probabilities. But if not, such calculations are meaningless.

My claim is that on the basis of hard *empirical evidence*, we have to say that *it is not possible*. Hurricanes and lightning destroy structured things; they do not create them. Everyone has seen evidence of this little, simple fact because nobody has ever observed lightning create houses instead of destroying them. Moreover, nobody ever will because the nature of random material processes is that they break down every comprehensive order over time. This phenomenon, of course, corresponds entirely to the physical principle that the entropy (the lack of order on the fundamental level) of a system is necessarily growing until an *ordering principle* changes the process; for example, due to an external and stable energy flow, some kind of new structure starts to grow in the system.

My explicit claim that the *nature* of random material processes ensures that every comprehensive order is broken down over time is based on the conviction that, in reality, it is simply *impossible* that a random hurricane can create a Boeing 747. It is not the question of chance and thus a matter of making exact probability calculations to explain how life was formed at the beginning; instead, it is our conceptualization of the *principles* of the process *on the basis of our natural human and scientific experiences of this kind of processes.*

It is necessary only due to *logic* that there is a possibility for a random hurricane to create a Boeing 747. It is also necessary only due to logic that if I jump out the window, there is a possibility that I will fly. Logic, however, is not reality. In reality, it is a question of empirical evidence, not logical possibilities. Therefore, if we set aside the empirical evidence and immediately attempt to answer the question through calculations of probability and chance, then in reality, we do nothing besides making the impossible possible. With a deceptive magic trick, we substitute the logical possibility in the place of an impossibility of reality. Or to be harsh, thanks to the magic of numbers and to the so exact and scientific probability calculations, we start to believe in the magical power of random winds and lightning—or random mutations. And since any lightning, wind, or genetic mutation in the DNA are strictly deterministic physical process, even the meaning of our words "random mutation" becomes blurry; it is the reason that we have to examine this problem in more detail in chapter 4.

So the question is: why does Dawkins (and the neo-Darwinians) so "scientifically" look over the empirical evidence and deal with the problem as a question of chance and probability calculations? And why do we tend to believe them?

First, in their eyes, due to the Laplacian ideal of objective knowledge, this approach of exact probability calculations is far more scientific than asking what we believe based on our natural human experiences. This problem, concerning the knowledge ideal of modern science, will be the topic of the next chapter.

Second, starting in the 1960s, experimenters have attempted to recreate life in the laboratory from non-living chemicals by random events—for example, by random electric discharges. But no matter how many times they tried, the experiments always failed. It is serious scientific evidence against the neo-Darwinian concept; however, they look over it, claiming, "It has not yet succeeded, but this does not matter because the next experiment might."

Third, most importantly, they think in a *false dichotomy*. They say that there are two options: creation by a Higher Intelligence or creation by random material processes. God or randomness, there is no third option. It means that every other explanation easily becomes God himself which, of course, cannot be accepted in scientific discourse. It is also the reason that the hard empirical evidence of failed experiments to recreate life do not matter because if these negative results would in fact be accurate (which they are, of course), in their eyes, it would mean that life was created by God. That is obviously not possible, so the negative results of the experiments have to be false.

But let us ponder for a moment: what is the real difference between *God as a magical factor*, which cannot be scientifically observed, and a supposedly once-happened, *mysterious, random event* that cannot be repeated? (Which, by the way, also means that it cannot be scientifically observed and examined.) The picture of a random lightning bolt striking down from the sky and creating life or the image of a random, mysterious hurricane sweeping through a junkyard, leaving behind an operable Boeing 747, ready to fly, eloquently portrays the logic and real meaning of the neo-Darwinian concept regarding the origin of life. Logically, due to the dichotomy, it is precisely the same as God breathing the secret power of life down from the skies. Only they do not worship God but rather the demon of Laplace.

Finally, as we have seen—and this is the real point—they have materialist philosophical conviction. According to dualist creationism, life and man were created by God. According to materialist neo-Darwinism, life and man were created by random material processes, the mystical first event, mutations, and the mechanism of natural selection. According to emergentism, life and man were the achievements of emergent evolution, which means the workings of mutations and natural selection as well as the free acts of living beings, according to the ordering principles of life and evolution. It is the reason that I dare to say that emergentism alone conveys the true meaning of evolution.

1.3 Personal Reality from Personal Knowledge

In the middle of the twentieth century, Michael Polanyi explicated his theory about human and scientific knowledge in his book, *Personal Knowledge*. The main point of his book was that we finally have to leave behind false idealisms about our knowledge—especially the Laplacian ideal of objective knowledge—because they strangle science, leading to a moral inversion and political idealism that threatens our freedom and future. To this end, he focused on objectivism and Marxism.

I believe that the most dangerous ideas are the false dichotomies we employ in our thinking. For example, you have to choose neo-Darwinism because the only other theory is vitalism—and everybody "knows" that vitalism is "unscientific." The origin of life must be the consequence of a random material event; otherwise, you smuggle God into the picture. You have to choose materialism because the only other real option is dualism. This is the reason that emergentism also has the propensity to become unscientific or, when tamed, becomes a new kind of so-called non-reductive materialism.

These dichotomies are a consequence of absolute idealist thinking about our knowledge. It means that we assume that truth is something absolute, outside space and time; thus, it can be described by precise scientific concepts or theories, and any different concept—dealing with, e.g., the imperfect (non-absolute) knowledge of living beings—goes into the opposite category, labeled as wrong and unscientific. Accordingly, neo-Darwinians regard vitalism, God, dualism, and even emergentism in the same way: as something "unscientific." In other words, due to the subjective versus objective dichotomy, concepts outside of neo-Darwinism are based on naïve, subjective, traditional beliefs and not on objective, scientific, and critically examined evidence.

Personal knowledge wants to break this thinking. There is no absolute objective knowledge or perfect critical method, and our natural human experiences and personal beliefs (including religious beliefs) are not just naïve, subjective fantasies. It means that both scientific knowledge and our common knowledge are based on our natural tacit skills, our personal point of view, and our traditional beliefs about reality. The simple reason for this is that our skills, beliefs, and points of reference are our evolutionary heritage, and we have no divine ability to reach an ideal, objective knowledge. It is not enough to say, "Sure, evolution," or, "Sure, there is no objective point of view," as we often do, and then do everything in the same old way; instead, we have to face the real meaning and consequences of these facts.

So when Polanyi or I criticize neo-Darwinism or any other scientific school, we do not criticize science itself; on the contrary, we want to defend science and society from false traditional beliefs embedded in science and society. Science itself is a methodology, the most crucial methodology of Western civilization. I do not question that, for example, neo-Darwinism is scientific, and I do not question that materialism, as a fundamental framework for understanding reality, is a legitimate ontological position. I only claim that it is false in the same way that I claim that mainstream understandings about what constitutes scientific knowledge—both in the positivist and the relativist (post-modern) sense—are false.

I like to emphasize this difference between epistemology and ontology because both positivism and relativism, which are different kinds of materialism—and the most influential philosophies in science today—tend to pretend that there is no real difference between the question about knowing (epistemology) and the question about reality (ontology). For example, just because in certain areas (especially, of course, concerning the material conditions of evolutionary development) neo-Darwinism is a highly successful biological theory, it does not follow that the general ontological belief of neo-Darwinians is true. Similarly, physics is a highly successful science, but it does not necessarily follow that everything is physical (which, by the way, is a code name for material meaning that physics must be necessarily materialist). The two giants of the new mechanical physics of the seventeenth century, Isaac Newton and René Descartes, did not think so at all. Materialism became influential only at the beginning of the twentieth century.

However, it is true that a specific methodology—for example, the Laplacian ideal of objective knowledge and the critical method of doubt—could become profoundly connected to a particular ontological conviction. In the next chapter, I will show, for example, how objectivism has become a kind of epistemological materialism or, in other words, how scientific objectivism became a cradle from which materialism was raised.

According to Polanyi: "Truth lies in the achievement of a contact with reality—a contact destined to reveal itself further by an indefinite range of yet unforeseen consequences."[7] The reason for this—as well as the reason why reality cannot be described precisely using objective criteria—is because reality is not absolute or eternal but rather is always changing as an integral part of space and time (just as, for example, life and human beings have gradually emerged from the primordial matter of Earth, utterly changing its reality). Polanyi focused on knowledge, but if his theory of personal knowledge is true, there will be several "unforeseen consequences" of it as well. I try to achieve his vision of these unforeseen consequences in this book, *Personal Reality*.

Personal reality is the ontology of personal knowledge. Polanyi himself already made this clear in the last chapter of *Personal Knowledge*, but he never really concentrated on it:

> We must face the fact that life has actually arisen from inanimate matter, and that human beings—including the teachers of mankind who first shaped our knowledge of rightness—have evolved from tiny creatures resembling the parental zygote in which each of us had his individual origin. I shall meet this situation by re-establishing within the logic of achievement, the conception of emergence first postulated by Lloyd Morgan and Samuel Alexander.[8]

According to this commitment, my primary goal is to break the false ontological dichotomy that more and more suffocates science and society today. In the Preface, I talked about three ontological positions, but in science and society, because we are stuck thinking in a false dichotomy, we recognize only two: dualism and materialism.

---

7. Polanyi, *Personal Knowledge*, 147.
8. Polanyi, *Personal Knowledge*, 381–82.

It is our natural human experience that reality has many faces and at least two of them can be well-recognized. In archaic times, those two faces were known as a kind of spirit and a kind of body. Plato defined them philosophically as Ideas of the spiritual world and bodies of our shadow world, and Christianity believed him. Aristotelian philosophy and science, which only became influential in the Middle Ages, tried to leave this dualism behind, in a sense, with a hierarchical view of reality. But then, modern critical philosophy and science, which were born especially from the efforts of René Descartes and Galileo Galilei, re-established Plato's dualism in a new form: mind and matter. Materialism is also the consequence of modern critical philosophy and science, and its point is that it doubts the existence of minds or souls—that is, the reality of our natural experiences about ourselves and our free nature. According to materialism, there are no minds, no souls, no free will, and no morality. These are just vacant, naïve terms; there is only matter. Emergentism seeks to break this dichotomy of modern critical thinking and establish our natural belief in the existence of our personal souls in the framework of the concept of (emergent) evolution. This is the reason that Polanyi gave the subtitle "Towards a Post-Critical Philosophy" to his *Personal Knowledge*.

Emergentism was established by Samuel Alexander, but it never became a real independent philosophical school. First of all, it was swept away by the rising power of materialism, and secondly, neither of the two important followers of Alexander could acknowledge his starting point: reality in its fundaments is space and time. Lloyd Morgan took a way that could easily be understood as a kind of dualism, while C. D. Broad took another approach that could be interpreted as a new kind of (non-reductive) materialism. The dualism versus materialism dichotomy broke the new school at its birth instead of allowing the new school to break the dichotomy.

Polanyi has some followers but, according to the anecdote, perhaps his most well-known follower, Marjorie Grene—who was at his side as he wrote *Personal Knowledge*—urged him to forgo the last chapter, the only one about personal reality and evolutionary emergence, because of its harsh critique of neo-Darwinism and, "of course," everybody knows that neo-Darwinism is good science. Personal knowledge, however, means nothing without personal reality because without evolutionary emergence, the term evolution loses its original meaning in the fatal embrace of the neo-Darwinian theory. In consequence, personal knowledge loses its own tacit roots, the only roots that can give it reality and true meaning.

We are at the beginning of a long, hard road, but my goal is to establish the concept of personal reality that, according to my belief, we are the children of evolution. Paraphrasing Polanyi's words, I cannot hope to do more in this book than to convince like-minded persons with my straight points and arguments that we have to break the dichotomy. Materialism and neo-Darwinism are not what is scientific; materialism is simply false and misleads us all.

In Part One, "Personal Knowledge," I will follow Polanyi's thread of thought closely, showing the meaning of personal knowledge; therefore, I will mostly argue against epistemological materialism (objectivism). First, I will show that if we are consistent, then objective knowledge is in fact meaningless. Finally, I will turn back to the question of randomness and its consequences to our evolutionary origin with which I started this book.

In Part Two, "Emergence," I will establish the concept of emergence. I will show that the concept of reduction is not the antithesis of emergence. On the contrary, there is an emergentist method of reduction, too, which complies with the actual scientific practice of life sciences much more than the idealistic materialist concepts. I will also argue that twentieth-century physics and Albert Einstein's theory of relativity is not materialist ("physicalist") at all but instead supports Samuel Alexander's theory about the reality of time and thus his concept of emergent reality; therefore, in this part, I will mostly argue against scientific materialism (positivism).

In Part Three, "Evolution," I will show the real meaning of evolution in detail, arguing against biological materialism (neo-Darwinism). My point will be that both biological and cultural evolutions are the emergence of knowledge; for example, replication of unicellular beings is not a material process—solely in its conditions—but rather the duplication of existing knowledge in a living being. Indeed, this book is nothing less than the cultural emergence of knowledge from *Personal Knowledge* by my heuristic efforts according to the most fundamental ordering principle of science, truth. We will see that the driving force of evolution is time and that our freedom and Christian morality are rooted in our evolutionary origin.

Finally, in Part Four, "Personal Reality," I will conclude by examining the consequences of personal reality to our actual personal life in Western societies; therefore, I will mostly argue against moral and political materialism (relativism and neo-Marxism). As I mentioned in the Preface, I do not believe that we have time to delay in understanding our past if we are to gain a real and hopeful vision of the future. If we do not believe that time is real—as materialism does not—we must not be surprised that we will lose our future.

On one more final note, since real meaning is rooted in our tacit evolutionary origin (3.4) and there are no logically coercive, explicit arguments that anyone has to necessarily acknowledge (11.5), my arguments will be circular (3.6), gradually deepening our understanding of the meaning of our starting point for those who are open to the truth that we are the children of evolution. It is not random that an excellent book always has to be read once more. I hope that at the end, these hermeneutic circles will strengthen this truth. So I will use inside references, as you can see in this paragraph, to make it easier to find the more detailed discussions of certain claims or arguments in the book.

1.4 Conclusion

My conclusion here will be short; there is not too much yet to conclude. When I was a child in the eighties, I watched David Attenborough's series about life on Earth and evolution, and I believed him. Then, I was shocked at university when I understood that "objective" science only speaks about evolution but does not want nor even dares to face the real meaning and consequences of it. As a result, science itself even tries to deny it.

However, if we are not created in the image of God, then there is no objective point of view over our personal lives, and it is simply not possible that we have the power to reach the objective knowledge of the Laplacian demon, which, according to the ruling scientific dogma, is the only knowledge that is scientific (2.2). Relativism has already shown that it is only a façade (11.2), and as concepts like evolution, free will, and morality lose their real meanings, everything becomes more and more formal; scientific achievement is measured by vacant, meaningless metrics; bureaucracy and ideology become the "norm" at universities; and you cannot even speak the truth—it is now simply not your job. If we do not, at last, acknowledge our real albeit imperfect evolutionary powers to reach knowledge and truth, these ideological movements, strengthened by scientific reluctance and materialism, will destroy free thinking, free science, and free society. I was born in a communist dictatorship, and I do not want to die in a new kind of one.

Perhaps our future is not in the Heavens, as traditional dualism thought, but the moral fundaments of our free societies still lie in our traditional Christian values. To have a real future of our own, we have to understand both our biological and cultural past (evolution) and need to preserve our Christian moral dynamism and values without the concept of God, which is perhaps the hardest challenge Christianity has ever had to face. Then, we can imagine and realize a hopeful and free vision of a future among the stars.

2

The Laplacian Ideal of Knowledge

2.1 Preface

In one of his works, Pierre-Simon de Laplace mentioned a super-intellect that, at any given moment, can grasp the place, velocity, and any other fundamental property of all of the objects in the universe. Since this super-intellect is also perfectly familiar with the laws of mechanics, it can deduce from these two factors all possible past and future states of the universe. Later, Laplace's super-intellect was renamed to Laplace's demon, but it is still used to define the real possessor of the ideal objective knowledge in almost every scientific discipline to this very day. At first sight, this can be seen as a harmless metaphor, but in fact, it is a perfect, almost artistic formulation of one of the most important tacit convictions of modern critical philosophy and science. By determining our concept of knowledge, Laplace's demon has severe consequences both on science and society.

First of all, it is essential to see that Laplace's vision of perfect knowledge is based on the logic of Newtonian mechanics—it can only be true if the Newtonian worldview is true. It has to be asked, then, whether the Newtonian worldview is really true. It ruled the scientific community in the nineteenth century, when Laplace defined his super-intellect, but after the rise of quantum mechanics and Albert Einstein's theory of relativity at the beginning of the twentieth century, can it still be regarded as true? At this point, the only sure thing is that Laplace's demon continues to be mentioned in science and philosophy as if Einstein, Bohr, Heisenberg, etc. never lived and the theory of relativity and quantum mechanics did not change any fundamental part of the Newtonian worldview. Is this really the case? This is the scientific face of the question.

The other one is philosophical, which also has two different sides. What are the epistemological preconditions of the ideal objective knowledge of Laplace's demon? In other words, what are the tacit presuppositions of Laplace concerning the workings of knowing? How does the demon think and by what kind of logical and intellectual tools and methods is it able to reach this ideal knowledge? What is the nature of this ideal objective knowledge? This last question leads to the other side: what are the ontological preconditions of the ideal knowledge of Laplace's demon? That is, what are Laplace's tacit presuppositions concerning reality? What does the nature of the universe (including the nature of space, time, matter, etc.) have to be due to this ideal? And finally, what is the true nature of Laplace's demon?

The authority of Newton is enormous; every pupil learns in elementary school that he was the best of all scientists and his mechanics is the basis of numerous professions. The ideal objective knowledge of Laplace's demon is an integral part of an old, long-lived scientific tradition; however, by consistently answering these questions, we will see that Laplace's demon is not the possessor of the ideal knowledge, but, in fact, knows nothing which we would ever care about.

2.2 The Knowledge of the Demon According to Laplace

Here is the famous mention of the demon in Laplace's own words:

> We may regard the present state of the universe as the effect of its past and the cause of its future. An intellect which at a certain moment would know all forces that set nature in motion, and all positions of all items of which nature is composed, if this intellect were also vast enough to submit these data to analysis, it would embrace in a single formula the movements of the greatest bodies of the universe and those of the tiniest atom; for such an intellect, nothing would be uncertain, and the future, just like the past, would be present before its eyes.[1]

In his short first sentence, Laplace explicates his view that the universe is deterministic. According to the ruling, so-called Copenhagen interpretation of quantum mechanics, this statement can be strongly challenged, but for now let's assume that the universe is deterministic. This assumption is fundamental for the knowledge of Laplace's demon since if there were indeterministic events which happen without any causes, then the demon could not be able to predict any future states of the universe. However, this problem is not yet solved by adopting this assumption because even if the ruling Copenhagen interpretation of quantum mechanics is not acknowledged, the predictability of a deterministic universe can still be questioned.

---

1. Laplace, *Philosophical Essay*, 4.

Accordingly, the Copenhagen interpretation is an ontological concept about a fundamental feature of the world, while the latter problem concerns an epistemological concept, and the two are not the same at all. Perhaps the universe is entirely deterministic, contrary to the ruling Copenhagen interpretation, but we are still not able to predict its future states because the method by which science tries to achieve this goal does not comply with the nature of the determinism of the universe; the universe can be deterministic in different ways. I will return to this problem later (2.4) and again, in greater detail (9.7). For now, I have just wanted to emphasize that Laplace's concept of determinism is a particular kind of idea that corresponds, of course, to the principles of Newtonian mechanics.

In his long, second sentence, Laplace supposes an intellect, a demon that, at any given moment, knows all fundamental properties of all of the objects in the universe as well as all the fundamental forces that "set nature in motion." Then, he claims that if the demon has the capacity to handle this data, it will also be able to predict any future and past states of the universe. This ideal knowledge is, of course, neither available to us nor can science be identified with it in practice, but it presents a clear vision of how science should work. It defines, therefore, the nature of the suitable scientific method by showing an ideal. For example, it determines which natural phenomena are scientific and thus has to be examined (e.g., Higgs boson, hypnosis, or strings) and which have to be ignored (e.g., witches, animal magnetism, or human spirits). So the stated point of this ideal is to clarify the difference between *true, objective, scientific* knowledge and *false, subjective, naïve* beliefs. Laplace's demon is the perfect manifestation of the knower at the objective side of the subjective versus objective dichotomy.

Now, we need to ask what was tacitly presupposed by Laplace in his definition; that is, what both the *epistemological* and *ontological* preconditions of his ideal are. First, let's see what Laplace has already told us.

First of all, he explicitly claims that the demon's knowledge referring to the universe is a huge set of data that has to be substituted into a "single formula," by which the demon can calculate all the past and future states of the universe. In consequence, the demon's knowledge is perfectly *exact* and *explicit*. If it wants to be able to calculate all past and future states of the universe, then it will need such strictly exact and explicit data and formula from which all of its assertions will follow by a *logically coercive power*. Its knowledge cannot be the least bit unspecified or tacit; otherwise, it could know nothing with perfect certainty. To put it in other words, a few small mistakes in the current data or only one in the formula could cause total misrepresentations of any past or future state of the universe. Therefore, the demon's knowledge is perfectly exact and explicit, and it needs nothing else in addition to calculate all the past and future states of the universe.

The ontological consequences are these: the universe is *nothing more than what the demon can describe with his knowledge*; otherwise, Laplace could not claim that "for such an intellect nothing would be uncertain," neither past nor future. Since if there were, for example, "dark matter"—I mean unknown things for the demon—these unknown things would influence the course of events in the universe and the demon's calculations would prove to be wrong. But according to Laplace, this is not the case. His demon possesses complete and perfect knowledge of the universe. The universe includes, therefore, merely such kind of objects that can be described in purely exact, explicit ways.

Now, the question is what the nature of this kind of objects is. Or, in other words, which scientific discipline theorizes and examines this kind of objects? The answer is, of course, *fundamental physics*. It is important to emphasize that it is *fundamental* physics and not physics as such because physics in general can examine any comprehensive phenomenon which cannot be specified perfectly at all (5.3). Comprehensive phenomena (e.g., a planet, a frog, or a human person) are individual, always changing, complex objects and only some of their characteristics can be described by exact, numeric parameters and mathematically formulated exact principles (laws)—that is, by physics. However, the objects of fundamental physics, at least in principle, are perfectly universal, constant, point-like entities that possess merely such so-called primary properties that can be described and defined by exact, explicit laws and parameters. Of course, it needs to be examined later what fundamental physics—that is, quantum mechanics—really is, in practice, compared to this ideal (2.4), but for now, let's remain at the philosophical problems.

The next question we should ask is this: what about the case of comprehensive phenomena which cannot be specified by exact, numeric parameters? What is supposed about these phenomena by Laplace? He does not say anything explicitly, but he handles them in the same way as fundamental particles. He apparently thinks that the demon can easily treat both of "the movements of the greatest bodies of the universe and those of the tiniest atom." However, different comprehensive phenomena not only have many different kinds of movement (even in the case of lifeless gas giants), but also, in the case of the Earth, there are a lot of these various movements—for example, the movements of frogs, machines, human beings, etc., as well as other comprehensive characteristics, for example, feelings, thoughts, moral values, and beliefs of living beings—which cannot be specified precisely at all. It follows that Laplace can claim that his demon can treat all the movements of the universe *if and only if* he tacitly supposes that the specific characteristics and movements of these comprehensive phenomena, which cannot be specified precisely, *are not real*.

In consequence, comprehensive phenomena are real only to the extent that their movements and characteristics can be described in exact, explicit ways—that is, to the extent that the descriptions of their specific characteristics and movements can be identified with the purely exact and explicit descriptions of the parts from which they are built up. This is the problem of *reduction*. Reduction is a scientific method by which it can be shown that a comprehensive phenomenon is only a set of lower-level parts and nothing more (2.5, 5.3). For the demon, these parts are "tiny atoms"—that is, the theorized entities of fundamental physics, which, according to the ruling ontological interpretation, are purely material. It seems that this ontological hypothesis complies with Laplace's intents perfectly. Therefore, from the ideal objective knowledge of Laplace's demon follows a *materialist ontology* that claims that there exists only such kind of fundamental material parts which can be specified precisely and only such kind of comprehensive phenomena the exact descriptions of which can be identified with the exact descriptions of their parts by which the demon calculates the past and future states of the universe.

The last question that has to be answered at this point is where the movements and characteristics of the comprehensive phenomena come from which cannot be specified exactly. In other words: what are these movements and characteristics, according to the ideal knowledge of the demon if, in reality, they do not exist? The answer is simple: they are *illusions*, just as, for example, it is merely our subjective illusion (impression) that the Earth is standing motionless under our feet while the Sun is orbiting it by mad pace. It means that these phenomena are *purely epistemological*, only the consequences of our limited human knowing; we falsely perceive what is moving and what is motionless, what is real and what is not. And this, "of course," is just one example that natural human knowing is subjective, thus, we should follow the ideal knowledge of the demon that never would have made such a mistake. The question is why it never would have made such a mistake.

2.3 The Knowledge of the Demon According to Polanyi

In contrast to Laplace, Polanyi describes the knowledge of the demon as follows:

Assume, for the sake of argument, that we posses a complete atomic theory of inanimate matter. We can then envisage the operations of a Universal Mind in the sense of Laplace. The initial positions and velocities of all the atoms of the world being given for one moment of time, and all the forces acting between the atoms being known, the Laplacean Mind could compute all future configurations of all atoms throughout the world, and from this result, we could read off the exact physical and chemical typography of the world at any future point of time. But we now know that there is a great and varied class of objects which cannot be identified, and still less understood, by establishing their complete physical and chemical topography, for they are constructed with a view to a purpose which physics and chemistry cannot define. So it follows that the Laplacean Mind would be subject to the same limitation: it could not identify any machine nor tell us how it works. Indeed, the Laplacean Mind could identify no object or process, the meaning of which consists in serving purpose. It would ignore therefore the existence not only of machines but also of any kind of tools, foodstuffs, houses, roads, and any written records or spoken messages.[2]

First of all, Polanyi summarizes the knowledge of the demon which we have already seen by Laplace's own words. Then, he emphasizes that the demon's knowledge does not refer to the whole world—as Laplace claims—but rather only to the fundamental particles of the universe; only this kind of objects can be specified by exact, perfectly explicit parameters. It follows that it also refers to those comprehensive objects which can be identified by a set of these fundamental particles or, to put it into Polanyi's words, which can be identified "by establishing their complete physical and chemical topography." Perhaps it is a little bit surprising at this point, but Polanyi can also speak about physics and chemistry (and not just about fundamental physics) because, according to him, the comprehensive objects of physics and chemistry can be specified exactly and their descriptions can be identified perfectly with that of the material particles of fundamental physics (5.6).[3]

Finally, Polanyi claims that the demon's knowledge means nothing concerning higher-level, comprehensive phenomena. The ontological side of the claim is that there are such comprehensive phenomena in the universe which, although they have a material basis, are not material at all. Polanyi is an emergentist, he consistently believes in the existence of souls and persons. The epistemological side of the claim is that based solely on

2. Polanyi, *Study of Man*, 48–49.
3. Polanyi, *Personal Knowledge*, 391.

its ideal knowledge, the demon *cannot even identify* higher-level, comprehensive phenomena.

Polanyi's first example is a machine that is, of course, the object of engineering, not of physics or chemistry. Then, he emphasizes the role of-purposes which, according to him, are the main reasons why the demon cannot identify the comprehensive phenomena in question. This is the most trivial example for understanding the problem because in the Laplacian universe, due to Newtonian mechanics, there are no purposes at all. Therefore, if there are objects with a purpose in the real universe, as it can easily be argued, then the demon will have no concepts or intellectual tools to describe and identify these purposes. Nonetheless, it is only the surface of the problem which could lead to several misunderstandings, too; the point itself is much more concerning.

Consider Polanyi's words: "A complete physical and chemical topography of a frog would tell us nothing about it as a frog, unless we knew it previously *as a frog*."[4] To understand this assertion, we have to examine the real nature of the demon because therein hides the reason why "a complete physical and chemical topography" in itself—that is, the ideal fundamental knowledge of the demon—means nothing concerning any comprehensive phenomena, both emergent and material ones.

So what is the demon? First of all, it is *not a person* but rather a *bodiless spirit* (intellect) that at any given moment possesses the exact descriptions of all the fundamental material parts of the universe. From this data, it can deduce all the past and future fundamental states of the universe. According to the Laplacian ideal of objective knowledge, the demon knows everything and his knowledge is purely explicit. It follows that, in turn, he does not and most importantly *cannot possess any tacit or personal knowledge*.

What would happen if the demon possessed personal knowledge, that is, the demon's knowledge was based on tacit evolutionary roots just as much as the knowledge of real human persons in the evolutionary system of Earth? Then, the demon could not be a bodiless spirit; its knowledge would become limited by bodily skills and perceptions, anchored to a certain point of space and time. Therefore, it would suffer from exactly the same "subjective illusions" as the knowledge of human persons. The main point of personal knowledge is that we cannot see the whole universe at a given moment as the demon does but rather, *inevitably, only from a certain point of view* (center), based on our evolutionary heritage—that is, from our body, here and now. We also have no pure, deductive power to calculate the past and future states of the universe; rather, our knowing is limited by and based

---

4. Polanyi, *Personal Knowledge*, 342.

on tacit bodily skills and senses. Polanyi definitely explicates this already on the first page of the main text of *Personal Knowledge*:

> For, as human beings, we must inevitably see the universe from a center, lying within ourselves, and speak about it in terms of a human language shaped by the exigencies of human intercourse. Any attempt rigorously to eliminate our human perspective from our picture of the world must lead to absurdity.[5]

This means that our *center*, which is our inevitable *point of reference*, is necessary lying within and works by our body. Our body simply cannot be "vast enough"—as Laplace puts it—to process all the data of the whole universe. As a matter of fact, according to the rules of formal logic, we can only process a few datum, deductively speaking. We do not infer from exactly defined (focal) parts to other exactly defined (focal) parts but rather tacitly integrate from (subsidiary) parts to (focal) comprehensive wholes, then orient ourselves in the world by these orderly comprehensive wholes (3.3). It follows that, contrary to the demon, we do not see fundamental material parts at all. Nobody has ever seen, for example, an up quark by which the demon calculates due to "the complete physical and chemical topography" of the universe; rather, we see machines, frogs, planets, peoples, etc.—that is, according to the Laplacian ideal of objective knowledge, different kinds of comprehensive, orderly wholes in an utterly illusory way. To be honest, it is absolutely true that we are not perfect; sometimes we are clearly wrong, failing to identify what is moving and what is motionless under our feet (as the great Copernicus found out). However, we will soon see that the demon is, in fact, wrong in *every* case (2.4).

So the demon's knowledge, contrary to our knowing, could be "perfect" and ideal just because *it is not rooted in a kind of tacit evolutionary heritage*. Something or somebody cannot be at the same time a bright and perfect super-intellect—that is, a bodiless spirit over and above the whole universe—and a fallible person with limited bodily skills at a given point in space-time. As a matter of fact, when Laplace says that if his demon were "also vast enough" to process all the data of the whole universe, it is completely misleading that he could then conclude all the past and future states of the universe since by this claim, he tacitly supposes that the center of the demon is also in a body—only in a huge body. But if this were the case, then his demon could not be able to do what Laplace wants it to be able to do. It is much more telling when he says "for such an intellect, nothing would be uncertain and the future, just like the past, would be present

---

5. Polanyi, *Personal Knowledge*, 3.

before its eyes." The demon, of course, has no eyes; this is only figurative speech, but it is literally true that if it finished his calculations, then, according to the ideal, it would know everything that could be known and all states of the universe, past, present, and future, could be seen *as present* before its perfect intellect. The demon is, in fact, a beast *outside of space and time*. He is simply not part of the very material universe that he observes. And if it "did" what it had to do, according to Laplace's intentions, then it would never be able to do anything else. I will examine the consequences of this problem in the next subchapter.

My point is only the consequence of the fact that although the demon possesses a perfect, completely explicit knowledge of all fundamental material parts of the whole universe, it *solely possesses this kind of knowledge*—and not the limited, personal knowledge of human beings. At this point, the question should be asked: how could it recognize any comprehensive object of the universe if it did not possess the tacit skills and senses of human beings by which the parts—e.g., the individual photons coming from the different parts—can be integrated into comprehensive, orderly wholes? The "complete physical and chemical topography" of a comprehensive object (that is, the Laplacian ideal of objective knowledge) is by definition *not the same* as the tacit recognition of a comprehensive object (that is, the personal knowledge of human beings), even if we assume that the content or reference of the two types of knowledge is exactly the same. Nobody can learn from a quantum mechanical textbook how to recognize a frog—even if a frog is, in fact, nothing more than a pile of quarks and electrons—and nobody can learn from Newton's *Principia Mathematica* how to build a machine—even if engineering is based on the principles of Newtonian mechanics. We recognize a frog by our tacit bodily senses and skills which were acquired as we grew up (ontogeny) based on the evolutionary heritage of our phylogeny, and we can build a machine based on our cultural heritage of craftsmanship and engineering as, for example, James Watt did. The demon does not possess these kinds of knowledge by definition. Therefore, *it cannot recognize or identify any comprehensive wholes of the universe*, neither frogs nor machines, neither planets nor stars; its knowledge concerns only the fundamental parts. In consequence, it knows nothing that ever would interest us in real life—not including nuclear physicists, of course.

So concentrating on purpose, Polanyi is, in fact, not really harsh on the demon because he tacitly enables it to recognize higher-level but material—that is, physical and chemical—phenomena. However, the point is that without the previous tacit recognition of an object, the perfect and "complete physical and chemical topography" means nothing, even in the case of lifeless planets and stars. Cosmology is not fundamental physics (7.4). Tacit knowledge always has to come before the explicit topography—that is, before any explicit knowledge; otherwise, there is no meaning at all. I will illustrate this crucial consequence of personal knowledge with a detailed example in subchapter 2.5 and detail the whole phenomenon in subchapters 3.3 and 3.4, but for now, let's see the ontological side of Polanyi's claim.

What would be the consequence of the demon's knowledge concerning reality if its knowledge were real and true? Since without personal knowledge, it would not be able to recognize any higher-level comprehensive phenomena, *none* of these phenomena could be part of the real universe. Not just those that cannot be specified precisely, as we have seen at the end of the previous subchapter, but also, in fact, all of the higher-level, comprehensive phenomena. It follows that these phenomena would have to be regarded *as mere illusion*s of imperfect human knowing—as would our every other subjective impression—all starting with the fact that we once naïvely believed that the Earth was standing still under our feet. Yes, it literally means that *every* comprehensive, orderly phenomenon is merely an illusion: every machine, every frog, every planet, every star, and every human person. The *consistent* ontological claim of the materialist Laplacian ideal is that we are only our own subjective illusions. Yes, you are your own illusion, too. This is the reason that Polanyi finished his thread of thought with these words: "Any attempt rigorously to eliminate our human perspective from our picture of the world must lead to absurdity." Contrary to the materialism of the Laplacian ideal, Polanyi's ontological claim is simple: we are what we seem to be: *comprehensive, orderly wholes composed of matter*. This whole book is about to reveal the most profound meanings of this simple fact.

Perhaps it is still hard to believe, but now we can see that the ideal objective knowledge of the demon leads to absurdity. The question is why this simple truth is not so obvious for us, why is it so hard to believe, and most of all, why do scientists and philosophers still tend to follow the Laplacian ideal of objective knowledge? First, they conceal this fact by *deceptive substitutions* (2.5), and if they, at least partially, notice it, they will still never choose the one alternative they generally see: naïve, subjective, and unscientific beliefs coming from superstitions and religion. In the next chapter, through Polanyi's *Personal Knowledge*, I will show that subjectivity versus objectivity—as well as knowledge versus belief—is a false dichotomy and there is a third option, which, in fact, is the real fundament of science, philosophy, and human knowledge. Before I unfold the meaning of deceptive substitutions in detail, let us see the physics of the demon that has always been put aside to this very point.

2.4 The Physics of the Demon

I noted in the Preface that the Laplacian ideal of objective knowledge is based on the worldview of Newtonian mechanics and that Laplace's demon is used in science and philosophy as if the rise of Albert Einstein's theory of relativity and the rise of quantum mechanics at the beginning of the twentieth century did not produce any significant change to the Newtonian worldview. In the second subchapter, concerning the fact that the knowledge of the demon refers to the theorized entities of fundamental physics—which is, of course, quantum mechanics and its successors today—we stated that we will have to examine this problem later. Accordingly, the question is this: although quantum mechanics was initially developed due to the Laplacian ideal, does it still comply with the strict requirements of this ideal?

Not at all. As a matter of fact, quantum mechanics is not even a classical scientific theory in the sense that it might tell us what the exact parameters of the fundamental material parts are and by which the demon could then calculate its answers. It does not even tell us, for example, that the fundamental parts are particles or waves. This strange, contradictory claim of quantum mechanics can, of course, be accepted from a practical point of view, but not from a philosophical one: if the fundamental parts are both waves and particles at the same time, then the ontological reasons of this strange fact must be explained in detail, which has not yet happened. Moreover, quantum mechanics (or, at least, the ruling Copenhagen interpretation of quantum mechanics) has left behind these theoretical problems; instead, it has become a set of practical, operational principles by which experiments can be set up and the *probabilities* of different expected results can be predicted more precisely. In this sense, quantum mechanics is a highly successful intellectual tool, but as a theory, it never really tells us what factually happens in the real universe. This philosophical deficiency was the main reason why Einstein never fully accepted the Copenhagen interpretation of quantum mechanics.

Our actual fundamental physics is highly successful in practice, but it does not comply with the Laplacian ideal because it does not provide any unambiguous data by which the demon could precisely calculate the past and future states of the universe. Yet, this fact did not question the ideal. The reason is twofold.

First, quantum mechanics has left behind this ideal only partially. The methods of quantum mechanics still comply with the Laplacian ideal since it uses exactly defined data and explicit formal equations by which it calculates any future states of quantum systems. The only main difference is that it uses *probability statements* concerning the events and not unambiguous ones (3.4). Of course, the indeterministic interpretation of quantum mechanics is tightly connected to this fact, which I will discuss a little bit later at the end of this subchapter.

Quantum mechanics has left behind only the ontological part of the Laplacian ideal—at least partially—and not its epistemological vision, especially its scientific methodology. This change happened mostly due to the influence of Ernst Mach's positivism, which tried to reject every ontological claim in science at the end of the nineteenth century and the beginning of the twentieth century (3.2). This kind of philosophical thinking was desirable for many physicists at that time because of the particular practical problems of experimentation with which early quantum mechanics had to face. Then, in the twenties and thirties, the ruling Copenhagen interpretation of quantum mechanics and the new, most successful third wave of positivism were born shoulder to shoulder in the same German-speaking scientific community.

Positivism is a kind of Laplacian critical philosophy that denies the ontological side of the Laplacian ideal to be able to embrace its epistemological side more easily (3.2). At the same time, it is just as tacitly materialist as the Copenhagen interpretation of quantum mechanics because, in the name of science, it usually rejects non-material phenomena, stigmatizes only metaphysical and non-materialist theories as unscientific, and, most importantly, it tries to *reduce* the descriptions of every comprehensive phenomenon to exact, fundamental scientific statements. From this intention, the idea was born in the mind of Rudolf Carnap, perhaps the most influential figure in third wave positivism, to call their ontological position *physicalism*. But this explicit word is only a deceptive substitution for their real and tacit ontological conviction: materialism. The term physicalism conceals this fact, suggesting that physics and science would necessarily be at their side (5.3). At the start of the twenty-first century, positivism is still the ruling philosophy in the natural sciences and physicalism is the ruling ontological conviction in Anglo-Saxon analytical philosophy.

The second reason that the Laplacian ideal is not questioned in physics is that since the eighties, despite the practical and theoretical problems of twentieth-century physics—that is, the existing contradictions between the two fundamental theories of general relativity and quantum mechanics—most theoretical physicists have chosen not to abandon their ideals but rather to fully return to the Laplacian ideal, hoping to find a cure for these problems by the more consequent application of the ideal itself. I refer here to the rise of "string theories." According to string theories, everything is composed of tiny, oscillating, multi-dimensional strings which can be described in perfectly exact, explicit ways; therefore, at least in principle, by substituting this data into the formulas of string theories, all past and future states of the universe can be perfectly calculated after all. If this project were successful, then twenty-first-century physics could fully return to the Laplacian vision of the world in the ontological sense as well. However, in spite of three decades of intense work by many excellent physicists, string theories still cannot make any meaningful new predictions based on the concept of their nine- and ten-dimensional small strings, still suffering from several significant methodological and philosophical problems. It is not random that, in practice, everybody still uses the equations of quantum mechanics. After so much effort, time, and money spent on string theories, this result is a serious concern.[6] Nonetheless, if the Laplacian ideal of objective knowledge is false, then string theories will never be successful (4.6). I mean this strictly in terms of truthfulness; in the sense of institutional or academic results, they are indeed highly successful.

The other leading fundamental theory of physics has some major consequences concerning the Laplacian ideal as well. According to Albert Einstein's theory of relativity, simultaneity is always in question (6.3). Different observers from a different time, place, and velocity could also find the time sequence of events different. For one observer, an event (A) that occurs before another (B) could also take place after the same event (B) for a different observer. Furthermore, neither time nor space is absolute but rather depends on the situation of the given observer—that is, what his or her point of reference is in the universe. For example, as the famous twin paradox pictures it: time on Earth and time observed from a fast spaceship will go differently. Moreover, observation itself is highly limited, not only because of human imperfections but also because it can only be carried out at the maximum speed in the universe—that is, at the speed of light. Anybody who looks up at the nightly sky does not see how Sirius is doing at the moment but rather how it appeared eight years ago.

Laplace, however, claims that his demon can "see" all the objects in the universe at a given moment and can calculate from this data all the past and future states of the universe. According to Einstein, there is no simultaneity of the present, the concepts of past and future are relative, and every observation is limited to the speed of light. If these facts had no consequence for the ideal knowledge of Laplace's demon, it would mean that the facts of the theory of relativity are just as illusory as the impression that the Earth is standing motionless under our feet. Yet, among physicists, the Laplacian ideal of objective knowledge still keeps itself above water.

---

6. See, for example, Lee Smolin's excellent work on the problem (Smolin, *Trouble With Physics*).

I believe that the reason for this strange, contradictory situation is that it is not clear what the philosophical meaning of Einstein's theory of relativity is (6.7). According to positivism, the ontological explanation of scientific theories has to be avoided. Furthermore, this practical approach can solve the problem that, at the ontological level, Einstein's theory is in complete contradiction with Newton's. As a fundamental institution of Western civilization, science wants to avoid facing the fact (especially before the eyes of the public) that twentieth-century physics replaced Newtonian physics just as Copernicus, Galilei, and Newton replaced the physics of the so-called "dark" and superstitious Middle Ages in the seventeenth century. If we do not understand the philosophical meanings of the so-called Copernican and Einsteinian Revolutions, then the detailed, critical analysis of these historic events could quickly lead to relativism, which, at the beginning of the third millennia, now questions even the most essential fundaments of science itself (11.2). Although physicists and other scientists try to defend science, their old arguments—based on the Laplacian ideal of objective knowledge—are useless against the new and rigorous arguments of the relativists, which are, in fact, based on the more coherent application of the same ideal on the history and social structure of science (11.5). Of course, in a practical sense, it is true that general relativity is the extension of Newtonian mechanics, solving some extreme situations where speed, mass, or both are huge, but this is true only in a practical sense and when we set aside what Newton and Einstein claimed about the nature of space, time, light, and matter—that is, when we hush up the ontological meanings and consequences of these theories and let in the relativist approach, which takes any practical definition of science into pieces by its detailed analyses of the practical working of science itself as a social and historical institution. Instead, we should face the fact that Laplace's demon is a Newtonian beast, not an Einsteinian one.

In the previous subchapter, we have seen that Laplace's demon is a beast outside space and time, and now we can understand the real meaning of this conclusion. It can "see" the whole universe at a given moment because there is simultaneity of the present—that is, the concept of the present is absolute. At any given moment, everything in the universe has the same date. This is true, of course, to all past and future moments too. Time is absolute and the objects in the universe do not influence its flow. The demon can "see" the whole universe at a given moment because there is no speed limit to its observations. In the seventeenth century, no one knew that the speed of light is finite, and, according to Newton, the speed of light certainly does not limit the "spread" of gravity—which is infinite. Since space is also absolute, distances that, according to Einstein's theory, can be different for different observers do not distort the demon's "vision" as peculiar "gravitation lenses."

Laplace said, "For such an intellect, nothing would be uncertain, and the future, just like the past, would be present before its eyes." If I ask—but not in relation to Laplace's demon—who is that being to whom nothing is uncertain, and the future, just like the past, is present before his eyes? The answer is simple: God. He is the only one who can exist outside the universe. It is quite fascinating to me that scientists, who easily can declare any claim that questions the dogma that everything in the universe is material to be "obscure" and "unscientific" and who proclaim that Einstein was the brightest mind of all, tend to follow a Newtonian beast that is, in fact, a grotesque picture of God. I think Steven Hawking's famous words perfectly describe this strange and inconsistent situation: "If we do discover a complete theory . . . it would be the ultimate triumph of human reason—for then we would truly know the mind of God."[7] I could also paraphrase Richard Dawkins in that it seems physics is taught as though Darwin never existed.

The "complete theory," or with other popular term, the "theory of everything," is, of course, nothing else but the "single formula" of Laplace's demon—that is, a certain name for the Laplacian ideal of objective knowledge by which everything can be described exactly and by which all past and future states of the universe can be calculated perfectly—to finally "know the mind of God." However, remember Laplace's words: "If this intellect were also vast enough to submit these data to analysis, it would embrace in a single formula the movements of the greatest bodies of the universe and those of the tiniest atom." In reality, he describes a super-computer that can calculate everything and does nothing else rather than God; at most, only the instantaneous observational "skills" of the demon are divine, so it is a strange, mythical computer-God. Nevertheless, it follows that later we also have to examine the real meaning of the knowledge of machines and computers to see the essential difference between the knowledge of living beings and machines (8.5).

The Laplacian vision of the universe has another severe consequence that I would like to introduce with an example before I finish this subchapter with the problem of determinism. I mentioned a few pages earlier that the central historic event which grounded the birth of the Laplacian ideal is called by historians of science the Copernican Revolution. I will examine its meaning in the next chapter (3.2), but its main scientific message is usually presented like this: if we rely on our subjective, bodily perceptions, then we will naïvely believe that the Earth is standing motionless at the center of the

---

7. Hawking, *Brief History of Time*, 193.

universe; however, if we follow the critical scientific thinking of Copernicus, we can recognize that the Earth is not in the center of the world at all, but in reality, it revolves around the Sun (and the latter is motionless). Set aside the fact that the Sun is not the center of the universe and moves just as much as the Earth does (in this literal sense, Copernicus's theory is just as false as Aristotle's old one); the main point here is that, according to the Laplacian ideal, in fact, *neither* the Sun *nor* the Earth *is moving*.

Remember Laplace's words once again. They are telling now, too: "The future, just like the past, would be present before its eyes." The demon is outside the universe. He is not part of space or time and both time and space are absolute. It means that the space and time relations of objects in the universe can be described by exact parameters due to a four-dimensional, Cartesian coordinate system. Consequently, the calculations of the demon concerning any past or future state of the universe are nothing more than to define the new space parameters depending on the new time parameter, which is simultaneous, all over the universe, at any given moment. Of course, all other fundamental parameters can be defined in this way as well. Therefore, when the demon has finished his calculations—which are, by the way, done in zero time because the demon is outside of time—then all past and future states of the universe "would be *present* before its eyes." This is the way in which time loses its real unique characteristics (e.g., irreversibility) and becomes a simple *fourth dimension of space*. There is no past and no future for the demon, only presents, existing beside each other—just as the points of space are beside each other—in one simultaneous moment.

This result is also the consequence of Newtonian mechanics, which treats time as a vacant, space-like, and *reversible* factor (6.2). Moreover, for the demon, even the sequence of time parameters lost its original meaning because it can calculate any state of the universe from any other state due to different time parameters: everything is "present." In consequence, time becomes space-like, even in this originally unique characteristic, and instants of time do not build on each other anymore, as one peculiar instant after the next (as anybody can experience this fact), but instead, time instants become as distinct as space points in a dimension. They are not gradually built on but rather simply beside each other. This means that our natural experience of a person—at first as a baby, then a little child, after that an adolescent, then a young adult, before they finally become a grown-up—is just as illusory as our impression that the Earth is standing still under our feet. According to the Laplacian ideal of objective knowledge, the flow of time is only an illusion. *Nothing is moving.* Everything is a "present" part of the four-dimensional block of the universe. This timeless concept of the universe is the reason that the concept of evolution has also lost its real meaning (1.2). Without time, there is neither real ontogeny nor real phylogeny. Contrary to Newton's vision, an always present fourth dimension of space is not time at all. If someone ignores the philosophical meaning of Einstein's theory of relativity, particularly concerning the nature of space and time, regarding it as mere mathematical expansion or precision of the Newtonian theory, then the four-dimensional universe can easily be kept—we only need to use a "little bit" more complicated, non-Euclidian mathematics to accurately describe its parameters due to the invisible and strange curvatures of space and time (6.5).

When we speak about the motions of Earth or the growing up of a child—since these processes are not part of the Laplacian ideal of objective knowledge—if we still think this ideal could tell us anything about the real meanings of these processes, we, in fact, secretly substitute meanings from our personal knowledge in the place of the exact parameters of the calculations of the demon, thereby misleading ourselves. This phenomenon is called a "deceptive substitution" by Polanyi. But before that, let's see to our last problem in this subchapter: the question of determinism.

At the beginning of the second subchapter (concerning the Copenhagen interpretation of quantum mechanics), I said that the universe could be deterministic in different ways. I will return to this problem in detail later, focusing on its relationship to the concept of evolution (9.7), but the main point already can be seen. According to the Laplacian ideal, due to the *nature of space*, the determinism of the universe is a purely *mechanical* determinism, as everything has its own, precisely-defined place in the four-dimensional space-"time" of the block universe. There are no free acts and there is no free will—both of them are purely subjective illusions. This concept is, as we have seen, the consequence of Galilei and Newton, as they started to measure time as a strange fourth dimension of space, so that time is nothing more than a physical correlation between a given distance and the speed of the object that covered that distance. In some case, this interpretation is, of course, entirely legitimate, but the Laplacian ideal of objective knowledge regards *everything* in this way. The Copenhagen interpretation of quantum mechanics thinks in this kind of determinism, too, only it denies it.

The other kind of determinism comes from the *nature of time*. If time is real and not just a space-like, measured correlation between different states of material objects in the block universe, then time will determine what comes next. This determination, however, cannot be measured and calculated exactly—that is, future events cannot be predicted in the same way as the demon calculates the nature of space; rather, this determination is due to the unique nature of time. In consequence, in the mechanical sense, it is *not* determinism at all. It is *not* indeterminism either. Of course, the mechanical, physical state of the universe influences the future but does not determine it because there is real time too. Time determines, in the actual mechanical and physical (material) conditions, the future, that is, its own, active flow. *Future in its fundament is time, nothing else.* Therefore, it is true that a person's present and past determine his future, but, first of all, it is not a mechanical-material determination, and if time is not absolute—as Einstein's theory of relativity suggests—but everybody has their own past and present, then everybody can determine, based on his own time (past) and due to the given (present material) conditions, his or her own future. The way that a person does this is called free will.

My claim is that there is real freedom in the universe. It is not just an illusion, the determinism versus free will dichotomy is *false*. At this point, I cannot go into more detail, but I want to shed light on an important connection. Polanyi says: "As human beings, we must inevitably see the universe from a center lying within ourselves." This is the main point of personal knowledge. So when Einstein speaks about the fact that there is no absolute space and no absolute time—every point of reference has its own space and time, and from that point of reference, every other time and space seems to be different—they both, in fact, speak about the same thing. *There is no absolute point of reference*: the demon is not real. The Laplacian ideal of objective knowledge is false.

Nevertheless, according to Einstein, the speed of light is the same *for everybody*. Why, if there is no absolute point of reference? I will explain this strange characteristic of the universe in subchapter 6.4 by the nature of time.

2.5 Laplacian Faults or Deceptive Substitutions

Perhaps, or at least I dare to hope, it is now clear, to some degree, what a deceptive substitution is. But since it is one of the central concepts of personal knowledge, I am going to detail it in this subchapter. Since it is usually quite neglected, I am going to do it at a really slow pace, explaining the concept to its very core. The main point of this notion, I believe, is connected to the concept of reduction and thus to the correlation between comprehensive, orderly wholes and their parts. Nonetheless, I will now focus on the concept of deceptive substitutions or Laplacian faults and will not discuss the problem of reduction in detail until chapter 5 (especially subchapters 5.3 and 5.4), only after I have thoroughly established the concept of personal knowledge in Part One.

We have seen that, according to the Laplacian ideal, comprehensive phenomena are real only to the extent that their movements and characteristics can be described exactly, that is, to the extent that their descriptions can be identified with the purely exact and explicit descriptions of the parts from which they are built up. This is the fundamental meaning of the method of reduction by which it can be shown that a comprehensive phenomenon—for example, a bright emerald from South Africa—in spite of its significantly different appearance, is, in fact, as material as an electron.

Materialism claims that by reduction, it can be shown that *every* real, comprehensive phenomenon is material. This includes human persons, too, because, of course, nobody wants to regard human beings (and thus, him or herself) as unreal. Therefore, since only the perfectly exact descriptions of material parts comply with the Laplacian ideal of objective knowledge, solely these material parts—and those comprehensive phenomena which can be identified with them by reduction—can be regarded as real. This is the goal of the materialist project.

The claim that there are such comprehensive phenomena, which can be described exactly, and that these descriptions, due to the method of reduction, can be identified with the descriptions of fundamental material parts is perfectly acceptable from an emergentist point of view. Emergentism is a much more moderate ontological conviction than materialism. It does not assert that every comprehensive phenomenon is emergent compared to matter. Materialism claims that everything is material and thus has to be reduced to material parts. Emergentism only claims that there are both material and emergent phenomena.

Now, let's forget for a moment what we have seen so far and try to complete this project. How can someone identify material comprehensive phenomena *solely* by the one real, scientific knowledge of Laplace's demon? This question refers only to the epistemological side of the problem. A bright emerald, for example, is apparently a material object, but it is also a comprehensive, orderly whole; therefore, if we want to show *scientifically* that it is indeed material and not just naïvely believe that it is so, then we will have to reduce its description to the exact, scientific description of its parts. But if we cannot identify it solely on the basis of the ideal Laplacian knowledge, then we can*not* reduce it since, according to materialism, there is only one kind of true, objective, and scientific knowledge, while the tacit skills and personal knowledge of human beings are just false, subjective, and naïve beliefs, or, at most, practical experiences that should not play any role in real scientific knowing and the verification of scientific concepts and theories. Therefore, if someone is *consistent* with his materialist ontology and his ideal of objective knowledge, then personal knowledge *cannot play any role in the scientific method of reduction either.*

We have seen numerous times that the demon, according to Laplace's intention, can perfectly describe every fundamental material part in the universe by exact numeric parameters, but now, let us ponder how it could know from this and *only* this tremendous amount of explicit numerical data which one refers to the electron of a rock versus the electron of a tree? The exact data are like these:

1. $x_1=266,456,345$; $x_2=342,958,324$; $x_3=150,121,564$; $x_4=343,333,543$; $i=376,780$

2. $x_1=266,456,345$; $x_2=370,629,547$; $x_3=583,098,270$; $x_4=343,289,564$; $i=361,086$

3. $x_1=266,456,346$; $x_2=452,287,453$; $x_3=493,408,607$; $x_4=374,432,128$; $i=889,301$

4. $x_1=266,456,346$; $x_2=271,560,288$; $x_3=390,487,078$; $x_4=373,845,548$; $i=901,564$

5. $x_1=266,456,346$; $x_2=292,282,924$; $x_3=180,739,223$; $x_4=374,459,441$; $i=900,031$

6. $x_1=266,456,347$; $x_2=564,294,403$; $x_3=110,317,066$; $x_4=377,572,463$; $i=880,037$

7. ...

Does $x_1=266,456,345$; $x_2=342,958,324$; $x_3=150,121,564$; $x_4=343,333,543$; $i=376,780$ or $x_1=266,456,345$; $x_2=370,629,547$; $x_3=583,098,270$; $x_4=343,289,564$; $i=361,086$ refer to the electron of a rock? While you can ponder on these numbers until the end of time, you still will never know the answer because without the comprehensive concept of the rock and the personal experiences of the given rock as a comprehensive phenomenon, this question simply can*not* be answered. It also means that the concept and knowledge of the rock cannot be constructed from solely the knowledge of the exact parameters of the parts. Rocks (and any other material or emergent comprehensive phenomena) can be recognized and such concepts can be constructed *solely by natural human skills, senses, and personal knowledge.* The demon, by definition, does not possess this kind of knowledge. In Polanyi's words: "This ideal of universal knowledge is mistaken since it substitutes for the subjects in which we are interested a set of data which tell us nothing that we want to know."[8]

8. Polanyi, *Personal Knowledge*, 140.

So, if a self-proclaimed materialist were consistent (at least to a minimum degree) and he did indeed only use such ideal Laplacian knowledge that complies with the perfect and exact description of the material world during his scientific work, then he would never reduce anything—that is, *he would never scientifically prove about anything that it is indeed material in nature.*

The fact that they are not at all consistent means that they *substitute* their personal knowledge of comprehensive wholes in the place of the Laplacian knowledge *unnoticed*, then pretend as if they could ignore their natural tacit skills and personal knowledge, solving the problem solely on the basis of exact and perfectly explicit Laplacian knowledge. In the case of a rock, this means that they successfully reduce the higher-level description of the rock to the lower-level, exact, and numerical parameters of its fundamental material parts but "forget" the fact that they first identified the rock by their own natural human skills and senses (and cached it by their own hands). It is solely due to this knowledge that they even have any concept about rocks as comprehensive, orderly wholes in the first place. Therefore, natural tacit skills and personal knowledge are the *preconditions* of any exact and objective Laplacian knowledge. The evolution of human knowledge did not start with nuclear physics:

> The tremendous intellectual feat conjured up by Laplace's imagination has diverted attention (in a manner commonly practiced by conjurers) from the decisive sleight of hand by which he substitutes a knowledge of all experience for a knowledge of all atomic data. Once you refuse this deceptive substitution, you immediately see that the Laplacean mind understands precisely nothing and that whatever it knows means precisely nothing.[9]

A Laplacian Fault or deceptive substitution is a kind of magic trick *by which exact, perfectly explicit data and formulas get into the places of tacit experiences and concepts* (which are, in fact, based on personal knowledge), but we pretend as if the two kinds of knowledge perfectly correspond to each other. In consequence, there is no need for tacit skills and personal knowledge for real scientific knowledge, and our knowledge could be separated into two distinct, contradictory parts due to the objective versus subjective dichotomy.

When Polanyi introduced the concept of deceptive substitutions in the first chapter of his *Personal Knowledge*, his more detailed example for the concept was the *principle of simplicity*, in which a scientific theory is preferred in contrast to another one. According to Polanyi, however, the real

---

9. Polanyi, *Personal Knowledge*, 141.

meaning of simplicity cannot be defined and understood by explicit, objective criteria (as we like to pretend) if we do not also refer to the concealed *rationality of reality* behind the theories which, in fact, guides our choice and cannot be specified objectively. The theory of relativity and quantum mechanics will not be simple at the exact and objective level of their mathematics at all if we do not tacitly refer to their implicit, scientific rationality and philosophical meaning concerning reality.[10]

Perhaps it is worth mentioning that Polanyi introduces the notion of personal knowledge in explicit form through the concept of deceptive substitutions when he speaks about simplicity in the case of Albert Einstein's theory of relativity. He emphasizes that *scientific beauty* was mentioned by Einstein's followers several times as the reason why they chose Einstein's special relativity over H. Lorentz's dynamic ether theory (which complied with the experimental data as much as Einstein's one) or later, why they chose Einstein's general relativity over D. C. Miller's experimental results (when, of course, the latter also complied with the experimental data). According to him, the concept of beauty refers to that *inherent rationality of nature* which was revealed by Einstein's theory. This is exactly what we mean by using the term "scientific beauty." By using another term instead of it, however, we conceal this fact as though it were only about some incidental, aesthetic point; thus, we do not have to contradict the positivist dogma that there is no profound, inherent rationality in nature beyond the strict and exact data of fundamental material particles. But I will discuss the historical meaning of Copernicus's and Einstein's revolutions in detail at the beginning of the next chapter (3.2) and the philosophical meaning of the theory of relativity concerning the inherent rationality of nature in chapter 6.

Deceptive substitution is also when we acknowledge the fact that there is no real, objective viewpoint—as the Laplacian ideal of knowledge supposes it—and we still prefer one theory over another on the basis of, so to speak, which is "closer" or a major step "toward" the (non-existent) objective ideal. With this false openness, we are just flaunting our bright self-reflection to conceal that the basis of our scientific choices still remain the same absurd, objectivist ideal. It becomes absurd because we explicitly state that it is false and non-existent, yet we still follow it. Nonetheless, the real reason that this is also a deceptive substitution is that the real purpose of such scientific talk is to conceal the personal skills and intellectual passions by which we, in fact, make our scientific choices.

It is also a deceptive substitution when Laplace says that "the future, just like the past, would be present before its eyes," because, as we have seen

---

10. Polanyi, *Personal Knowledge*, 16.

in the previous subchapter, for the demon, there is neither future nor past—everything is at an infinite present, "before its eyes." Only Laplace himself knows from his natural experiences as a human person what time is, and he substitutes his personal knowledge in place of the demon's abstract, purely explicit knowledge to make sense to its knowledge.

From what we have seen in the first chapter, the case of neo-Darwinism is also a deceptive substitution. The neo-Darwinian theory is only the theory of change, but in their actual wording, they substitute the concept of evolution, thus concealing the truth before the public—and sometimes even before themselves. To substitute a logical possibility in the place of a real possibility of reality concerning the creation of life, as we have seen in the case of Dawkins's Boeing 747, is a deceptive substitution as well.

At first sight, perhaps these deceptive substitutions could be seen as white lies, but they are not. They conceal and sometimes even question the real tacit and personal fundaments of human knowledge and science. More importantly, they lead to the different forms of moral inversion which, in the context of society, had terrible consequences in the twentieth century. This problem will be discussed in chapter 12, after the detailed establishing of the concepts of emergence and evolution in Parts Two and Three.

I would like to finish this chapter with an explanation of a phrase that was used several times in this chapter. Perhaps everyone can recognize the meaning of this phrase with ease. In connection with it, I have said that, contrary to the materialism of the Laplacian ideal, the emergentist ontological claim is simple: we are what we seem to be—comprehensive, orderly wholes composed of matter. This whole book is about to reveal the most profound meaning of this simple fact.

The meaning of this "simple fact," however, is already highly problematic at the surface. Both a materialist and an emergentist can say that we are comprehensive, orderly wholes composed of matter, and in both cases, the claim seems to be true. But the only reason both of them can affirm this claim is that the explicit sentence—"we are comprehensive, orderly wholes composed of matter"—means nothing in itself. An explicit sentence becomes meaningful only by the tacit act of commitment based on our personal beliefs. I will discuss this in detail in subchapter 3.4. Someone can tacitly commit himself to something and thus affirm something based, of course, solely on his own personal beliefs. In the case of a committed materialist, this naturally means his *personal* materialist ontological conviction.

Therefore, if a materialist affirms this explicit sentence—"we are comprehensive, orderly wholes composed of matter"—he, in fact, means that *we are only a set of fundamental material parts and nothing more*. While an emergentist like Polanyi, for example, means that we are *more* than a set of fundamental material parts: *we are non-material, emergent wholes*. Based on the results of this chapter and to reveal one level of the complex meaning of this assertion, I should say that we are more than piles of spatially-arranged, fundamental material parts: we are emergent wholes, constructed by time, our evolutionary past, our present conditions and opportunities, and our future goals.

The committed materialist's conviction is based on a critical philosophy that, due to the subjective versus objective dichotomy, only regards that which complies with the Laplacian ideal of objective knowledge as knowledge—that is, exact, explicit, and formal or, in one word, *impersonal*. This approach leads to the rejection of the reality of personal knowledge and personal reality. Polanyi's conviction, on the other hand, is based on his post-critical philosophy that acknowledges the reality of personal knowledge and personal reality *by trust* because it recognizes that there is no consistent, critical method or objective knowledge of the Laplacian ideal. We have to trust our tacit senses, intellectual skills, passions, and natural beliefs; they are not just naïve, illusory superstitions, they are our evolutionary heritage.

2.6 Conclusion

At the beginning of the modern era, a conceptual dichotomy was formed that separated objective, scientific knowledge from any so-called subjective or personal beliefs. The ideal knower of objective scientific knowledge is a God-like being, outside space and time, who, according to a "single formula," calculates all past and future states of the universe from the perfectly exact data of the actual state of its fundamental material parts. This picture of perfect knowing (famously explicated by Laplace) is based on Newtonian mechanics, and if we leave out the God-like demon, it easily leads to the ontological concept of materialism because only the descriptions of fundamental material parts comply perfectly with this ideal, objective knowledge.

However, if we reconsider what the demon really knows, it will quickly turn out that it does not have any knowledge of comprehensive, orderly wholes at all—including machines, planets, frogs, and human beings—because it has no body, no tacit senses and skills, and no personal knowledge by which these kinds of comprehensive objects could be recognized. This materialist picture of the universe and this objectivist picture of knowledge are solely appealing to us because we are not consistent at all, unknowingly substituting our real, personal knowledge of the wholes in place of meaningless, explicit data. This invisible magic trick allows us to not have to face the real foundations of scientific and human knowledge.

It also means that we do not have to face our natural, personal beliefs, passions, and motivations, which are deeply rooted in our body and our evolutionary heritage. In consequence, for the sake of a false ideal, philosophy gradually loses its original aim and becomes a vacant albeit detailed analysis of the explicit surface (especially of language and arguments) or worse, it is distorted into moral inversion.

Personal knowledge is all about facing the real foundations of our scientific and cultural knowledge. Its main point is that there is no objective point of reference; we are not bodiless demons but rather human persons in a palpable body, and we can see and understand the universe only from our personal point of reference (center), based on our tacit bodily senses and skills. This fact of our personal reality, however, does not break the concept of truth and real scientific knowledge. Although the conceptual dichotomy of subjective versus objective is false, we have the natural, personal power to search for the truth and reach reality thanks to our billions of years of evolutionary heritage.

3

Personal Knowledge

3.1 Preface

Polanyi starts his train of thought in *Personal Knowledge* with a request to the reader: set aside all your beliefs and prior notions, no matter how natural they may seem to you, and imagine contrasting objectivity to subjectivity with perfect consistency. What is the meaning of this pure objective knowledge? How does the universe and human beings look from this pure objective point of view?

His answer is this: since pure objectivity cannot be biased at all, it cannot take into consideration any subjective viewpoints of human beings; therefore, from a consistent, objective point of view, every small, material part of the whole universe should be examined *in absolutely equal manner*. In this case, human beings would not get any time for scientific inquiry because the Solar System and the Earth are only tiny parts of the Milky Way among billions of other stars and planets. Of course, the Milky Way is also just one galaxy among billions of others.[1]

It does not matter how much scientists talk about the need for consistent objectivity, it is clear that there is no such scientist in the world who could and would want to contemplate the universe in this manner. In that case, neither the Earth nor another person could appear in scientific knowledge as a particular, exciting thing or being. We pay attention to specific things and creatures *only because of our so-called subjective, anthropocentric point of view*. Therefore, the pursuit of pure objectivity in science is unfounded because it ignores the real workings of human knowing, which is rooted in our natural, evolutionary interest toward the particular things and beings of our own environment.

---

1. Polanyi, *Personal Knowledge*, 3.

Polanyi, of course, speaks about the viewpoint of Laplace's demon and its absurd nature (2.3). But if the Laplacian ideal of objective knowledge is false, then the question inevitably will arise: what is the real nature of scientific knowledge? And what is the real meaning when scientists talk about objectivity—what they are hiding?

> The purpose of this book is to show that complete objectivity, as usually attributed to the exact sciences, is a delusion and is, in fact, a false ideal. But I shall not try to repudiate strict objectivity as an ideal without offering a substitute, which I believe to be more worthy of intelligent allegiance; this I have called 'personal knowledge.'[2]

3.2 The Tacit Roots of Scientific Discovery

Polanyi shows the real meaning of objectivity with the example of the Copernican revolution. According to the modern understanding of science, the previous medieval, Aristotelian/Ptolemaic, and Earth-centric worldview—which was a religious, superstitious, and anthropocentric subjectivism—was superseded by the Sun-centric worldview of modern, objective science. Thus, science transcended the narrow point of view of man and his subjective, illusory impression that the Earth is standing still under his feet. By pure scientific rationality, it was revealed that the Earth revolves around the Sun (with huge velocity) and not vice versa. Man lost his place at the center of the universe and became one of the many incidental existents at the edge of the world.[3]

The Copernican view of the universe, however, is just as far away from a pure, consistent objectivist viewpoint as the Aristotelian/Ptolemaic one. As much as the Earth is not the center of the universe, neither is the Sun—both of them are insignificant specks of dust in the vast universe. The great, scientific step of Copernicus does not go toward this direction but rather toward a *more abstract* personal knowledge.

> In a literal sense, therefore, the new Copernican system was as anthropocentric as the Ptolemaic view, the difference being merely that it preferred to satisfy a different human affection.[4]

---

2. Polanyi, *Personal Knowledge*, 18.
3. Polanyi, *Personal Knowledge*, 3.
4. Polanyi, *Personal Knowledge*, 4.

Copernicus chose the new Sun-centric view not because he wanted to occupy a more pure, consistent, and objective stance, but rather because he preferred the *theoretic* Sun-perspective over our natural *experience* that the Earth steadily and immovably stands under our feet. Copernicus *had no empirical evidence at all* on the side of his theory—as a matter of fact, the apparent empirical evidence supported the old, Aristotelian view—but he still committed himself to the Sun-centric view because it provided him deeper *intellectual enjoyment* than the old, earthbound one. Nonetheless, in a sense, it can be stated that the Copernican view is more objective than the previous Aristotelian one; not on the basis of pure objectivism but rather because it was a step toward a "more ambitious anthropocentrism."[5]

> It becomes legitimate to regard the Copernican system as more objective than the Ptolemaic only if we accept this very shift in the nature of intellectual satisfaction as the criterion of greater objectivity.[6]

It is important to note that the basis of this new, Polanyian sense of objectivity is such personal aspiration—an *intellectual enjoyment* or *passion* based on the scientist's intellectual skills (3.3)—which, according to modern understandings of science, is subjective and thus has to be rejected. For Polanyi, however, these intellectual passions and skills cannot be subjective; otherwise, they would not be able to lead to more objective scientific theories—not even in a weaker sense. At this point, however, Polanyi's goal is only to establish that although there is no ideal knowledge (in the sense of pure, consistent objectivity), the selection of the Copernican theory did not happen randomly or solely by subjective factors:

> [The Copernican theory's] excellence is not a matter of personal taste on our part but an inherent quality deserving universal acceptance by rational creatures. We abandon the cruder anthropocentrism of our senses—but only in favor of a more ambitious anthropocentrism of our reason.[7]

According to Polanyi's example, if we abandon our commitment that the Earth is at the center of the universe—which is based on our natural experience of the Earth, standing still underneath our feet—then we can get a Copernican theory that is not only satisfactory for us but also for every other possible intellectual beings in the Solar system (that is, of course, if they also abandon their previous commitments, based on their natural

---

5. Polanyi, *Personal Knowledge*, 5.
6. Polanyi, *Personal Knowledge*, 4.
7. Polanyi, *Personal Knowledge*, 4–5.

experiences, that Venus, Mars, etc., is standing still underneath their feet): "Since [Copernicus's] picture of the solar system disregards our terrestrial location, it equally commends itself to the inhabitants of Earth, Mars, Venus, or Neptune, provided they share our intellectual values."[8]

We can acknowledge that the Copernican theory is better, more rational, and more objective than the previous, geocentric one, but we also have to deny that this bright, scientific achievement is the consequence of the objectivism of modern science or was based on the critical scientific method and strong empirical evidence. If this is true, however, then a question will inevitably arise: if the Copernican theory has nothing to do with pure objectivity and the empirical observations of that time, then how can—and, for that matter, *should*—it be regarded as a much better theory than the previous one?

The answer is this: due to its *inherent rationality*, the new Copernican theory can make contact with reality in new ways that become apparent for the scientific community by newer manifestations of reality. In this case, it means Kepler's, Galilei's, and Newton's additional concepts and theories and those new empirical observations which only became possible by the new approach of Copernicus. The Copernican vision of reality was verified by these additional theories and empirical observations *way after* Copernicus's death in the seventeenth century:

> We accept [the given theory] in the hope of making contact with reality; so that, being really true, our theory may yet show forth its truth through future centuries in ways undreamed of by its authors.... In this wholly indeterminate scope of its true implications lies the deepest sense in which objectivity is attributed to a scientific theory.[9]

Although Polanyi's concept of personal knowledge breaks with the objectivism of modern science, and later, it was proven by new discoveries that, for example, the Sun is not the center of the universe and the planets do not move in circular orbits at all, he can still claim that the Copernican theory is true and more objective than the false, Aristotelian one. These latter facts concerning the discoveries after Copernicus's death are the reason that objectivism cannot be consistent; otherwise, it should reject that the Copernican theory was a scientific development toward objective truth.

We will see later that this is exactly the consistent conclusion that has been drawn from the detailed, critical analysis of the history of science by relativists in the second half of the twentieth century. In this sense, relativism

---

8. Polanyi, *Personal Knowledge*, 4.
9. Polanyi, *Personal Knowledge*, 5.

is but a more consistent, critical approach (11.3). It does not reform science and does not propose a new concept of objectivity (and, thus, of the truth); rather, it merely questions the fundamental beliefs and values of science.

Due to his new concept of personal knowledge, Polanyi, however, can hold the fundamental beliefs and values of science consistently. For him, the sign of truth is not that a theory complies perfectly with actual empirical observations and a pure, objective ideal but rather that it makes contact with reality in new ways that allow for further discoveries and additional theories—as we can see from the history and development of science. Science has the power "to make contact with reality in nature by recognizing what is rational in nature."[10]

It follows, according to Polanyi, as we have already seen, that pure, consistent objectivism *entails materialism* (2.3). If objectivism wants to reject the belief that humans, their personal point of views, their peculiar intellectual skills, and their passions are unique and fundamental to scientific knowing, then it will also have to deny that human beings are different compared to other matter in an ontological sense. Thus, human beings are pure material objects, just as any other part of the universe (e.g., interstellar gas).

According to Polanyi, however, materialism is contradictory because it presupposes a knower who is able to access pure, objective knowing but also consequently can*not* be material; otherwise, he would be like any other human being, only able to observe the universe from his specific point of view (center), anchored in his material body (2.3). So, besides objectivism, Polanyi also rejects materialism. For him, reality is something more, something hidden, which cannot be specified perfectly at a given moment but instead will emerge and be revealed gradually, for example, with the help of scientific theories. The knowing (and rational) person is an integral part of reality. For him, the goal of science (and philosophy) is not only to observe and describe reality in the most exact way but to understand it more and more deeply—which means the exploration and explanation of hidden rationality in nature. Thus, according to Polanyi, reality has both *material* and *rational* manifestations.

From this point of view, Polanyi claims that there are only two major traditions in science concerning the inherent rationality of nature in opposition to each other: the *Pythagorean* and *Democritian* ones.[11] The former initially presupposed that numbers are a part of nature, thus, there is necessarily some kind of rationality hiding in reality, while the latter emphasized the material aspects of reality. To differentiate between these major tradi-

---

10. Polanyi, *Personal Knowledge*, 6.
11. Polanyi, *Personal Knowledge*, 6.

tions, Polanyi's asks whether the given tradition acknowledged that there is inherent rationality in nature or not. The otherwise fundamental question regarding the exact nature of this hidden rationality due to a particular minor tradition plays no role in this differentiation. Contrary to this, the usual categories of the history of philosophy for different philosophical traditions are based on particular ontological and methodological differentiations among these traditions.

According to Pythagoras and his followers, reality itself is nothing but numbers. Plato called himself a Pythagorean in the sense that he acknowledged that reality itself was composed of hidden rational entities, but he regarded these entities not as natural numbers but rather as Ideas, composing a different, purely rational world. Aristotle changed Plato's theory only to the extent that, according to him, there are not two distinct worlds; rather, the hidden, inherent, and rational Forms are, in fact, in the things themselves, and these two—matter and Forms—compose all earthly objects. Since Polanyi also claims that there is a hidden, inherent rationality in nature, he is part of the Pythagorean tradition as well. In his view, however, this intrinsic rationally cannot be identified with numbers or Ideas but rather dynamic, emergent principles and comprehensive, orderly wholes, according to the emergentist tradition.

The mechanical worldview of Descartes and Newton, which became dominant in modern science, is primarily based on the Democritian tradition. According to this worldview, numbers and mathematics are no longer inherent parts of nature but rational (intellectual) tools, the use of which, in turn, remains fundamental for science. Therefore, for this scientific approach, reality is nothing more than the totality of incidental, material objects. These objects, however, are located in an explicit, absolute, and purely theoretical *space-time* that entirely complies with Euclidian geometry. Consequently, the scientific understanding of this space-time and the laws which determine the motion of material objects in its abstract framework *are necessarily based on* the rational tools of numbers and mathematics. It means that although rationality itself is no longer an inherent part of nature, by the intellectual powers of scientists, it still has a pivotal role in science to treat the absolute, Euclidian *background* of nature.

The discovery of non-Euclidian geometrics in the nineteenth century, however, led to the rejection of the reality of mathematics: mathematical propositions became simple, contentless assertions (tautologies). For many mathematicians and scientists, it meant that there is no true geometry of reality; the different geometries are only human creations, based on arbitrarily chosen axioms. It was the first time in the history of human thought when the hidden, inherent rationality of nature was consistently denied, so the Democritian tradition was held in a pure form.

In consequence, a new *positivist* school, led by Ernst Mach, was formed in Wien, rejecting every scientific assertion that concerned any kind of rationality in nature. According to them, scientific theories are only useful, exact summaries of scientific experiences. Mach's critique of Newton's theory of space-time clearly impacted Einstein, and his positivist concepts of science also significantly influenced Niels Bohr and the development of the Copenhagen interpretation of quantum mechanics. In philosophy, Mach can be regarded as the predecessor of the Vienna Circle and the logical positivists (the third wave of positivism). The last remnants of the Pythagorean tradition also vanished.

In Mach's view, Newton's theory of absolute space-time, based on Euclidian geometrics, is a meaningless, silly metaphysics that must be expelled from science. It has nothing to do with real, observable phenomena and its foundation is merely an arbitrary system of geometrical axioms and theorems which have no real contact with reality. Real scientific theories have to be grounded on exact, experimental data. According to the positivist interpretation of the history of science, Einstein did nothing with his theory of relativity but answer the negative outcome of the Michelson-Morley experiments, which could not detect the movements of Earth in contrast to the ether.

Polanyi, however, shows that this is not the case at all. He even asks Einstein himself, who acknowledges that the Michelson-Morley experiments had little importance in the discovery of relativity theory. Instead, his thinking was led by different *intuitive speculations* concerning the nature of light—for example, how the universe would look like from the perspective of a light beam if someone could ride it, that is, *not from an* objective point of view.[12]

Albert Michelson and Edward Morley performed their famous experiment in 1887. It was later repeated by Morley and D. C. Miller with more precise instruments. Originally, the investigation aimed to define the velocity of Earth compared to the ether that fills up Newtonian space-time. At that time, light was considered a wave that spreads through the absolutely motionless ether. According to this concept, since the Earth is orbiting the Sun and, thus, not at rest, if the velocity of light can be measured in perpendicular dimensions, the results would have to be different compared to the Earth due to its revolving motion in the absolutely motionless ether. However, the results were significantly less than they were expected.

---

12. Polanyi, *Personal Knowledge*, 10.

It is interpreted by the traditional history of science that this led to the rejection of the concept of ether and Einstein's theory of special relativity (according to which the speed of light is absolute and the motions of other objects are relative; therefore, the results of the Michelson-Morley experiment would have to be the same in every dimension). The situation was much more complicated, however, because Hendrik Lorentz's dynamical ether theory explained the results of the experiment just as precisely as Einstein's theory of special relativity did—that is, the rejection of the concept of ether was not only based on the experimental results. Furthermore, it happened despite the fact that it led to numerous theoretical problems. For example, according to Einstein, light is both particle and wave at the same time—a definite conceptual contradiction—and light is such a wave that it has no medium in which it could spread through, another serious, conceptual problem.

Moreover, the experimental results, which were repeated primarily by D. C. Miller over 100,000 times during the next three decades, did not show that the Earth was motionless compared to ether (that is, that the speed of light is an absolute constant) but rather that the speed-difference was significantly smaller than it should have been due to the revolving motion of the Earth around the Sun. Therefore, the results of the experiment, in fact, did not verify Einstein's concept that the speed of light is the same in every inertial frame of reference. The results of D. C. Miller's experiments, however, as Polanyi emphasizes, were ignored by the scientific community without any well-established explanation, regarded as simple measurement errors.

The situation is highly similar to that of the Copernican theory. The old Aristotelian/Ptolemaic theory could explain the observed movements of the planets just as Lorentz's dynamical ether theory could explain the results of the Michelson-Morley experiment. And as Einstein's theory led to some serious conceptual problems concerning the nature of light, the Copernican theory could not explain the reason for the movement of the planets—contrary to the Aristotelian theory, which could. The scientific community still chose the Copernican theory and then the Einsteinian one. This is the reason that Polanyi says that Einstein's followers accepted the theory of relativity not because of any objective experimental evidence but rather because of the *intellectual beauty* and *rationality* of the theory (2.5).[13] That is, due to the new—and, at that point, hidden—manifestations of reality which, on the one hand, would solve the conceptual problems and, on the other, would confirm the original theory, they thought that the Einsteinian theory would lead to further theories and new empirical observations

---

13. Polanyi, *Personal Knowledge*, 14.

According to Polanyi, Einstein did not show that Newton's concept of space-time is meaningless because it is based on arbitrarily-chosen Euclidian geometry instead of observable scientific data (as Mach thought); rather, Einstein showed that the Newtonian concept is *false*. He did this *by intuitively grasping a deeper meaning of rationality in nature*. Newton's theory of space-time is, in fact, based not only on Euclidian geometrics but also *on the nature of ordinary human experience*, according to which objects are always observed before a strict material background. This material background was abstracted by Newton as an absolute, Euclidian framework of space-time behind the material objects of reality (6.2).

Einstein, however, supposed that in the case of the whole, material world, there is no such background, theorized from natural human experience, in which fundamental material objects can appear (e.g., light in the ether). It means that Einstein supposed—at least tacitly—that on a cosmic scale, where the question of the movement of light was concerned, ordinary human experience (which was adapted to earthly conditions, of course) should have been ignored *just as Copernicus supposed* that regarding the real, cosmic movement of the planets, the ordinary, earthly, human experience of the Earth as standing still under our feet should have been ignored. Instead, Einstein based his intuitive approach *on a more profound rationality of nature*.

Einstein started to use non-Euclidian mathematics in physics to describe the changes in time and space generated by material objects which, according to Polanyi, in contrast to the positivist view, was a significant step toward the Pythagorean tradition. With this step, Einstein corrected two errors: the first is that the followers of Newton still tried to understand the deeper rationality hidden in nature through a Euclidian geometrics firmly based on ordinary human experiences, and the second is that the positivist followers of Mach tried to fix this mistake by rejecting all kinds of rationality in nature.[14]

We will see in chapter 6, however, that although Einstein could grasp a deeper meaning of reality concerning the nature of space and time intuitively, because of the strong positivist influence of his time and the fact that he was concentrating on the exact mathematical formulation of his theory, he could never really explicate this deeper meaning of reality or the real consequences of his fantastic vision. He died lonely, still trying to reach this goal against the whole scientific community, ruled by positivism.

I think it is worth mentioning that Polanyi cites Kepler in detail to show how visible his mystical and passionate commitment to a Sun-centric

---

14. Polanyi, *Personal Knowledge*, 16.

worldview is, which, in contrast to the positivist picture of science, perfectly complies with the true nature of scientific discovery (11.5). Polanyi's quotations come from Kepler's *Harmonices Mundi*, that is, *The Harmony of the World* (Book V, chapter 10, and Preface):

> Of what sort vision is in the sun, what are its eyes, or what other impulse it has . . . even without eyes . . . for judging the harmonies of the (celestial) motions . . . for those inhabiting the earth; not easy to conjecture . . . in the sun there dwells an intellect simple, intellectual fire or mind, whatever it may be, the fountain of all harmony.
>
> What I prophesied two-and-twenty years ago, as soon as I discovered the five solids among the heavenly orbits—what I firmly believed long before I had seen Ptolemy's Harmonics—what I had promised my friends in the title of this fifth book, which I named before I was sure of my discovery—what sixteen years ago I urged to be sought—that for which I have devoted the best part of my life to astronomical contemplations, for which I joined Tycho Brahe . . . at last I have brought it to light, and recognized its truth beyond all my hopes. . . . So now since eighteen months ago the dawn, three months ago the proper light of day, and indeed a very few days ago the pure Sun itself of the most marvelous contemplation has shone forth—nothing holds me; I will indulge my sacred fury; I will taunt mankind with the candid confession that I have stolen the golden vases of the Egyptians, in order to build of them a tabernacle to my God, far indeed from the bounds of Egypt. If you forgive me, I shall rejoice; if you are angry, I shall bear it: the dice is cast, the book is written, whether to be read now or by posterity I care not; it may wait a hundred years for its reader, if God himself has waited six thousand years for a man to contemplate His work."[15]

Polanyi notes that Kepler "even went so far as to write down the tune of each planet in musical notation."[16]

3.3 The Tacit Roots of Personal Knowledge

Polanyi draws attention to the unspecified parts of skills through the detailed examination of the structure and inner workings of them. He regards these skills (e.g., swimming, cycling, playing the piano, various crafts, cotton

---

15. Polanyi, *Personal Knowledge*, 7.
16. Polanyi, *Personal Knowledge*, 7.

spinning, and the use of industrial equipment) and scientific knowing as the same concerning unspecifiability. So according to his intention, cycling—his most well-known example of tacit knowledge—is not just an example of the workings of practical skills but also that of the intellectual and scientific:

> Science is operated by the skill of the scientist, and it is through the exercise of his skill that he shapes his scientific knowledge. We may grasp, therefore, the nature of the scientist's personal participation by examining the structure of skills.[17]

Human skills are guided by different *rules*. For example, if someone wants to swim, he will have to learn the appropriate technique of respiration and keep more air in his lungs during swimming than usual. If someone wants to ride a bicycle, he will have to learn how to turn the handlebar with small, careful movements in the direction he starts to fall in order to regain his balance. These principles are not generally known and, in themselves, they have no significance at all. They become meaningful merely during the performance of a skill. Polanyi's detailed examples are swimming, cycling, and playing the piano.[18]

Of course, it is possible to describe how a falling cyclist regains his balance with exact, mechanical equations. This might even have significant scientific value, but during cycling, it has no use. Nobody can ride a bicycle by calculating such mechanical equations in his mind. On the contrary, if these complicated equations divert our attention, we will inevitably fall. In the same sense, if the pianist turns his attention to the depression of keys and does not pay attention to the piece as a comprehensive phenomenon, then his performance will fall apart. If we start to concentrate on the pronunciation of particular sounds, we quickly lose the meaning of a given word. Say the same word—for example, "cabbage"—again and again, concentrating on its particular sounds; at the end, the word will mean nothing and its meaning will disintegrate into pieces.

The reason for this phenomenon is that our attention has only *one focus*. The artist is still aware of several different things, however, because awareness also has *multiple scopes*. According to this fact, Polanyi differentiates between two kinds of awareness: *focal* and *subsidiary*. The two awarenesses are mutually exclusive—that is, one pays attention to something either focally or subsidiary.[19]

---

17. Polanyi, *Personal Knowledge*, 49.
18. Polanyi, *Personal Knowledge*, 49–51.
19. Polanyi, *Personal Knowledge*, 55.

During the act of a skill, the comprehensive act itself is the focus of our attention (focal awareness): the cycling, the swimming, the playing of a piece, the pronouncing of a word, etc., itself. At the same time, one is aware of every tool, tangible part, and rule through which the act is accomplished as a comprehensive whole (subsidiary awareness). He does not pay attention to these parts directly; rather, he is aware of the bicycle as a tool, his muscular movements as tangible parts, and the rules of keeping more air in his lungs, how to regain his balance, etc. subsidiarily.

Contrary to the rules of an act, the other subsidiary parts and tools can be specified relatively well by turning the focus of our attention on them. As we have seen, however, then the original act itself will stop and a new, *knowing* act will start. If someone does not know an act of skill as a comprehensive whole, he will never be able to learn that skill through the detailed analysis of its parts—no one learns to ride a bicycle from a mechanical textbook but rather by continuous practice as a child in the garden. According to Polanyi, this fact is the reason that an act logically cannot be specified by its parts. The learning of an act is a *tacit, practical* process.[20]

Since the nature of the process by which a focal, comprehensive whole is formed from the subsidiary parts is tacit, Polanyi calls this *tacit integration*. Accordingly, the structure of skills can be depicted as follows:

subsidiary parts → tacit integration → focal whole

This integration cannot be specified by formal logic since formal logic creates explicit, deductive relations among focal parts, whereas during a comprehensive act, one is only aware of the parts subsidiarily:

> This difference between a deduction and an integration lies in the fact that deduction connects two focal items, the premises and consequents, while integration makes subsidiary bear on focus.[21]

This is the reason that comprehensive, orderly wholes cannot be deduced from focally explicated parts. Moreover, as we have seen, destructive analyses based on formal logic and explicitly specified parts tear any comprehensive act into pieces. Therefore, this integrating processes has a necessarily *tacit nature* because one is only aware of the parts subsidiarily and has to integrate his comprehensive act *tacitly*.

The difference between deductive inference and tacit integration is the following:

20. Polanyi, *Personal Knowledge*, 56.
21. Polanyi, "Logic and Psychology," 32.

subsidiary parts → tacit integration → focal whole → goal

focal part(s) → explicit deduction → focal part(s)

Tacit integration is an *irreversible* process. This means that during the process, something new comes into being that cannot be specified by its parts. Contrarily, an explicit deduction is a *reversible* process, where the premises are also the logical consequence of the conclusions. It follows that tacit integration complies with the nature of time, while explicit deduction complies with that of space (6.2). There are several other methods in science that, according to the Laplacian ideal, follow the logic of the latter. Polanyi emphasizes the role of destructive analyses. Destructive analysis, according to Polanyi, is a method of knowing which tries to understand and explain the meaning and workings of a given phenomenon or act by the detailed examination of its focal parts. Therefore, the point of this method is that it is focusing on the parts and tears down the given phenomenon or act into the smallest possible pieces.[22]

Polanyi asserts that this method is essential in science. On the one hand, it is useful to demonstrate the falsehood of certain phenomena, skills, and methods (e.g., homeopathy), and on the other, the detailed knowledge of the parts could deepen our understanding of the given phenomenon and strengthen the given skill. At the same time, he draws attention to the dangers of this method because an excessive belief in it could quickly lead to the false concept that everything can be deduced from its material parts—which, according to Polanyi, is a total misunderstanding of the real workings of science. And if a new scientific skill (for example, mesmerism [2.5]) is conceptually misunderstood by its discoverers, then the systematic demonstration of these conceptual contradictions in the explanation of the new skill can even lead to the rejection of the skill itself, despite the fact that it is working perfectly.

On this ground, Polanyi differentiates between *personal* and *objective* facts. All knowledge referring to a comprehensive, orderly object or a meaningful act is a personal fact. This means that, for example, the recognition that someone is riding a bicycle is a personal fact because it does not refer to subsidiary, exactly specifiable, tangible parts but rather to an integrated, comprehensive act. Then, through destructive analysis, it can be decomposed into such tangible (or even material) parts, which, according to their relatively more objective nature, can be called objective facts (e.g., the concrete muscular and neurological movements of the body during cycling). It follows, on the one hand, that personal facts are the preconditions of

---

22. Polanyi, *Personal Knowledge*, 51.

destructive analyses and more objective facts, and, on the other, that there are no entirely objective facts: even the elementary particles of quantum mechanics do not seem to be altogether specifiable.[23]

Polanyi determines tools not by their structural parts and material compositions but rather by their roles in human acts—that is, what their positions are in the tacit structure of human skills: subsidiary parts → tacit integration → focal whole. It connects the concepts of body and tool in a fundamental way: "Our appreciation of the externality of objects lying outside our body, in contrast to parts of our own body, relies on our subsidiary awareness of processes within our body."[24] According to him, an external object is what is focally observed and localized during a knowing act. If something is not seen in this way, then it will not be considered an object; nonetheless, it could still be entirely real and play an important, subsidiary role in an act (for example, as a tool).

A person's body observed focally is also an object. No one usually considers his body in this way, however, and we are aware of it *only subsidiarily*. This means that a person's body is normally used as an *internal tool* to reach different goals—that is, from this point of view, it is used exactly as any other *external tool*, for example, a hammer to get the nail into the wall:

> Our subsidiary awareness of tools and probes can be regarded now as the act of making them form a part of our own body. . . . While we rely on a tool or a probe, these are not handled as external objects. . . . We pour ourselves out into them and assimilate them as parts of our own existence. We accept them existentially by dwelling in them.[25]

The phenomenon Polanyi speaks about is called "embodiment" or "extended cognition" in the philosophical literature. It means that the mind extends into the body and even *beyond* it, into external objects, in a sense that the mind, contrary to the traditional Cartesian concept, is not another extensionless substance (as the body is an extended material substance) but rather works in the body, by the body, and can even expand beyond the boundaries of the body. It follows that the mind cannot be identified with the body, as materialism holds (which, in fact, means that mind does not exist). By his concepts of focal and subsidiary awareness, Polanyi gives a new interpretation to the phenomenon of embodiment. The concept of subsidiary awareness allows a new explanation for how different bodily or

---

23. Polanyi, *Personal Knowledge*, 63.
24. Polanyi, *Personal Knowledge*, 59.
25. Polanyi, *Personal Knowledge*, 59.

external parts become parts of the mind while they still keep their own nature, as focal objects.

So our body is just as much a tool as a hammer, except that it cannot be thrown away—although there are such psychotic patients who feel another way and sometimes even try to get rid of certain body parts. This is the case when somebody is alienated from his own body—not just during a focal knowing act *but also in a subsidiary way*: he does not feel that one of his body parts is an integrated part of his person anymore.

Normally, we also learn to use our body as a subsidiary, internal tool. Learning to use those muscles and joints of which perhaps we are not at all focally aware is an essential part of child development. Later, however, during a yoga course, for example, we can learn more about the many different muscles and joints in our body, and by a focal analysis, we can deepen our knowledge of our body. Through the gradual practice of this knowledge, that is, by the extension of our subsidiary awareness of our body, we acquire new bodily skills.

Perhaps it is worth noting that if we could get rid of all our external tools (that is, all houses, dresses, machines, etc.) that would also mean the end of our life. During the last few millions of years, our external tools have become just as integral a part of our life as our internal tools—that is, our body and our language (10.7).

Human beings, of course, have not only hammer-like, tangible tools but intellectual tools as well, which play a fundamental role in scientific skills and knowing:

> Hammers and probes can be replaced by intellectual tools; think of any interpretative framework and particularly of the formalism of the exact sciences.[26]

Someone is aware of words during an act (e.g., a talk) in precisely the same way that they are aware of a hammer when they hit a nail into the wall—that is, subsidiarily. Of course, words are useful for other things, like getting informed or getting in touch with others, but the way in which we use them is exactly the same as tools. Since scientific knowing is mainly based on human languages and their conceptual categories, such presumptions are, in reality, just as important for science as any particular scientific method or theory:

> Our language includes the numerals and the elements of geometry, and it refers in these terms to laws of nature whence we can

---

26. Polanyi, *Personal Knowledge*, 59.

pass on to the roots of these laws in scientific observations and experiments.[27]

Like the tool, the sign or the symbol can be conceived as such only in the eyes of a person who relies on them to achieve or to signify something.[28]

According to what we have seen so far, the following categories can be given for tools:

	Internal	External
Tangible	body	artificial tools
Intellectual	spoken language	written language

Table 1: Tangible and intellectual tools.

Written language cannot be classified as its own category since every tool of written language is also an external, artificial tool and, of course, every written language is—at least partially—a spoken language, too. Furthermore, it is important to note that, in a sense, every spoken language is an extended version of bodily signs—that is, unarticulated voices and body language (10.7)—in the same way that artificial tools were initially made to be a direct extension of the human body. This means that ultimately every highly explicit and sophisticated scientific method or practice is *based on deep bodily skills, sensibilities, and passions*. In the twentieth century, human technology and scientific knowledge has allowed the connecting of spoken languages with artificial tools and the organized installations of artificial tools in the human body.

To use an intellectual tool successfully, one has to *trust* that it is just as capable to do its task as he believes that a hammer is capable of getting a nail into the wall. If he thinks that the given tool or concept is not capable of doing the task or solving the problem in question, then he will simply not use them. Trust is necessary because during the act, the tool is in the subsidiary position of awareness. It is just as tiny a part of the comprehensive human act as any part of the body—that is, the acting person is not aware of it focally. Without trust, the (tangible or intellectual) tool is merely an alien object, and if someone pays attention to it focally, it can become an object

---

27. Polanyi, *Personal Knowledge*, 59.
28. Polanyi, *Personal Knowledge*, 61.

of critical examination. It is the primary precondition of the critical method and destructive analysis that one has to back away a few steps and examine the object focally *without trust*.

Therefore, language, as an internal intellectual tool, has to be trusted. If someone uses language, they cannot doubt it; rather, they *must accept it without criticism*. It means, according to Polanyi, the assimilation of the conceptual and explanatory framework of that language. Intellectual tools can only be used as tools by trust and without criticism in a subsidiary position of awareness.

It follows, according to Polanyi:

> The supposed pre-suppositions of science are so futile because the actual foundations of our scientific beliefs cannot be asserted at all. When we accept a certain set of pre-suppositions and use them as our interpretative framework, we may be said to dwell in them as we do in our own body. Their uncritical acceptance for the time being consists in a process of assimilation by which we identify ourselves with them. They are not asserted and cannot be asserted, for assertion can be made only within a framework with which we have identified ourselves for the time being; as they are themselves our ultimate framework, they are essentially inarticulable.[29]

That is, the real foundations of scientific beliefs and theories cannot be asserted because a conceptual and explanatory framework, in which any assertion can be made, is a necessary precondition of any assertion, and these foundations are the preconditions of any such framework. Consequently, the real foundations of scientific beliefs and theories are such inarticulate—that is, tacit—intellectual tools which were accepted uncritically and were internalized and embodied in a subsidiary position of awareness. It does not mean, however, that we cannot talk about them, but if someone partly explicated them during a critical examination after he had backed away a few steps, he would not find them convincing at all. The reason for this is that during a critical examination, as we have seen, according to the nature of any critical examination, he has to make them external, in a focal position of awareness, so he has to alienate himself from them. The real foundations of scientific beliefs and theories, however, gain their meaning only in practice, in a subsidiary position of awareness, just as any other rules for acts of human skills.[30]

---

29. Polanyi, *Personal Knowledge*, 60.
30. Polanyi, *Personal Knowledge*, 61.

Polanyi regards the acting person as a kind of *center* (2.3). This center is the focus point of that being who, during his acts and by his subsidiary awareness, assimilates and controls his (tangible and intellectual) tools, the different rules of the act, and the material parts and conditions which are necessary for his acts. Without these, the focal, personal center is powerless. So, a person is not a tangible object but rather a comprehensive, emergent center of existence, who acts due to his own means and by his own tools. Accordingly, we can depict the complete structure of human skills in the following way:

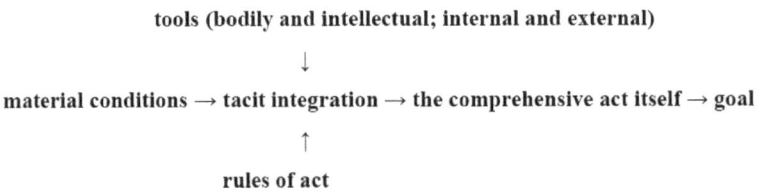

Figure 2. The structure of human skills.

The rules of an act are also fundamental for determining the workings of craftsmanship. On the one hand, it means that they can only be examined to some extent focally and, on the other, that they only gain their real meaning in practice; therefore, craftsmanship itself can only be acquired in practice.

Practice also excludes the critical method and destructive analysis because for the sake of acquiring a new craftsmanship, one has to accept both the unarticulated rules of the act of that craftsmanship and the peculiar situation in which he can learn that craftsmanship (by example and practices) uncritically. It follows that craftsmanship can only be acquired in such institutions where the apprentice accepts the authority of his masters, trusts them unconditionally, and follows the traditions of that institution. If he does not do these things, tries to use critical methods against his masters and his institute, or tries to learn the rules of the act of that craftsmanship by destructive analysis (when perhaps even his masters could not explicate those rules perfectly), then he will acquire nothing and will soon find himself outside the institution:

> These hidden rules can be assimilated only by a person who surrenders himself to that extent uncritically to the imitation of another. A society which wants to preserve a fund of personal knowledge must submit to tradition.[31]

31. Polanyi, *Personal Knowledge*, 53.

> This reliance is a personal commitment which is involved in all acts of intelligence by which we integrate some things subsidiarily to the center of our focal attention. Every act of personal assimilation by which we make a thing form an extension of ourselves through our subsidiary awareness of it, is a commitment of ourselves; a manner of disposing of ourselves.[32]

So, to use an object as a tool, one has to trust it and assimilate it into his person in the sense of subsidiary awareness—it is the act of commitment itself (3.6). This is also true, of course, for any intellectual tool or rules of an act. We internalize and assimilate language, words, and concepts as intellectual tools and laws and morals as the rules of acts, committing ourselves to them uncritically. Our bodily and intellectual skills are based on these subsidiary, assimilated tools, which, consequently, one is aware of only subsidiarily. Such tools can only partially be articulated focally and gain their real meaning only in practice. Therefore, skills can only be learned in traditional institutions through trust and personal knowledge—including science, as a kind of high-level, intellectual craftsmanship. These skills work only if one acknowledges both his bodily and social reality uncritically. Here lies the roots of those (tangible and intellectual, internal and external) tools and rules of an act which, after assimilation and embodiment, allow him to reach his ends.

> It is the act of commitment in its full structure that saves personal knowledge from being merely subjective. Intellectual commitment is a responsible decision, in submission to the compelling claims of what in good conscience I conceive to be true. It is an act of hope, striving to fulfill an obligation within a personal situation for which I am not responsible and which therefore determines my calling. This hope and this obligation are expressed in the universal intent of personal knowledge.[33]

3.4 The Tacit Roots of Explicit Sentences

Polanyi differentiates between two kinds of statements in regards to clarity: *unambiguous* statements and *probability* statements. His example of an unambiguous statement is the formula of Newtonian mechanics. In principle, if the physical parameters of the actual state of a given object are known, any possible future and past states of an object can be calculated by a few exact formulas. However, this knowledge can only be regarded as purely

---

32. Polanyi, *Personal Knowledge*, 61.
33. Polanyi, *Personal Knowledge*, 65.

objective *if someone does not take into account the application of mechanical formulas to empirical facts*:

> The derivation of data and checking of data that bridge the gap between our instrument readings and the magnitudes figuring in our formulae can never be fully automatic. For any correlation between a measured number introduced into an exact theory and the corresponding instrument readings rests on an estimate of observational errors which cannot be definitively prescribed by rule.[34]

Real scientists, contrary to the ideal demon of Laplace, have no instant, perfect senses or skills for knowing. The instruments by which they generate the data going into their mechanical formulas are also not perfect. *Random* measurement errors occur regularly and have to be corrected by different kinds of evaluation methods. In other words, since the process of data collection is not guided by the unambiguous formulas of Newtonian mechanics, there are only probability statements referring to these errors. There is no unambiguous, always valid rule or method for how the occurring mistakes have to be corrected. Therefore, when there are contradicting results during the verification of a scientific theory, scientists must rely on their personal judgment—which, of course, is the normal way how science is done.

In contrast to classical mechanics, in most of the sciences, there is only an option for probability statements. Polanyi's examples are quantum mechanics and one of the experiments of Charles Darwin. In these cases, there is no possibility for explicating scientific knowledge in an unambiguous way but rather only *in relation to some probability*. In the case of quantum mechanics, it means that there is no definite data or exact equations—as in the formulas of Newtonian mechanics. For example, concerning the place of an object, there is only probability data for what the exact probability is that the given object would be in this, that, or any other possible location:

> Probability statements can never be strictly contradicted by experience, even if we assume that all external perturbations and all observational errors are entirely eliminated.[35]

This means that in the case of quantum mechanics and similar scientific practices, the personal evaluation of scientific experiences of the theory will be necessary even if one does not take the previously detailed problems and errors of measurement into account.

34. Polanyi, *Personal Knowledge*, 19.
35. Polanyi, *Personal Knowledge*, 21.

So, according to Polanyi, probability statements are useful for scientific considerations not because they objectively synthesize the scientific experiences (as positivism claims) but rather because they give an opportunity for scientists to personally evaluate the theories and compare them to measurement data:

> If no strictly objective restriction can be derived from the assignment of this probability, we may expect to find in it instead some guidance to our personal participation in the event to which the probability statement refers.[36]

Polanyi gives the example of rolling dice. In a strict sense, no experience can contradict the statement: "The probability of a double six is 1/36." It does not refer to clear future events—which could refute it—but only to future *possibilities*. Therefore, in the purely objective sense, *it cannot be in conflict with any experience*. Cast two dice and the result is a double six. This is not surprising at all and does not contradict the statement that the probability of a double six is 1/36. Cast again and the result is another double six. The probability of these two double sixes is only 1/1296. Let's continue, and the result—once more—is a double six. The probability of this series is now 1/46,656. This third double six is very surprising. In a strictly objective sense, however, it still complies with our probability statement *just as* the first double six did; it is one of the *possible* outcomes. Nonetheless, we are still really amazed, and if someone casts three double sixes, one after another, during a typical dice game, we might start to suspect that he is cheating and his dice are loaded.

So, the fact that the series of three double sixes is surprising does not mark any conflict between experience and the exact probability statement concerning this series; rather, it is *the expression of our personal evaluation that is connected to this kind of random event—this and only this personal participation establishes a relation between experience (reality) and the probability statement*:

> I ascribe universal validity to my appraisals of probability, in spite of the fact that they make no predictions which could be contradicted by any conceivable events.[37]

Since it cannot be decided by strict, objective criteria which events are too improbable to treat as the consequence of real, hidden factors, it has to be determined by personal evaluation. There is, however, no

---

36. Polanyi, *Personal Knowledge*, 21.
37. Polanyi, *Personal Knowledge*, 22.

objective rule for when this personal evaluation has to happen or the exact probability for when an event is to be regarded as the consequence of real factors (and not just some random fluctuation), which should then be unfolded and explained.

Darwin had to face this problem exactly when he wanted to determine whether the difference between the heights of plants in cases of cross-fertilization and self-fertilization is due to the nature of these processes or merely the consequence of some random processes. So, after how many "double sixes"—that is, how big does the size difference between cross-fertilization and self-fertilization have to be—to conclude that this difference is the consequence of some "loadedness"—that is, a real principle of nature—hiding behind the results?

Of course, it is also possible—and, moreover, it is necessary—for science to create formal rules and methods for this kind of scientific examination, however, these rules and methods do not replace but rather solely support the personal evaluation of the results. In Polanyi's words: *"But such formalization is likely to go too far unless it acknowledges in advance that it must remain within a framework of personal judgment."*[38]

If a scientist, according to some objectivist conceptual and explanatory framework, claims that these formal rules and methods are sufficient to decide a scientific question of this kind, then it is simply a deceptive substitution (2.5). Since *in practice* he still evaluates the results of formal methods on the basis of his personal intellectual skills and participation, and only *in his theoretical reflection* on his works, he would say that his work complies with an objectivist framework. This means that by his objectivist interpretation, he conceals his personal participation in the process. Polanyi explains this kind of deceptive substitution with the following example.

According to R. A. Fischer, who was perhaps the most important figure in laying down the foundations for neo-Darwinian theory, a statistical method can be given concerning Darwin's experiment by which it can be shown that the probability that cross-fertilization increases growth is more than 95 percent. This explicit sentence, however, has no connection with our experience in itself; rather, it is only a probability statement, referring to a certain possibility. The non-personal, *objective probability* of this statement is not the same as the *meaning* of the statement *based on a personal judgment* that cross-fertilization increases the growth. Therefore, the explicit sentence means nothing in itself. It only expresses the degree of one's personal conviction concerning the given statement numerically. It has no real meaning because no experience can contradict it, and no experience can contradict it because the whole statement, in fact, is this: the probability

---

38. Polanyi, *Personal Knowledge*, 19.

that cross-fertilization increases growth is more than 95 percent, and the probability that it reduces it is less than 5 percent. The statement is perfectly objective and non-personal, but it has nothing to say about reality, therefore, in itself, it does not correspond to any scientific practice.[39]

So the real scientific statement—which, of course, was also meant by Darwin himself—is that cross-fertilization *increases* the growth of plants. It follows that experience *can* contradict it, but *this is exactly the source of its meaning*. It is not an unambiguous statement of classical mechanics, made absolute and without exception, but rather only a biological statement, verified by the statistically analyzed results of Darwin's experiment. During this evaluation process, scientists have to judge which results can be accepted as evidence and which cannot on the basis of their personal, intellectual skills and passions; there is no other option. The conviction of a scientist regarding the truth of the statement follows from this process (science in practice). Consequently, the probability of the statement refers to the degree of this conviction, which, however, cannot be identified with a non-personal probability statement.

Therefore, the rephrasing of the real scientific statement—that cross-fertilization *increases* growth—into an objective, non-personal statement—the probability that cross-fertilization increases growth is more than 95 percent—is only a deceptive substitution, concealing the personal judgment of the scientist. It makes no real claim concerning reality but rather merely explicates a possibility. In practice, of course, everybody would understand what the original statement claims is that cross-fertilization *increases* growth. Everybody *must* understand it in this way because the non-personal rephrasing means nothing in itself. It follows that an assertion of a statement on the basis of a sincere conviction is more than its pure content. "An unasserted sentence is no better than an unsigned check; just paper and ink without power or meaning."[40]

We can say anything about objectivity and exactness to scarify on the altar of Laplace's demon, but a sentence gains meaning solely by a tacit act during which we personally commit ourselves to the fact that cross-fertilization increases growth—that is, in reality, its probability is 100 percent.

According to this analysis of scientific practice, Polanyi claims that every articulate assertion has two composite parts: 1. *sentence*; 2. *tacit act*. The sentence is an *explicit formula*. The tacit act is a *commitment* by which a person asserts the sentence. It follows that the explicit sentence gets meaning and refers to an aspect of reality *only by* the person's tacit commitment:

---

39. Polanyi, *Personal Knowledge*, 24.
40. Polanyi, *Personal Knowledge*, 28.

"Only a speaker or listener can mean something by a word, and a word in itself can mean nothing."[41] It can be depicted in the following way:

explicit sentence + tacit commitment → an aspect of reality

The sentence "snow is white"—or, for that matter, "snow is red"—means nothing in itself. It will mean something and become true—or, in the case of "snow is red," it will become false—if and only if a person refers to an aspect of reality by it. Without this reference, both sentences are only vacant, explicit phrases. It follows that referring to reality is not merely another explicit sentence; otherwise, nothing would change with the original "snow is white" or "snow is red" statements but rather a *tacit commitment* that, according to our beliefs, reality is in a kind of state, that is, snow is white or red. This act of commitment is not explicated; it is simply not part of the explicit sentence "snow is white."

Therefore, if a person has not committed himself to the content of his sentence, it will remain a vacant, explicit sentence and cannot become a meaningful assertion about reality. The phrase "snow is red" is just a sentence, not an assertion—unless someone indeed believes that snow is red. Consequently, a lie is also not an assertion about reality but rather only an *act of speech*. Of course, someone can be wrong, but then he has to assert that snow is red frankly. A sentence can be part of an assertion or not, but based solely on the explicit form, it cannot be decided which case it is. This can only be decided based *on the tacit context*.

A sentence from a scientific paper or an encyclopedia also has no meaning in itself—no matter how precisely or exactly they were explicated. They will gain this sense if and only if somebody asserts them according to his tacit convictions and previous experiences. It follows that two persons do not and cannot understand exactly the same thing under an assertion explicated in a sentence. It could merely happen if they had exactly the same tacit convictions and previous experiences. However, this does not mean that there is not and cannot be meaning between two persons; the basis for understanding is not perfect objectivity but rather common, tacit convictions and similar experiences.

Polanyi differentiates between the *confident* or direct and the *skeptical* or oblique use of a word or a sentence. According to the former case, someone asserts a sentence honestly with commitment, while, according to the latter one, he suspends his assertion to examine its (explicit and tacit) contents.[42]

41. Polanyi, *Personal Knowledge*, 252.
42. Polanyi, *Personal Knowledge*, 250.

We have seen in the previous subchapter that articulation and language are not self-standing, based on some mental principle, but rather are based on skills—that is, a person can articulate his thoughts, beliefs, feelings, etc. solely by his tacit bodily and intellectual skills. After acknowledging the evolutionary origin of human beings, this fact can be considered as trivial, but the consequences are not trivial at all: *tacit knowledge is the precondition of all articulate, explicit sentences and thought.* That is, every assertion is based on tacit acts.

Modern science, however, still tries to describe all aspects of reality as explicitly as possible—for example, explaining a person's acts through detailed neurological and physiological descriptions (this is also true, of course, for all cognitive processes of the mind). But if Polanyi's examination about the logic and tacit nature of affirmation is well-established, then it is the total misunderstanding of these processes. Since any affirmation is not just an explicit sentence but also a tacit act, it cannot be asserted by another detailed, descriptive sentence, only *referred* to (in the denotative sense). Or, it can be done again—that is, it can be confirmed with another tacit act in the existential sense (see below). This means that an *act* cannot be asserted, only an explicit sentence which describes an act. "Snow is white," in itself, is an explicit sentence. Snow is white, however, is an affirmation—a tacit act referring to an aspect of reality—due to the fact that the talking person has committed himself to its truth. It is the reason that it has denotative meaning.

"Peter rides a bicycle" is an explicit sentence that *can* be asserted. Peter's act itself, however—that he, in fact, rides a bicycle—*cannot*. Therefore, the two are trivially not the same. Nonetheless, if modern science, according to the Laplacian ideal of objective knowledge, starts to describe Peter's tacit act with more and more detailed, explicit sentences—for example, by the language of neurobiology—and starts to believe that the set of these highly detailed, explicit sentences can be complied with Peter's real tacit act, then the exact scientific description of Peter's act can be "valid" *only if* modern science disregards Peter as a free-acting person and instead regards him as a set of neurobiological processes. Unfortunately, this is the way modern science thinks today.

It also follows that the sentence "snow is white is true" (contrary to "snow is white") is not just a vacant, explicit sentence—even in itself—but rather a declaration of a person's commitment. Therefore, if somebody completes an explicit sentence (e.g., "snow is white") with the phrase "is true," then the original sentence is no longer just a sentence, asserted or not as somebody wishes, but it necessarily becomes an assertion, which is confirmed at once by the word "true."

The main consequence of this is that it is entirely meaningless to ask whether "snow is white is true" is true or not because it is not simply a sentence which can be asserted but rather a personal commitment to an aspect of reality which is just as *tacit* an act as riding a bicycle. Riding a bicycle is, of course, another type of personal act, different in some respects than confirming an act of affirmation with the word "true," but both of them are personal acts, and this is the reason that they cannot be true nor false. It is entirely meaningless to ask if Peter's bicycle riding is true or false because it is an act which, according to the nature of acts, is *successful* or *unsuccessful*, not true or false. One can only ask whether the sentence "Peter is riding a bicycle" is true or not—if, of course, somebody asserts it—and this assertion is true or false depending on the fact if Peter is successfully riding a bicycle or not. We will see in chapter 5 that reduction by which it can be decided that a comprehensive, orderly phenomenon is material in nature or not is also a kind of personal act. Thus, if we do not face this fact, we will utterly misunderstand its nature and real meaning; unfortunately, this is exactly the situation in science and philosophy, dominated by objectivism and positivism.

Polanyi claims that there are *two significantly different types* of linguistic expressions. The first type includes those normal expressions by which a person can compose sentences and assert something. The second one consists of those linguistic expressions that confirm or reject the use of the expressions of the first type—that is, these expressions of the second type do not compose sentences but rather *realize acts*.[43]

Polanyi differentiates among three different kinds of meaning: *existential, representative*, and *denotative*.[44] *Every kind of order has existential meaning*. In the more important case, it means that material parts exist in a comprehensive system which has its own ordering principles and meaning. For example, in the case of cycling, the ordering principles are the rules of the act of cycling, and the existential meaning of cycling is that somebody is riding a bicycle. In the case of a frog, the ultimate ordering principles are the ordering principles of life and evolution, and the primary existential meaning of the frog is that it lives and acts according to its own nature. Orders made by human beings (e.g., a portrait) generally have some representative meaning, too—that is, they convey messages. If this message is articulated by language, then the order will also have denotative meaning. For example, we will soon see that the Wales lettering in the next chapter's main example is not just a pile

---

43. Polanyi, *Personal Knowledge*, 255.
44. Polanyi, *Personal Knowledge*, 58.

of pebbles that have their own existential meaning but also conveys concrete, intellectual content for the arriving passengers.

So, according to the logic of affirmation, meaning is not based on the explicit content of sentences but *on the tacit acts of persons*. Affirmation is just as much an act as any other personal act. At the same time, due to its peculiar nature, affirmation gains a specific kind of meaning. Every tacit act of a person has existential meaning according to the person's commitment. The assertion of a sentence, however, is such a personal act that has not only existential meaning but because it refers to an aspect of reality, has denotative meaning, too. The traditional philosophy of language only regards the denotative meaning as real. The reason for this deficiency is that merely this kind of meaning can be connected to explicit sentences and thus, according to the objectivist ideal of knowledge, impersonalized. It can be depicted as follows:

assertion of an explicit sentence → denotative meaning

assertion as a tacit act → existential meaning

Contrary to Polanyi, the traditional philosophy of language tries to determine the meaning and usage of linguistic expressions in a formal, impersonalized way. Polanyi brings up several arguments against it.

We have seen that Polanyi differentiates between the confident and the skeptical usage of sentences. The latter is essential for the modern critical method (2.5), but a question still has to be asked: how can one decide whether a person uses a word or sentence confidently or skeptically? Polanyi claims that it can *only* be done by the tacit component because exactly the same, explicit content is used both in the confident assertion and in the skeptical articulation of "snow is white." That is, only the tacit body language, tone, or the context can help to decide this question, not some kind of objective criterion.[45]

To evade this argument, the most typical solution for the problem is the so-called "ostensive definitions." By these practical definitions, seemingly objective connections can be made between linguistic expressions and different aspects of reality if somebody who knows the expressions points to the referred objects:

> Accordingly, in formulating a definition, we must rely on watching the way the art of using a word is authentically practiced; or more precisely, watch ourselves applying the term to be defined in ways that we regard as authentic. . . . The formalization of

---

45. Polanyi, *Personal Knowledge*, 250.

meaning relies therefore from the start on the practice of unformalized meaning.[46]

This means that all ostensive definitions are based on the appropriate usage of language and on the trust between master and learner—that is, on a kind of craftsmanship (3.3). In other words, when somebody starts to learn a new language (by ostensive definitions, lexical explications, etc.), he does not use that language and its expressions skeptically but rather confidently, and he acknowledges that the given society uses that language correctly. In this sense, his confidence in the meaning of the expressions of that language is *a tacit act of social loyalty*. The determination of linguistic expressions by ostensive definition is, therefore, not the least objective.

On the other hand, asks Polanyi, what would the consequences be if the expression of language was perfectly exact, impersonal, and precise? The answer is this: since reality is always changing, words would gradually lose their meanings because they would not be able to grasp the different, changing aspects of reality. Therefore, "only words of indeterminate meaning can have a bearing on reality."[47] Furthermore, such perfectly formal and precise expressions would lose contact with persons, too, because "any strictly formal operation would be impersonal and could not therefore convey the speaker's personal commitment."[48]

So, according to the objectivist approach, if anybody were to *consistently* follow the criteria for perfect exactness and preciseness, that would mean the final elimination of their own persons:

> Any philosophy that sets up strictness of meaning as its ideal is self-contradictory. For if the active participation of the philosopher in meaning what he says is regarded by it as a defect which precludes the achievement of objective validity, it must reject itself by these standards.[49]

This means that, according to the Laplacian ideal of objective knowledge, the person and his tacit commitments are ignored in the structure of affirmation—that is, meaning is restricted to the territory of explicit sentences. Therefore, only those aspects of reality which can be grasped by explicit expressions are acknowledged as real. But since the nature of a person and his commitments are tacit, if objectivism were consistent, they could not be regarded as real. This final step, however, cannot be done

---

46. Polanyi, *Personal Knowledge*, 250.
47. Polanyi, *Personal Knowledge*, 251.
48. Polanyi, *Personal Knowledge*, 252.
49. Polanyi, *Personal Knowledge*, 252–53.

because the person and his tacit commitments are the preconditions of every assertion; objectivism is not consistent at all, it just builds a façade by deceptive substitutions (2.5). In chapter 5, we will see in the case of the concept of reduction that this argument can also be formulated against materialism in a more general sense (5.7). It follows that materialism cannot be consistent either; it should otherwise deny the existence of those persons who claim that materialism is true, which is simply contradictory and—in Polanyi's word—absurd.

According to Polanyi, one does not have to examine the impersonal, explicit sentences, which, in themselves, are in fact meaningless, but rather the *personal acts* and *tacit commitments* by which someone meaningfully asserts a sentence. This examination of personal acts, tacit commitments, and, in the most important case, self-examination *has to be the aim of philosophy*. It obviously cannot be objective, however, since it is about our most personal beliefs and convictions:

> Nothing that I shall say should claim the kind of objectivity to which, in my belief, no reasoning should ever aspire; namely, that it proceeds by a strict process, the acceptance of which by the expositor, and his recommendation of which for acceptance by others, include no passionate impulse of his own.[50]

3.5 The Tacit Roots of the Critical Method of Doubt

In the philosophical tradition, the term "critical philosophy" usually refers to the philosophy of Immanuel Kant and his followers. The term "critical," however, is used in a much broader sense, and critical thinking is opposed to "obscure," dogmatic thinking (although, what the latter means exactly strongly depends on the given speaker). Furthermore, the concept of critical is tightly connected to the concept of skeptical.

Polanyi uses the concept of critical philosophy in a broad sense. He regards every philosophy that tries to establish human knowledge and knowing on objective foundations—and, in consequence, rejects belief (one of the two main intellectual skills of human beings)—as critical. In his words: "The critical mind repudiated one of its two cognitive faculties."[51] He refers to St. Augustine, for whom belief was the foundation of any knowledge, and contrasts him with John Locke, who degraded belief into mere lack of knowledge:

---

50. Polanyi, *Personal Knowledge*, 256.
51. Polanyi, *Personal Knowledge*, 266.

> We must now recognize belief once more as the source of all knowledge. Tacit assent and intellectual passions, the sharing of an idiom and of a cultural heritage, affiliation to a like-minded community: such are the impulses which shape our vision of the nature of things on which we rely for our mastery of things. No intelligence, however critical or original, can operate outside such a fiduciary framework.[52]

According to this approach, modern critical philosophy was formed in the seventeenth century and René Descartes and his methodological skepticism played the leading role in the process. Polanyi calls his own philosophy *post-critical*, in opposition to critical philosophy, because he establishes it on *fiduciary* grounds. Polanyi concludes what the aim of *Personal Knowledge* is as follows:

> This book tries to serve a different and, in a sense, perhaps more ambitious purpose. Its aim is to re-equip men with the faculties which centuries of critical thought have taught them to distrust. The reader has been invited to use these faculties and contemplate thus a picture of things restored to their fairly obvious nature. This is all the book was meant to do.[53]

Polanyi explains the point of the critical method in the following way:

> The method of doubt is a logical corollary of objectivism. It trusts that the uprooting of all voluntary components of belief will leave behind unassailed a residue of knowledge that is completely determined by the objective evidence. Critical thought trusted this method unconditionally for avoiding error and establishing truth.[54]

According to the subjective versus objective dichotomy of objectivism, *belief is subjective* while *knowledge is objective*. Therefore, any kind of knowledge that is based on personal beliefs is subjective—that is, not real knowledge at all—and has to be regarded *by doubt*. Only those kinds of knowledge which can be justified objectively—that is, which *can stand the tests of all kinds of doubt*—should be accepted as real

The primary goal of critical philosophy by the method of doubt is to overcome "medieval superstitions" and to build a free, brave new world based on critical thinking. It also means, however, the questioning of traditional principles and institutions, including the principles of freedom

---

52. Polanyi, *Personal Knowledge*, 266.
53. Polanyi, *Personal Knowledge*, 381.
54. Polanyi, *Personal Knowledge*, 269.

and morality, since these principles and institutions are not based on critical knowledge but gradually became part of the fundamental beliefs and traditions of free, modern societies during the long course of cultural evolution (10.8; 12.2).

According to Polanyi, no one ever, in fact, wanted to execute the program of critical philosophy consistently; indeed, it is not even possible.[55] The reason for this is that every system of knowledge is based on such *fundamental beliefs* or axioms that were accepted tacitly, by trust, before the construction of those systems. This is even true for such exact systems of knowledge as mathematics as well. Polanyi shows this fact by the discovery of non-Euclidian geometry. Therefore, since the fundamental beliefs or axioms of a system of knowledge are *preconditions* for any verification and argumentation in that system, they themselves cannot be verified and argued—not even by the so-called perfect method of doubt; they should be believed or tacitly acknowledged by trust.

Those who consider themselves strictly critical of everything in reality do not know or ignore their own fundamental beliefs. This false self-image cannot be fixed as it is usually done in the name of self-reflection—recognizing that there are serious, subjective mistakes in one's thinking regarding the critical method ("humans are not perfect")—since the acknowledgment of such fallibility of the critical method, in fact, means that, according to strict, consistent objectivist criteria, he knows nothing.[56]

Polanyi claims that the roots of critical doubt not only go back to the sixteenth and seventeenth centuries but even further, way back to the primitive animal past of human existence. The common phenomenon when someone hesitates during a certain act what to do next is called by him implicit or *tacit doubt*. According to him, this deeper doubt is the foundation of explicit doubt of the formal systems of knowledge, and, to an extent, it determines every articulate assertion. If there were no tacit doubt, then there would be no explicit doubt either—just as Laplace's demon never doubts anything although it is the ideal of critical thinking (2.3).

It does not follow, however, that critical doubt has to be rejected in every case. Polanyi only argues that human thinking and systems of knowledge cannot be based on the critical method of doubt since real human thinking and knowledge are based on trust. As a matter of fact, Polanyi's harsh critique of the critical method is also a kind of doubt; it is merely not directed against the fiduciary fundaments of human thinking but a particular method of thinking. Polanyi gives several examples for when the method

---

55. Polanyi, *Personal Knowledge*, 269–70.
56. Polanyi, *Personal Knowledge*, 271.

of doubt is useful. One of those examples is his differentiation between contradictory and agnostic doubts. Every assertion can be re-explicated in the way of doubt, contradicting the original statement. This is the case of contradictory doubt, which is fundamental in science. Suppose that someone has the conviction, "I believe p," and explicate it according to contradictory doubt, "I doubt p." Then, rephrase it into a positive affirmation, "I believe not-p," and show that not-p is not possible. By this method, the original conviction, "I believe p," can be confirmed—even in the case when there is no direct evidence to support it.

Polanyi claims that the fiduciary character of doubt is most apparent in the case of so-called "reasonable doubt." It is clear that even the critical thinker himself does not want to doubt everything because this would not lead to real knowledge but rather agnosticism—that is, to the conviction that real knowledge is not possible for human beings. Furthermore, dogmatic thinkers also doubt such beliefs which cannot be complied with their dogmas. For example, they doubt the fundamental beliefs of critical thinkers who believe that reasonable doubt is the source of all real knowledge. Therefore, since there is "dogmatic doubt," too, it is *necessary* to differentiate between reasonable and dogmatic doubts, where the former is "well-grounded" and "systematic" and the latter is "unfounded" and "naïve."

> To urge that doubt must be reasonable is to rely on something that cannot reasonably be doubted—that is, in legal phrase, a 'moral certainty.'[57]

It means that in the case of certain beliefs, one suspends the critical method of doubt. However, it is not done based on the method itself because the method of doubt, at least theoretically, can be used against every kind of belief; rather, it is based on something else, outside the consistent application of the method, which, consequently, is a concealed, uncritical belief or conviction grounded on trust. Since the critical thinker does not and cannot doubt everything, he, in fact, relies on such beliefs and convictions during his doubt that he does not doubt but in which he trusts. In the positive sense, reasonable doubt can be separated from unreasonable doubt only by such fundamental beliefs that are *truer* than the fundamental beliefs of unreasonable doubts. Accordingly:

> Natural scientists can be said to be more critical than astrologers only insofar as we regard their conception of stars and men as truer than that of the astrologers.[58]

---

57. Polanyi, *Personal Knowledge*, 274.
58. Polanyi, *Personal Knowledge*, 274.

It follows that the method of doubt plays a positive role in science only in the sense that it can *stabilize* and *defend* the true beliefs and convictions of science against the attacks and doubts of another, false system of knowledge. The fundamental beliefs and truths of science, however, are not in the least the consequences of the application of the critical method of doubt.

Polanyi uses the example of Franz Anton Mesmer to show these limits of the critical method. The phenomenon of hypnosis was definitely rejected by critical science *for almost a century*—despite the fact that Mesmer and his followers verified it with *repeated* and visible *experimental evidence*. Today, however, this phenomenon is an integral part of critical science; for example, it is routinely used in different medical and psychological practices.

Mesmer was a German physician in the second half of the eighteenth century. He was the first to use the technique of hypnosis extensively and successfully during his practice. He thought, however, that hypnosis was related to the magnetism of the human body and thus he named it "animal magnetism." Scientifically, it was still a significant step forward because in contrast with former mystical and religious explanations of the phenomenon of hypnosis, he tried to interpret it by *scientific* concepts. Although his interpretation included such ideas as, for example, the notion that the tide-like, inner processes of the body are the consequences of the movements of the Sun and the Moon, which is clearly false today (he tried to apply Newton's theory in this respect).

During hypnosis, magnetic objects were moved by Mesmer over the patients' bodies and placed on them; moreover, it occurred that the patients had to drink liquids with different magnetic powders, affecting the animal magnetism of their bodies to reach healing. Besides these methods, Mesmer's treatments also included some primitive parts of hypnotic suggestions, but Mesmer himself regarded these hypnotic elements of the process as only the secondary consequences of animal magnetism.

Mesmer was accused of quackery by the scientific community in the name of skepticism and critical thought. After an ominous case, he even had to flee Vienna. The reason for this consequence is that his concept of animal magnetism and the strange psychological nature of hypnosis went against such deep mechanical convictions concerning the nature of reality in his era that even the most evident and palpable experimental facts of hypnosis were rejected by critical science. Almost a century had to pass before the phenomenon of hypnosis was acknowledged and allowed to re-enter the realm of science.

The question of hypnosis is now solved. But since there were several similar examples of critical science over the centuries, it can be supposed that there are still such phenomena which are rejected because of the method of doubt in the same way as it was done in the case of hypnosis. On the basis of these examples, it can be claimed that the method of doubt was poorly executed and despite this fact, if one does not assert that, in turn, it is used perfectly today, then it follows that the method of doubt still necessarily leads to significant mistakes and unfounded scientific convictions. It means that the critical method of doubt as a principle for scientific knowing is in itself not well-established. Therefore, there is an opportunity and a need for a post-critical philosophy.[59]

In consequence, "the practice of scientific skepticism, in respect to allegations rejected by science, consists in upholding the current scientific view of their subject matter"—and nothing more. Polanyi, however, reminds us that stability is a fundamental characteristic of science. It worked well for centuries, so do not underestimate its importance.[60]

Polanyi examines doubt against religion in detail because the critical method was originally used against Christian dogmas. Polanyi claims that religion "is an indwelling rather than an affirmation."[61] Therefore, its point is not the affirmation of the existence of God, as it is generally treated, but rather the immersion in a peculiar system of knowledge as an intellectual tool—that is, the *indwelling itself*. This religious process of immersion can be identified with the process of when a swagger-cane as a tool becomes part of someone's hand, only it realizes at a higher existential level (3.3).

> God cannot be observed, any more than truth or beauty can be observed. He exists in the sense that He is to be worshipped and obeyed, but not otherwise; not as a fact—any more than truth, beauty or justice exist as facts. All these, like God, are things which can be apprehended only in serving them.[62]

This means that "God exists" is an affirmation of a complex, tacit commitment just as the "snow is white is true" is an affirmation of the tacit commitment that "snow is white" and not an affirmation of an explicit fact, referring to an aspect of reality as "snow is white" (3.4). It follows that it cannot be doubted explicitly but only rejected as a conviction or as truth. It can be doubted only tacitly. In this sense, Christians always doubt it to some extent because this tacit doubt is an integral part of the Christian faith.[63]

---

59. Polanyi, *Personal Knowledge*, 274.
60. Polanyi, *Personal Knowledge*, 276.
61. Polanyi, *Personal Knowledge*, 279.
62. Polanyi, *Personal Knowledge*, 279.
63. Polanyi, *Personal Knowledge*, 280–81.

Christianity and the committed search for God cannot be disproved or understood by explicit facts. A Christian ceremony means nothing to someone who does not believe in God and is not a Christian. Nonetheless, there are such factual testimonies in the history of Christianity which strengthen and confirm the Christian faith, and during the last centuries, critical philosophy successfully disproved a significant part of these testimonies. However, since the worship of God is rather an indwelling, a commitment toward God, it cannot be refuted by disproving these factual testimonies or by any other scientific experiments, but it can be weakened because factual events which did not happen, of course, have no meaning concerning supernatural or any other kind of system of commitments. Biblical criticism is successful not because of the refutation of Christian faith but rather because of the refutation of these factual testimonies:

> It destroyed the religious meaning of things without fully compensating for this loss by a different meaning, and the total volume of belief, from which all meaning flows, was effectively reduced.[64]

We have seen that every affirmation is based on a person's tacit commitment; explicit sentences in themselves mean nothing (3.4). In this sense, *belief is nothing else but a tacit commitment toward reality*—that an aspect of reality has a peculiar nature, character, property, etc.—and the roots of belief stem *from human evolution*, not from divine creation. Therefore, religious faith is a type of natural human belief when someone's tacit commitments work inside an explicit religious conceptual and explanatory system. The primary role of religious traditions were to provide the intellectual tools by which human societies could explicate their fundamental tacit commitments. Of course, the consequence of this process was that what societies think about the universe, their place in it, and their goals were strongly determined by religion.

According to Polanyi, we have to be thankful that critical philosophy destroyed the religious dogmas and static societies of the early modern era and thereby made thinking freer. We were clearly not created in the image of God. We will not find the source of belief and meaning in these old dogmas. But we do not have to be grateful that critical philosophy has not provided any meaningful answers to the most fundamental questions of human life; moreover, it has explicitly rejected and stigmatized these questions as unscientific many times. At the end, we do not have to be thankful at all because due to the Laplacian ideal of objective knowledge, the final

---

64. Polanyi, *Personal Knowledge*, 286.

consequence of this process is that our scientific picture of the universe has become meaningless:

> The book of Genesis and its great pictorial illustrations, like the frescoes of Michelangelo, remain a far more intelligent account of the nature and origin of the universe than the representation of the world as a chance collocation of atoms. For the biblical cosmology continues to express—however inadequately—the significance of the fact that the world exists and that man has emerged from it, while the scientific picture denies any meaning to the world, and indeed ignores all our most vital experience of this world.[65]

The universe, however, is not meaningless at all. There is life in the universe. Human beings emerged from its primordial, material beginnings to not only give meaning to the world through their languages but also by their lives and existences. Most of all, they can reveal and understand the inherent hidden rationality of reality (3.2). In contrast to this, the objectivist-materialist approach merely offers a meaningless universe of deterministic-random material parts and, of course, those deceptive substitutions by which it conceals this meaningless picture of the world before society (2.5).

These are the necessary consequences of the critical method of doubt because "all truth is but the external pole of belief, and to destroy all belief would be to deny all truth. . . . Objectivism has totally falsified our conception of truth by exalting what we can know and prove while covering up with ambiguous utterances all that we know and cannot prove, even though the latter knowledge underlies and must ultimately set its seal to all that we can prove."[66] Truth cannot be asserted without belief. The affirmation of truth is a commitment to a particular meaning that an aspect of reality has a certain nature, process, character, etc. Without belief and commitment, there remains but a set of meaningless facts of the parts. Therefore, rationality is not based on pure doubt but fiduciary roots.[67]

Internal pole *External pole*

tacit commitment (belief) → **an aspect of reality (truth)**

Figure 3. The two poles of commitment.

65. Polanyi, *Personal Knowledge*, 284–85.
66. Polanyi, *Personal Knowledge*, 286.
67. Polanyi, *Personal Knowledge*, 297.

Polanyi emphasizes once more that universal doubt, according to the true nature of the Laplacean ideal, destroys all meaning because no one can doubt his every concept and belief at the same time:

> What [the critical thinkers] actually want is not expressed but concealed by their declared principles. They want their own beliefs to be taught to children and accepted by everybody, for they are convinced that this would save the world from error and strife. . . . Since the skeptic does not consider it rational to doubt what he himself believes, the advocacy of 'rational doubt' is merely the skeptic's way of advocating his own beliefs.[68]

Polanyi then cites Bertrand Russell: "Thus rational doubt alone, if it could be generated, would suffice to introduce the Millennium." That is, the upcoming brave new world. According to Polanyi, the real meaning of this prophecy should be explicated in this way: "The acceptance of rational beliefs such as my own would suffice to introduce the Millennium."[69] But by this honest wording, modern scientism would have to give up the illusory principle of doubt. It would lead to the disdained situation where critical philosophy would have to face its own fiduciary fundaments.

According to Polanyi, the early rationalists of the seventeenth and eighteenth centuries stood up against religious dogmatism, rightfully using the critical method of doubt. Fortunately, in that era, this method did not yet attack their tacit beliefs and convictions. At the beginning of the twentieth century, however, the method of doubt became utterly useless against the new revolutionary dogmatisms of Marxism and National Socialism because the critical method had already undermined the fundamental beliefs and convictions of modern rationalism. Modern rationalism and philosophy can stand up against the revolutionary menace only by their true beliefs and the traditions of the eighteenth and nineteenth centuries because these revolutionary systems also use the critical method of doubt against rationality and science. So if modern rationalism, science, and philosophy still try to use the critical method against these menaces, that will undermine the true beliefs of rationalism and modern societies even more, strengthening these revolutionary systems. "Modern fanaticism is rooted in an extreme skepticism which can only be strengthened, not shaken, by further doses of universal doubt."[70] One can stand up against fanaticism merely by trust (12.5).

Concerning the tacit nature of assertions, we have seen that, according to Polanyi, the primary aim of philosophy should be the examination of

68. Polanyi, *Personal Knowledge*, 297.
69. Polanyi, *Personal Knowledge*, 297.
70. Polanyi, *Personal Knowledge*, 298.

personal commitments and tacit beliefs. The reason for this is that human persons have billions-of-year-old evolutionary and thousands-of-year-old cultural roots which fundamentally determine their present, their thinking, and their goals. The tacit acts which give meaning to explicit sentences cannot only be examined by strict, skeptical methods in a confident way. To ignore these tacit fundaments degrades any assertion into an empty, meaningless phrase. In consequence, nobody can start with a clean sheet, and the fortress of philosophy cannot be constructed following the ideal of critical objectivity and formal preciseness because it would mean nothing. Self-reflectively, Polanyi at first applies this program to his *Personal Knowledge*:

> I must admit now that I did not start the present reconsideration of my beliefs with a clean slate of unbelief. Far from it. I started as a person intellectually fashioned by a particular idiom, acquired through my affiliation to a civilization that prevailed in the places where I had grown up at this particular period of history. This has been the matrix of all my intellectual efforts. Within it I was to find my problem and seek the terms for its solution.[71]

> Our tacit powers decide our adherence to a particular culture and sustain our intellectual, artistic, civic, and religious deployment within its framework. The articulate life of man's mind is his specific contribution to the universe; by the convention of symbolic forms, man has given birth and lasting existence to thought.[72]

In Polanyi's view, modern scientism based on the critical method "fetters thought as cruelly as the churches had ever done."[73] It follows that the rejection of objectivism and modern scientism—as well as the restoration of our trust in our personal commitments and beliefs—does not mean a reversal to the dogmatism of the Middle Ages in any sense. On the contrary, we have to accept that we have deep, evolutionary roots, which, in turn, allow us to make contact with reality without any consistently objective criterion—that is, they enable us to formulate well-established, true, and scientific assertions about nature.

The critical method of doubt is not the real foundation of knowledge. Every conceptual and explanatory system has its own, fiduciary basis that is never doubted because if someone questioned everything—even their own fundamental beliefs—then they could assert nothing consistently. But, in fact, no one tries to follow this consistent path of the critical method. The

---

71. Polanyi, *Personal Knowledge*, 252.
72. Polanyi, *Personal Knowledge*, 264–65.
73. Polanyi, *Personal Knowledge*, 265.

method of doubt stems from the nature of objectivism, which, according to the false subjective versus objective dichotomy, regards every belief as subjective and merely accepts those statements as knowledge which have been proven by some impersonal, explicit process. Objectivism, however, ignores the fact that without the prior acknowledgment of certain fundamental principles or axioms, no process of verification or argumentation can be accomplished—that is, certain fundamental principles per definition have to be acknowledged on the basis of trust even in the case of the most exact sciences and mathematics.

The method of doubt was originally focused on medieval and early modern religious dogmas; therefore, its role was *not to establish* the fundamental principles of philosophy and scientific knowledge at all but rather to *stabilize* and *defend* them. The rejection of religious dogmas and the liberation of thinking were wonderful achievements of the modern era. Belief, however, cannot be identified with religious dogmas because it is a natural, human commitment toward reality by which any truth can be affirmed at all. The explicit rejection of every kind of belief due to the critical method of doubt necessarily leads to the weakening and concealing of the real, fiduciary principles of knowledge. This process poisoned twentieth-century Europe, and it can be halted only if philosophy and science sets an example to the whole Western world and honestly returns to their real, tacit, fiduciary foundations.

3.6 The Tacit Fundament of Personal Beliefs: Commitment

As we have seen in the previous subchapters, the objectivist approach wants to build knowledge on such fundaments which cannot be doubted—that is, those which have withstood the proof of any possible critic. According to Polanyi, however, it is an impossible endeavor, and reflecting on this fact he acknowledges that his own approach to knowledge is necessarily *circular*: "Any enquiry into our ultimate beliefs can be consistent only if it presupposes its own conclusions. It must be intentionally circular."[74]

This circularity could be broken if there were an approach to knowledge that would question its own fundaments before it would even accept these fundaments (to then start further inquiries based on these same fundaments). It would mean that (1) it is possible to reach knowledge without or at least before any fundaments or (2) there are such purely rational, fundamental beliefs (in this case, rather, axioms) which cannot be questioned—that is, which can be acknowledged *a priori*, so there is no

74. Polanyi, *Personal Knowledge*, 299.

need for further examinations in their case. Polanyi claims that neither of these cases is consistent. According to him, an honest philosophy (and science) has to face the fact that it has such *fundamental beliefs* that were acknowledged without any critical examination on the basis of an *acritical, fiduciary* act and that any philosophy can start on further inquiries only after this fiduciary act when they have fundaments upon which they can build any new knowledge.

In the case of the examination of fundamental beliefs, it means the *presupposition of the conclusions*—that is, the examination starts with the fundamental beliefs themselves, which have been acknowledged by a fiduciary act as the basis of any endeavor toward new knowledge, while at the end of the examination, we will arrive at such fundamental beliefs that, consequently, have been strengthened and deepened by this examination since the examination would have otherwise refuted its own fundaments (and thus itself). This deepening in meaning, however, is, of course, a new knowledge concerning our initial starting point—that is, the circle that we have just made has proven itself to be fruitful. In this sense, *Personal Knowledge* is a circle, and now, I will try to widen and deepen this circle with *Personal Reality*. Nonetheless, the point is that the fundaments of human knowledge are, therefore, such tacit beliefs that cannot be specified exactly, but can be explored and more and more understood by each philosophical endeavor, diving into their most profound meanings and evolutionary past.

"Logically, the whole of my argument is but an elaboration of this circle," says Polanyi.[75] It is the reason that he mentions: "I cannot hope to do more in this book than to exhibit a possibility which like-minded people may wish to explore."[76] In the strictly logical sense, he does not try to use coercive arguments because he denies the existence of such arguments. He can only hope that like-minded persons who accept the same fundamental beliefs will find his honest and consistent alternative persuasive and start this endeavor for new knowledge themselves.

First of all, Polanyi commits himself to the following fundamental belief: "I believe that in spite of the hazards involved, I am called upon to search for the truth and state my findings."[77] The mentioned hazards stem from the fact that the fundamental beliefs have been acknowledged by a fiduciary act and not by unquestionable critical methods, so, in principle, it can turn out any time that they are false or they are misinterpreted. This is the reason that although philosophy must trust its fundamental

---

75. Polanyi, *Personal Knowledge*, 299.
76. Polanyi, *Personal Knowledge*, 315.
77. Polanyi, *Personal Knowledge*, 299.

beliefs, it should always still be humble and ready to rethink even its most fundamental beliefs.

Perhaps the most crucial, fundamental beliefs of a philosopher and a scientist are *to search for the truth* and *to share the truth with others*. Maybe, or at least I dare to hope, for my readers, these fundamental beliefs of science and philosophy are trivial and natural. We will see, however, that in the twentieth century, they were questioned and at the end of the century, they were denied by critical philosophy (positivism and relativism). Thus, philosophy and science gradually start to lose their real fundaments in practice, too (11.2; 12.4).

According to the objectivist ideal of knowledge, only such knowledge can be regarded as truth which has stood the proof of the critical method of doubt—that is, unquestionable. As we have seen in the previous subchapters, objectivism is, in fact, not consistent at all, so in practice, it does not even try to follow its own ideal. Contrary to objectivism, Polanyi acknowledges that there is no unquestionable knowledge—that is, he accepts a concept of knowledge which is consistent and complies with scientific practice. Therefore, in contrast to cold critical examination, in reality, the discovery of truth happens in the following way:

> The personal participation of the knower in the knowledge he believes himself to possess takes place within a flow of passion. We recognize intellectual beauty as a guide to discovery and as a mark of truth.[78]

It means that the search for the truth is not based on a logically coercive, objective method but rather on *intellectual passions*. In other words, truth simply cannot be deduced by an explicit method from objective (focal) facts. It can merely be recognized, unfolded, and then acknowledged by tacit skills and intellectual passions—that is, the discovery of truth is a *kind of tacit integration*, based on several, subsidiary facts (3.3).

Polanyi differentiates between *personal* and *subjective* passions. A person merely endures his subjective passions and feelings. They are only passive, not part of those commitments which go beyond the person. However, the point of personal passions is exactly that they go beyond the person and actively encourage him, for example, to search for the truth. Therefore, the personal "transcends the disjunction between subjective and objective."[79]

A personal act is a kind of act which, on the one hand, is motivated and guided by individual passions and thus cannot be objective, but on the

---

78. Polanyi, *Personal Knowledge*, 300.
79. Polanyi, *Personal Knowledge*, 300.

other hand, it is also that which is submitted to such impersonal principles which are over and above the person—that is, due to these principles, a personal act cannot merely be subjective. It follows that the personal has two poles, both a *universal* and a *subjective* one, which are connected by the act of commitment.

The two poles of personal knowledge:

Passionate person → Commitment → Universal principles

For example, according to the nature of heuristic acts, the assertion that "I believe that snow is white" emphasizes the personal pole, while the "snow is white is true" emphasizes the universal pole, which generally arises in the act of persuasion. But in the sense of their point, the meaning of the two assertions is the same—that is, a person has committed himself to a truth ("snow is white") which is independent of him and universally valid. "According to the logic of commitment, *truth is something that can be thought of only by believing it*."[80]

The answer to the question why the nature and structure of personal knowledge are of this kind can be found in the evolutionary origins of human beings. Polanyi defines the territory of the personal in human intellectual life according to this fact:

1. Perception and satisfaction of appetites, which were mainly controlled by unconscious, personal judgments, lie at the lower end of this scale. (In case of perception, however, it happens from time to time that the automatic, passive processes were overruled by conscious intellectual acts.) Bodily processes under the intellectual level are, of course, tightly connected to the person himself, but these processes do not force the person to commit himself because they can be corrected, as it happens quite often. It means that the person does not identify himself entirely with the inarticulate person of the body to whom these lower-level desires and motivations belong. Therefore, the participation of the person in these processes is severely limited; it is rather the territory of the subjective.

2. For other reasons, the person's participation is also restricted in the highest-level intellectual processes. In mathematics (and partly in exact sciences), the intellectual processes were controlled by strict formal rules and principles that, in a sense, maim all real, personal activities and judgments. Therefore, it is rather the territory of the objective. Since this kind of thinking is at the highest level of the intellectual

---

80. Polanyi, *Personal Knowledge*, 305.

scale, it can be regarded as natural that the Laplacian ideal of perfectly exact and formal knowledge was born.

3. The real territory of the personal can be found between these two border zones. It is the territory of articulate problems that can only be solved, on the one hand, by tacit heuristic passions and, on the other one, in the framework of a coherent and explicit intellectual scheme. Polanyi claims that the best example for it is the scientific discovery itself: "From the first intimation of a hidden problem and throughout its pursuit to the point of its solution, the process of discovery is guided by a personal vision and sustained by a personal conviction."[81]

It means that although thinking goes forward in an explicit conceptual and explanatory framework, it also has to overcome the natural, logical gaps of the process by tacit, heuristic, and passionate efforts, and if it is necessary, it will have to reinterpret or modify the intellectual framework itself radically. According to this:

> While originality conflicts sharply with the ideal of a completely formalized intelligence, it also differs altogether from drive-satisfaction. For our appetites are ours, and it is ourselves they seek to satisfy, while the discoverer seeks a solution to a problem that is satisfying and compelling both for himself and everybody else. Discovery is an act in which satisfaction, submission, and universal legislation are indissolubly combined.[82]

So the satisfaction of a desire and the universal intention are the two endpoints of personal knowledge. However, universal principles can exist for someone if and only if the given person commits himself and submits his own personal acts and judgments to these universal principles. Without these principles, there remains merely the subjective satisfaction of desires. In other words, if there are no acknowledged and followed universal principles, knowledge will necessarily remain subjective, which leads to relativism. Universal principles, however, do not exist as (objective) facts but rather *as truth*. They will become valid solely by a personal act if someone commits himself to them. "Commitment is, in this sense, the only path for approaching the universally valid."[83]

It means that universal principles cannot be grasped in the same way as it can be done with tangible things—for example, with "snow is white," which can easily be stated by an explicit sentence and then asserted in the

---

81. Polanyi, *Personal Knowledge*, 301.
82. Polanyi, *Personal Knowledge*, 301.
83. Polanyi, *Personal Knowledge*, 303.

denotative sense. Universal principles can only be grasped in such ways which reflect the structure of affirmation of "snow is white is true"—that is, universal principles can only be grasped *by a tacit act in the existential sense* as a person commits himself to those principles at the same time (3.4). Without this, they will lose their meaning.[84]

The precondition of any *responsible, free act* is *a person's need for universality*. When a person acts only due to his desires, he is free only in the sense that he follows his *own* desires. He is not restricted by external forces and he does not have to be responsible for anybody or anything in his choices. However, the need for universality, acknowledged by a person, urges him to such constructive efforts that it will also coerce his actions: according to the universal intention of his commitment, he will freely act by his own will as he *has to* act.[85] "Here I stand and cannot otherwise," Polanyi cites Luther.[86] In other words: "The freedom of the subjective person to do as he pleases is overruled by the freedom of the responsible person to act as he must."[87]

So although he has no choices, if a person acts conscientiously, according to his responsible situation, he still freely chooses what he has to choose. In this case, the person is not restricted by external forces as well (as in the case of acts by subjective desires) since the person's choice stems from his *own* commitment and his *own* sense of responsibility. From another point of view, there are no free choices in the case of subjective desires either because the person's actual desires determine his decision entirely.

The main difference lies in the intentions of these acts and the natures of the two different kinds of determinations. In the case of subjective desires, a person's intention is merely to satisfy his own *bodily desire*, while in the case of a responsible free person, it is to satisfy his intellectual and moral desire, which go beyond his person and toward a *universal principle*. This difference is the reason that the former person is free only in a very limited sense, while the latter one is universally free.

The act of a responsible person is always heuristic since there are always indeterminacies and logical gaps in his acts. Consequently, he has to bridge these gaps by his own active, heuristic efforts (Polanyi's example is scientific discovery). This heuristic process, however, significantly differs from the nature of the passive act-determination of desires. The acts of responsible, free persons become determined by the fact that "they are submitting to the universal status of the hidden reality which they are

---

84. Polanyi, *Personal Knowledge*, 308.
85. Polanyi, *Personal Knowledge*, 309.
86. Polanyi, *Personal Knowledge*, 308.
87. Polanyi, *Personal Knowledge*, 309.

trying to approach"—that is, their acts are determined merely by a *future reality* (goal) that they want to discover or simply want to reach,[88] while the acts of the subjective person are determined by the *actual conditions* of his desires. This difference is, in fact, between a goal-directed and an effect-like determination, which are called "*a fronte*" and "*a tergo*" determinations by Polanyi. The former complies with the nature of time, and although desires work at the biological level, for a person who wants to submit himself to higher goals, their determination can be described as mechanical, so this latter determination complies with the nature of space (2.4). As I have already promised, I will examine these determinations in detail (9.7) after a detailed examination of the concepts of space and time in chapter 6, but we will understand the deeper meaning of Polanyi's words in the context of our evolutionary origin concerning the concept of truth only in subchapter 11.5.

So, merely the act of commitment establishes a relationship with reality.[89] If a person says a sentence, for example, "it is night," without any commitment—for instance, just for fun—then the content of the sentence can only comply with reality in that *random* situation if it is, in fact, night. However, if a person says this sentence with commitment, then the content of the sentence complies with reality *due to his personal experiences*. "Responsible action excludes randomness, even as it suppresses egocentric arbitrariness."[90] Of course, random events impact any responsible, free act, but they do not guide them.

The goal of problem-solving or scientific discovery is but the revelation of the hidden reality (3.2). These processes are heuristic in nature. It follows that they cannot be mechanistic or logically coercive since the continuously changing nature of reality excludes these possibilities:

> The implications of new knowledge can never be known at its birth. For it speaks of something real, and to attribute reality to something is to express the belief that its presence will yet show up in an indefinite number of unpredictable ways.
>
> An empirical statement is true to the extent to which it reveals an aspect of reality, a reality largely hidden to us, and existing therefore independently of our knowing it. By trying to say something that is true about a reality believed to be existing independently of our knowing it, all assertions of fact necessarily carry universal intent. Our claim to speak of reality serves

---

88. Polanyi, *Personal Knowledge*, 309.
89. Polanyi, *Personal Knowledge*, 304.
90. Polanyi, *Personal Knowledge*, 310.

thus as the external anchoring of our commitment in making a factual statement.[91]

If the major part of reality is not known, and this is the fact, then these hidden parts of reality will exist *independently* from human knowing and manifest themselves in unpredictable ways. And if assertions of facts now refer to those aspects of reality which originally existed independently from human knowing, then these assertions will be universally intended, and everybody will have to accept them as true facts. It follows: "In a heuristic commitment, affirmation, surrender and legislation are fused into a single thought, bearing on a hidden reality. . . . A result obtained by applying strict rules mechanically, without committing anyone personally, can mean nothing to anybody."[92]

This last quotation once again refers to the Laplacian ideal of objective knowledge (2.3). This "knowledge" is the consequence of perfect and logically coercive rules (the ideal equations of physics) but means nothing because Laplace's demon is a bodiless, purely rational spirit who, per definition, *cannot commit himself* to anything. He "knows" all the possible explicit sentences concerning reality, but without tacit skills, commitments, and universal intentions, he cannot assert these sentences. Therefore, the objectivist ideal of knowledge—the Laplacian supercomputer—knows, in fact, nothing. The system of perfect and exact explicit sentences "known" by it only means anything to human persons. Laplace's demon seemingly "owns" this knowledge only because of a deceptive substitution.

It follows that, according to Polanyi, scientific discovery is not a logically coercive mechanistic process but rather the *highest level of craftsmanship*. It is the highest level because it uses the most-improved tangible and intellectual tools. However, its point is also the same as that of the simplest craftsmanship: it is based on tacit human skills.[93] As every other intentional act, scientific discovery is also based on unconscious bodily functions and limited by inborn and gradually developed skills of childhood. Moreover: "Worse still, we are creatures of circumstance . . . and this reliance on the cultural machinery of our society continues through life."[94] So, scientific discovery is an active heuristic act, and since it is not logically coercive, it always includes the possibility of failure. In consequence, human persons can only believe in such things that could also be false.[95]

91. Polanyi, *Personal Knowledge*, 311.
92. Polanyi, *Personal Knowledge*, 311.
93. Polanyi, *Personal Knowledge*, 311–12.
94. Polanyi, *Personal Knowledge*, 322.
95. Polanyi, *Personal Knowledge*, 313.

From the fact that human persons can be wrong—that is, that there is no such scientific method that can necessarily lead us to the truth—and due to the different convictions of different persons, it does not follow, however, that there is more than one truth. In Polanyi's words: "Therefore, though every person may believe something different to be true, there is only one truth."[96]

3.7 Conclusion

Personal knowledge is about to consistently face the fact that we are the children of evolution. Objectivism and the critical method of doubt are based on the rational ideal of man that is, in fact, a strange and false picture of God. This ideal has led to the situation that modern critical philosophy and science have disavowed one of the two basic cognitive faculties of human beings: *belief*. Without the passionate commitment of the scientist to a sign of the truth, the critical picture of the process of scientific discovery becomes a fictional house of cards and the detailed critical analysis of the history of science will utterly destroy it, leading to relativism and the questioning of the fundamental beliefs and values of science itself.

Belief is not faith, according to Christian dogmatism; *belief is the fiduciary fundament of any human knowledge*. We will have to trust our sense of balance if we want to ride a bicycle; we will have to trust the hammer if we want to hit the nail into the wall; we will have to trust our language if we want to speak; we will have to trust our sense of scientific beauty if we want to discover a new theory; and we will have to trust our sense of reality if we want to understand the real meaning of a new scientific discovery—for example, the meaning of the theory of relativity.

Personal knowledge is about to face the fact that there is no objective "view from nowhere." We have to understand the universe from our personal point of reference, from our centers lying within our body. It is our starting point, our evolutionary heritage, and there is no clean sheet to start. In Polanyi's words:

> I believe, therefore, that as I am called upon to live and die in this body, struggling to satisfy its desires, recording my impressions by aid of such sense organs as it is equipped with, and acting through the puny machinery of my brain, my nerves, and my muscles, so I am called upon also to acquire the instruments of intelligence from my early surroundings and to use

---

96. Polanyi, *Personal Knowledge*, 315.

these particular instruments to fulfill the universal obligations to which I am subject.[97]

However, these bodily and intellectual skills, passions, and faculties not only define our starting point and our fundamental beliefs but also allow us to discover and understand our environment, our society, and the universe that surrounds us. In its main point, the scientist does nothing more than a young child or an animal in the woods: he tries to discover and understand the different aspects of reality due to his interests. He merely does this at a much higher intellectual level, with more advanced skills and tools, thanks to the technological and cultural development of Western civilization. If he wants to reach new scientific discoveries, however, he will have to trust his masters, his institutions, his scientific equipment, and, most of all, the inherited conceptual and explanatory framework in which he thinks. These are his fiduciary fundaments by which he has to start his work.

---

97. Polanyi, *Personal Knowledge*, 323.

4

The Meaning of Randomness

4.1 Preface

In science, perhaps the first thing that comes to our mind about randomness is the strange behavior of particles at the fundamental material level, according to the ruling, Copenhagen interpretation of quantum mechanics. As we have seen in subchapter 3.4, it cannot be unambiguously told what they will do next. For many scientists, this phenomenon suggests that there is a real randomness in nature which is maybe in connection with higher-level random phenomena—such as mutations in DNA or even the phenomenon of free will. However, according to Einstein's theory of relativity, there is no such randomness in nature: "God is not playing dice." This is one of the most severe contradictions between the two fundamental theories of modern physics.

In chapter 1, we have seen that, according to Dawkins and the neo-Darwinian theory, life originated from a random material event in the primordial soup more than four billion years ago, and the random processes of mutation and natural selection have determined the formation of life ever since. At the same time, since living beings are but comprehensive, orderly wholes, it follows that there is a strong connection between randomness and order. Even the casting of dice can create a kind of order if, for example, all of the dice show six on top. In subchapter 3.4, however, we have seen one of the experiments of Darwin in detail. The question was whether there is a real difference between the heights of plants in the cases of cross-fertilization and self-fertilization due to the nature of these processes or if the observable differences are only due to random processes—that is, if an observed, comprehensive order of plants is the consequence of some kind of hidden principle of nature or if it is just the consequence of random processes. This suggests that randomness cannot create real order or that, at least in different cases—a principle versus a random process—we have to speak about order in very different senses.

So, the question is: what is the connection between order and randomness? The examination of this problem will also shed light on the meaning of emergence—that is, in which sense can we speak of emergence in different cases of comprehensive, orderly wholes? During the chapter, I will use one of Polanyi's examples that I believe well-demonstrates the meaning of randomness and its connection to order and emergence (and, of course, to personal knowledge). At the end of the chapter, we will see the relationship between randomness, evolution, and personal reality, too.

In chapter 3 of his *Personal Knowledge*, Polanyi puts forward the mentioned example, according to which there are pebbles in a beautifully kept garden of a railway station arranged into words reading, "Welcome to Wales by British Railways."[1] Everybody who understands the given language would recognize this as a *meaningful, comprehensive pattern of order* and think that the careful stationmaster greets us in this way. Yet how can we know that this is the case if we have never seen the stationmaster arranging the pebbles in such a pattern? What if the pebbles are there in the garden and arranged as a consequence of, for example, a wild storm or a hurricane? How can we know for sure that such is not the case?

The answer that generally seems immediately evident to us entails computing the probability of the latter case: that is, the exact probability that a hurricane can randomly arrange pebbles into the specific pattern reading, "Welcome to Wales by British Railways." Since the result would be an awfully small number, we could calmly rule out this possibility and thereby strengthen our original impression that the stationmaster intentionally arranged the pebbles to greet us. However, the answer is not so simple and unambiguous, for a hurricane, of course, can create many other random, meaningless patterns of pebbles, the probability of which, in fact, would be an *equally small* number. Nevertheless, contrary to this fact, we would never claim that these meaningless pebble states are also the intentional work of the stationmaster. What is the source of this problem? Moreover, why do we state that any arbitrary state of pebbles by a hurricane is random whatsoever when the material processes of a hurricane—and thus the movements of the pebbles—are, in fact, entirely deterministic (according to the principles of physics)? Random equals deterministic?! Apparently not, but then again, what is the meaning of randomness?

---

1. Polanyi, *Personal Knowledge*, 33.

4.2 The Concept of Order

As we have seen, according to Polanyi's example, based on his personal experience of a journey, at the first station in Wales, there is a beautifully kept garden with pebbles, arranged by a careful stationmaster, to greet us: "Welcome to Wales by British Railways." Of course, everybody who understands the given language would at once recognize this as a *meaningful*, comprehensive *pattern of order* (figure 4). Contrary to this, for example, years later, because the careful stationmaster is retired, the pebbles are now randomly scattered all over the garden. Naturally, the pebbles have a kind of structure in this *randomly scattered state* as well, but *no meaning* at all (figure 5).

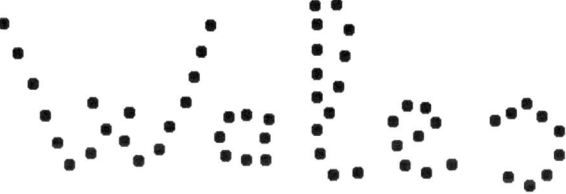

Figure 4. The Wales lettering.

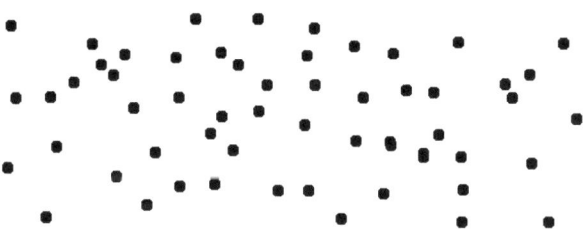

Figure 5. Random pebbles.

Nonetheless, *at the level of the pebbles*, there is no essential difference between the two cases. We see the same, well-defined pebbles, only in different positions. On a sheet of paper, we can map out the explicit location of every pebble, assigning exact numeric parameters to each of them in *both* cases—this is the exact, entirely explicit knowledge of Laplace's demon.[2] However, in themselves, these exact, numeric parameters could not deter-

---

2. If we ignore the fact, of course, that it is only an analogy and the pebbles do not comply perfectly with the ideal material objects—that is, particles of the knowledge of the demon.

mine which state of pebbles is meaningful and which is not, which is an orderly lettering and which is only a random pile of stones (2.5). Merely on the grounds of the explicit, numeric parameters, it could be vice versa, as there are several other, numerically-different states in which we would see the meaningful pattern of Wales lettering (multiple realizability: compare figure 6 to figure 4).

Figure 6. Multiple realizability.

There is no unambiguous, explicit formula to define the meaningful patterns of the Wales scheme in numeric parameters that would determine an exact boundary between meaningful and meaningless pebble states. The reason for this is that the meaningful Wales scheme is not only an explicit listing of numeric parameters at the level of the pebbles but also a *lettering* that we recognize as a *higher-level, comprehensive pattern of order*. As a matter of fact, in the second case of the randomly scattered pebbles, there is no pattern and we recognize *nothing* (figure 5). This fact, however, does not mean that we cannot get meaningful or even crucial physical knowledge of the meaningless movement of pebbles during another type of scientific investigation.

So, according to our explicit knowledge of the parts (the pebbles), the Wales lettering is not distinguishable; it is just one state of pebbles among many others. But if one says, "Yes, it has specific numeric parameters, contrary, for example, to the numeric parameters of the scattered pebbles," he has to explain why those specific parameters referencing the pebbles are distinguished. Why? The only reason is that these numeric parameters mark out a meaningful lettering, but the meaningful lettering is *already* a comprehensive pattern of order—that is, his answer is based on our knowledge of comprehensive, orderly wholes as well as on our knowledge of the random explicit parts. It will be a deceptive substitution if he persists in the idea that these numeric parameters are specific in themselves (2.5).

In the first case, we have two levels (figure 4): the higher-level of the Wales lettering and the lower-level of the pebbles. In the second case, however, we have only the level of the stones (figure 5). The pebbles are clear, *individual, tangible things*, while the Wales lettering has no separate, tangible body; rather, it is a meaningful, *comprehensive pattern of order*—at the level of pebbles, a specific listing of numeric parameters. The relationship between the two levels is *not symmetric* because there are random piles of pebbles without a meaningful pattern (case 2), but for the Wales lettering, the pebbles (or something else as a body of the lettering) are necessary *conditions* (case 1). This fact is the reason why the Wales lettering is an *emergent* phenomenon and the pebbles are its material body. *An emergent phenomenon emerges from its material conditions and cannot exist without it; an emergent phenomenon is a comprehensive, orderly whole in the random material conditions.*

If there is no way to differentiate between different types of pebble states and recognize the comprehensive Wales lettering of certain specific pebble states merely based on lower-level, explicit knowledge of the parts, then it follows that we recognize it based on other types of knowledge. In Polanyi's words, "Man has the power to establish real patterns in nature," [3] as we can recognize individual, tangible pebbles. We cannot define these comprehensive patterns of order in exact numeric parameters in the same way as the actual parameters of the stones, but we can clearly recognize them *by our natural tacit senses and skills*.

Therefore, on the one hand, we recognize higher-level, emergent patterns of order by our tacit powers and, on the other, we can make exact knowledge about the lower-level parts in numeric parameters, formulas, and equations, etc. These two kinds of knowledge have fundamentally *different natures*, but both of them are meaningful and important for us. The emergent knowledge concerns complex, *comprehensive* patterns of order (e.g., frogs, men, crystals, tornados, machines, etc.) and is *tacit*, while the physical one refers to simple, individual, quasi *point-like* entities (e.g., atoms, mass-points, quanta, DNA sequences, etc.) and is *explicit*. The reason why our emergent knowledge concerning the Wales lettering cannot be replaced by our explicit knowledge of the parts is that the latter simply *does not contain* the former—Laplace's demon has not and cannot have tacit knowledge concerning comprehensive, emergent phenomena (2.3).

In the previous chapter, following Polanyi's argument, we have seen that every kind of human knowledge is personal, however, "the degree of our personal participation varies greatly within our various acts of knowing"[4]— as in the case of our Wales example. On the basis of this fact, we can speak

3. Polanyi, *Personal Knowledge*, 37.
4. Polanyi, *Personal Knowledge*, 36.

about three different kinds of personal knowledge, which, as we will see soon, have considerably different meaning concerning reality:

1. *Objective facts*: in the case of the actual places of pebbles, the casting of three double sixes, or the movements of stars;
2. *Personal facts*: if a meaningful, comprehensive pattern is arranged in the pebbles or if one appraises the casting of three double sixes as an astounding, random event;
3. *Subjective mistakes*: if someone (as the astrologists) appraises the constellations as real, meaningful patterns or if someone thinks that a real, meaningful, comprehensive pattern of order (for example, the Wales lettering by the stationmaster) is aroused by mere chance.[5]

So, on the basis of our analyses, following Polanyi, we can claim that the recognition of order in nature is the achievement of two related personal judgments: "Every kind of human knowing, ranging from perception to scientific observation, includes an appreciation both of order contrasted to randomness and of the degree of this order."[6]

1. *The recognition of order*: we can distinguish order from randomness—that is, the orderly Wales lettering from the randomly scattered pebbles. In other words, we can find explanations for comprehensive, orderly wholes of nature, suggesting that they are not merely random and illusory—as the "Wales scheme," formed by a hurricane—but rather the consequences of some natural law or ordering principle.
2. *The appraisal of the deepness of order*: we can appraise the extent and deepness of an order. By this second personal skill, we cannot just explain the recognized comprehensive, orderly wholes of nature, but we can appraise the position of the given order within the scale of coherent existence.

To clarify the meaning of these two claims, in the next two subchapters, we have to investigate the problem and our Wales example from new perspectives.

4.3 The Recognition of Order

According to the Wales example, if someone finds a garden with pebbles, there are three possible options:

5. Polanyi, *Personal Knowledge*, 36–37.
6. Polanyi, *Personal Knowledge*, 38.

1. There is a recognizable, comprehensive pattern of order in the pebbles—a Wales lettering—arranged intentionally by the stationmaster.
2. There is no recognizable pattern of order in the pebbles.
3. There is a recognizable, comprehensive pattern of order in the pebbles—a Wales scheme—that is not the consequence of some intentional human activity but rather the material processes in the garden (e.g., a hurricane).

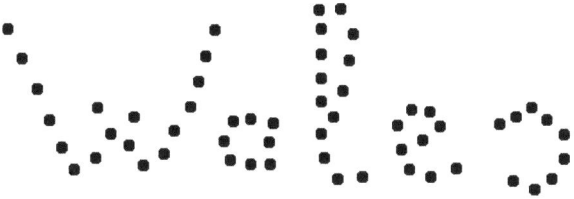

Figure 7. Case 1.

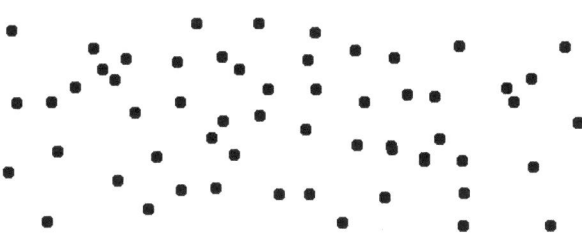

Figure 8. Case 2.

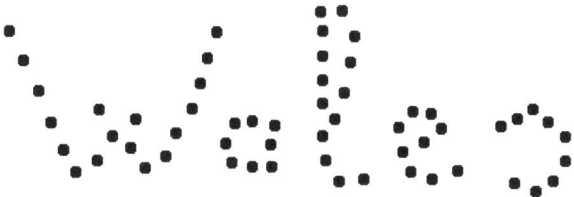

Figure 9. Case 3.

Suppose that, according to Polanyi's little story, someone arrives at the railway station and notices the Wales scheme in the garden. Immediately, he will think that it complies with case 1—that it was arranged intentionally by the stationmaster and is a meaningful, comprehensive pattern of order. Yet how would he know that this is for sure the case and the Wales scheme is not just the consequence of randomness?

As we have seen in the Preface, we are inclined to answer this question by referring to the tiny possibility that could lead to the Wales scheme without any human interference. It can be expressed numerically by relating the particular state of the pebbles of the Wales scheme to all possible states of the pebbles in the garden (one particular pebble state to x possible states—that is, 1/x) which would indeed be a very small number. Therefore, the Wales scheme was intentionally arranged by the stationmaster (case 1) because the probability of the other case (case 3) is awfully small.

However, this answer is not simple and unambiguous but instead highly problematic; the probability of a particular state of pebbles in the garden which has no recognizable pattern (case 2) would be exactly the *same* (one to all possible states, that is, 1/x) as the probability of the random Wales scheme (case 3). Nevertheless, contrary to this fact, no one would ever claim that this meaningless state of pebbles is therefore also the intentional work of the stationmaster. Moreover, no one would ever argue that it is the consequence of randomness—as it is claimed when the Wales scheme was not arranged by the stationmaster intentionally (case 3)—although *the probabilities are exactly the same* and *both of them were arranged by the same unintentional, physical processes in the garden.*

So, the questions are the following: when someone spots the Wales scheme, why does he believe that it complies with case 1? And why does he not notice that he argues for his belief inadequately, by probability calculations?

> We have assumed from the start that the arrangement of the pebbles which formed an intelligible set of words appropriate to the occasion represented a distinctive pattern. It was only in view of this orderliness that the question could be asked at all whether the orderliness was accidental or not. When the pebbles are scattered irregularly over the whole available area, they possess no pattern, and therefore the question whether the orderly pattern is accidental or not cannot rise.[7]

The answer to the first question is that we involuntarily regard the Wales scheme as unique compared to other pebble states (case 2). The basis

---

7. Polanyi, *Personal Knowledge*, 34.

of this judgment is our *personal knowledge* concerning different letterings, gardens, and railway stations. *Tacitly*, we *definitely know* that this Wales scheme is a lettering and was arranged by the stationmaster (case 1). We know because it is our natural, human experience that meaningful, comprehensive Wales letterings do not emerge by chance or by a hurricane from pebbles at appropriate places and on appropriate occasions. And if we still want explicit knowledge about the origin of the Wales lettering, we can get it quickly, without any hard and pointless explicit computing; we merely have to ask the stationmaster and he will tell us.

The answer to the second question is that we are arguing inadequately because, according to the Laplacian ideal of objective knowledge, we want to give a *non-personal* answer to the original question—that is, why we think that the Wales scheme was arranged intentionally by the stationmaster (case 1). To achieve this non-personal answer, we try to determine the so-called *a contrario* probability of our statement about the origin of the Wales lettering—that is, the probability that the Wales scheme was not arranged by the stationmaster (3.4). Our argument was deceptive, however, not only because the value of probability is exactly the same in all possible arrangements but also because it was based on our personal knowledge—that is, on the recognition of the comprehensive Wales scheme. Since if there were no recognizable scheme (case 2), the question that it was the consequence of randomness (case 3) or someone's intentional act (case 1), in fact, could not arise at all—thus numerically-expressed probabilities also could not be stated relating to it.

The reason that probabilities cannot be assigned to case 2 in itself is that it is precisely known, with 100 percent probability, that, in this case, the actual state of pebbles is the consequence of *deterministic* physical processes; and it is, of course, true for every other possible state of case 2. A value of probability can be assigned to any possible pebble state of case 2 *only if* it is *a contrario* contrasted to a peculiar possible state—for example, to the Wales scheme. *In itself*, every possible state is entirely determined either by physical processes or by the action of the stationmaster.

Suppose a new case, 1b, when there is a recognizable, comprehensive Wales scheme in the pebbles, arranged intentionally by the stationmaster, but the arriving person does not recognize it because, for example, he is Chinese and unfamiliar with the Latin alphabet. According to this situation, probabilities cannot be assigned to the Wales scheme as it was in case 2. This fact, on the one hand, shows the consequence of the lack of personal knowledge without which there is no question about probabilities at all, and, on the other, proves that the state of pebbles in the Wales scheme, once again, is *not the same* as the Wales scheme itself.

To explain this, let's consider the similarities and differences in the three original cases. In case 2, the particular state of pebbles is the consequence of deterministic physical processes just as the Wales scheme of case 3. Yet in case 2, no one would ever say that the state of pebbles is random, but in case 3, he would say exactly that. The contradiction, however, is only illusory since in case 3, the real meaning of the statement is not that the state of pebbles is random at the lower-level but rather that *the comprehensive, orderly Wales scheme is random at the higher-level*. That is, the assertion that the state of pebbles in the garden is the consequence of the lower-level, deterministic processes is, in fact, *correct in both cases*, only it is a vacant assertion because it was known with certainty (with 100 percent probability). The real meaning of the statement that the Wales scheme of case 3 is random—which, of course, is not known with perfect certainty—is that in contrast to case 1 of the intentionally arranged Wales lettering, *there is no specific order or ordering principle behind the particular state of pebbles*. Therefore, for the presumption of randomness—and thus for *a contrario* probability calculations—the prior assumption of ordering principles is needed.

Although it is well-established, perhaps this claim seems a little bit confusing because of the seemingly contradictory usage of the term "random." So let's take a closer look at the different cases of the usage of the term. Ernest Nagel, whose work, *The Structure of Science*, is still fundamental in the reduction and emergence debates, differentiates between five cases of chance or randomness:

1. Something happens unexpectedly rather than as the consequence of a deliberate plan; for example, two friends run into each other on the street.

2. No one knows the determining factors of an event or does not have enough knowledge of the factors to predict the determined event, so in practice, the event is random for us; for example, in principle, we can compute the result of a coin toss or rolling dice using Newtonian mechanics, but this is impossible to do before a football match.

3. An event is a consequence of the intersection of two independent, causal series; for example, a man walking on the street is hit by a flowerpot in a wild wind.

4. A given paradigm or "the context of inquiry" does not determine its object's every property; for example, the future positions of the planet Mars can be predicted precisely with the help of Newtonian gravitational theory, but to do any computing, we must first provide

the planet's initial position and velocity, which, of course, were not determined by the Newtonian theory.[8]

In these four cases, randomness is only a *relational* concept because here, *there are only deterministic events and processes* (coin tossing, dice rolling, a falling flowerpot, the movement of the planet Mars, etc.) and the events we call random are only the consequence of *the unique relationships of their determining factors or our insufficient knowledge of them*. Therefore, there is no "absolute" randomness or indeterministic processes; randomness and deterministic processes coexist well. In other words, a process that, in itself, is entirely deterministic (e.g., rolling dice), in relation with another process or system, could easily be random. W. Ron Ashby, in his *An Introduction to Cybernetics*, puts this: "By saying a factor is *random*, I do not refer to what the factor is in itself, but to the relation it has with the main system."[9] These words well reflect the approach of cybernetics and system theories which will be vital for us later. So, the question is: what are the entirely deterministic, determining factors in the case of the Wales lettering—the interrelations of which we call random?

Before considering the answer, let's look at Nagel's last case for randomness.

5. There are *no* determining factors or conditions for an event, so it happens *without any cause* (and we *know* that there is *no* cause).

In this case, randomness is not only a relational concept but also an *absolute* one. Nagel himself thinks that this absolute concept of randomness is contradicting,[10] as do Ashby, Einstein, and Polanyi himself. The main reason for questioning such absolute randomness is: how can we know *for sure* that an event has no cause and this is not simply the second Nagelian case of randomness, where we merely do not have enough knowledge about its determining factors? Nevertheless, this fifth case of randomness is not important for us in detail at this point, so I will investigate the problem later (4.6). What is important now is that randomness can be a relational concept. Therefore, if something appears to us as random, this does not at all mean that it is a consequence of some indeterministic or even supernatural process or factor, as someone might think if we start to speak about random, comprehensive phenomena compared to their material conditions in a minute.

---

8. Nagel, *Structure of Science*, 324–35.
9. Ashby, *Introduction to Cybernetics*, 259.
10. Nagel, *Structure of Science*, 335.

We have already seen a few times that when someone arrives at the railway station, he immediately and involuntary think that the Wales scheme has been arranged by the stationmaster (case 1), and if he learns that this is true, he will believe that the pebble state *is not random*; that is, it is a real message. But if this comes to be false (case 3), then he will believe that this specific pebble state *is random*, independent of the fact that, by the way, it has been arranged by entirely deterministic physical processes (e.g., a hurricane). Nevertheless, this does not mean that randomness equals determinism. It merely shows us the true meaning of the randomness of the pebbles in the garden. The pebble state in itself *at the lower-level* is deterministic in *both cases*, and the real question in our mind is the following: *is the Wales scheme determined only by lower-level, physical factors and principles or is it also determined by higher-level, emergent factors and principles?* In other words, can we understand the true nature of the Wales scheme only by our exact physical knowledge (case 3) or do we *also* have to use our higher-level, emergent knowledge concerning the intentions of the stationmaster and the meaning of the lettering in the context of the English language (case 1)?

If the Wales scheme is determined by *only physical factors and principles* (meaning that the pebble state is only the consequence of physical processes and due to physical laws), then the pebble state *is random* and without meaning, while if it is determined by *both physical factors and principles and emergent factors and principles* (meaning that it was created by the stationmaster, intentionally, using physical pebbles and according to the higher-level, ordering principles of English language), then it *is not random* and it has meaning.

Whether it is a consequence of some kind of higher-level, emergent *or* lower-level, physical processes, the real scientific question concerning the principles is not which is deterministic and which is random. To put it simply, the question is whether there is a higher-level, ordering principle or not. The random versus deterministic questioning is therefore a *false dichotomy* because the different kinds of determining factors and ordering principles are *all deterministic due to their own nature* and are all important and meaningful for us; we have to count, understand, and explain them *all*.

Nonetheless, in reality, if neither the intentionally arranged Wales lettering (case 1) nor the meaningless Wales scheme (case 3) is random and the term refers only to the lack of higher-level, ordering principles in case 3, then is there no real randomness in the example (and thus in similar cases of randomness)? No, in the relational sense, there is real randomness, because in case 1, when the lettering is determined by *both* physical and emergent factors, the *relationship* of these two determining factors is random. *This relationship*—and not something else—is what is indeed random. In this and only this random relationship, the otherwise deterministic, physical factors become the lower-level, *random conditions* of higher-level, emergent processes and principles. In consequence, it is *logically impossible* to explain the meaningful, comprehensive pattern of the order of case 1 *by only one* determining factor or principle.

We can explain a phenomenon using just one kind of principle if and *only if* we rely solely on our physical knowledge to determine the given state of the pebbles. In case 2, concerning the randomly scattered pebbles, this is undoubtedly the fact, but if there is a recognizable, comprehensive pattern to which a higher-level knowledge could refer, yet the knowledge of the higher-level pattern can be determined by our physical knowledge (case 3 of the fake Wales "lettering"), then, in fact, this is also the case (reduction). This still does not mean, however, that the two kinds of knowledge are identical. To recognize the fake Wales "lettering," we still need our higher-level knowledge concerning the "lettering," but in this case, we do not recognize a real, meaningful comprehensive pattern of order using our tacit powers. Instead, it is just an interesting, miraculous, and "random" phenomenon. If we think henceforward that it is a real, meaningful pattern, which emerged according to higher-level, ordering principles, then, we commit a *subjective mistake*.

Polanyi gives a detailed and telling example from his own scientific field for the workings of personal knowledge concerning the discovery of hidden, ordering principles in science. It is about the law of chemical proportions—that is, what the exact ratio of different elements in chemical compounds is. Once again, we remain in the field of exact sciences.

The law of chemical proportions can be determined by the detailed analyses of lower-level, material parts of the compound, which is, of course, a higher-level, comprehensive, orderly phenomenon composed from the parts. For example, salt is the compound of two different materials: sodium and chloride. In principle, the results could be any possible proportion (e.g., 378,954/984,758 or 366,544/786,454), because there is no such necessary rule that the ratio of elements have to be as simple as 1:1, 1:2, and so on. As a matter of fact, the scientists would have *much more objective* proportions if they had not supposed that the proportions had to be simple—due to some hidden ordering principle that was not known at that time. So, from this point of view, their choice could seem arbitrary. It means that according to the Laplacian ideal of objectivity, and based on the exact measurement of lower-level, material parts, they should have insisted on such results as 23/45 or 41/83 and should not have simplified them for subjective, arbitrary reasons to, for instance, 1/2. This insistence on the objectivist ideal, however, could have prevented the development of science because Dalton's atomic theory was, in fact, *based on this "arbitrary" concept* of simple chemical proportions; that is, the chemical proportion of 1/2 in H_2O, for example, is the consequence of the valency of different atoms. Later, Bohr and Rutherford only continued Dalton's work to explain the deeper meaning of this, at first sight, seemingly arbitrary system of simple proportions:[11]

> Dalton's discovery of the atomic theory was itself based on the evidence of simple chemical proportions and thus confirmed the intimations of reality contained in the appraisal of this orderly pattern.[12]

So, ignoring objectivity and exactness on the basis of their personal scientific skills and knowledge, when these chemists got nearly simple fractions for the proportions of elements in chemical compounds, they appraised that the roughly simple results of their experiments were not just the consequence of some randomness but rather, in fact, there is a hidden, ordering principle of simple, chemical proportions behind the exact data. We have to follow these early scientists to find the ordering principles behind life, evolution, and emergence.

It follows from the results of this subchapter that "the conception of events governed by chance implies a reference to orderly patterns which such events can simulate only by coincidence."[13] Polanyi's examples are the constellations by which the horoscopes calculate: astrology assumes that the particular, comprehensive orders of constellations are meaningful, but this assumption is false. They are *merely the consequences of* deterministic, physical movements of stars, just as the illusory Wales scheme in case 3 is the consequence of the deterministic, physical movements of pebbles. It means that the creators of horoscopes believe that they can grasp the manifestation of a hidden ordering principle in the constellations—as it was done, for example, by Einstein, in the case of space-time, with his theory of relativity—but in fact, they commit a subjective mistake because, in reality, the meaningless, deterministic movements of the stars display the wonderful patterns of constellation (for example, the W-scheme of Cassiopeia) *only by chance*.[14]

> Randomness [that is, the movements of stars and pebbles] alone can never produce a significant pattern, for it consists in the absence of any such pattern; and we must not treat the

---

11. Polanyi, *Personal Knowledge*, 40–43.
12. Polanyi, *Personal Knowledge*, 42.
13. Polanyi, *Personal Knowledge*, 36.
14. Polanyi, *Personal Knowledge*, 36.

configuration of a random event as a significant pattern, whether by attributing to it fictitiously a distinctiveness that it does not possess, as in the case of the scattered pebbles, or by granting it erroneously a specious significance, such as the fulfilment of a horoscope.[15]

Random, meaningless system	Orderly, meaningful system
the W-scheme of Cassiopeia	Wales lettering
there is no higher-level, ordering principle	there is a higher-level, ordering principle
↑ *determining interaction*	↕ *random interaction*
movements of stars	movements of pebbles

Table 2: The relation of random and ordered systems to lower-level, random systems.

This, of course, as we have seen, does not mean that the lower-level, background processes—that is, the movements of stars or pebbles—are random in themselves but only that they are random *in relation to* meaningful, comprehensive orderly phenomena. So, to make it perfectly clear, if I speak of deterministic, material processes, it will mean that I refer to them *in themselves*; but if there is an emergent, comprehensive orderly whole, I will refer to these *same* material processes *in relation to higher-level orders* as random, and both of my statements will be equally true. It follows that in a universal sense, it is true that *material processes are deterministic and*, at the same time, it is also true that *they are random* if there is any emergent, comprehensive phenomenon in the universe to make this latter assertion true, too.

Polanyi's critique against the *a contrario* method of R. A. Fischer (3.4) is based on this recognition, and it also grounds his argument against neo-Darwinism (4.7):

> To test the probability of such coincidences and hence the permissibility of assuming that they have taken place, is the method of Sir Ronald Fisher for establishing *a contrario* the reality of an orderly pattern.[16]

---

15. Polanyi, *Personal Knowledge*, 37–38.
16. Polanyi, *Personal Knowledge*, 36.

That is, for the sake of illusory objectivity, to allow the possibility that random astrological patterns can arise from stellar constellations in other ways than random ones, that a hurricane can create an illusory Wales scheme in ways that are not random, or, from a different perspective, that a real, comprehensive pattern can be the consequence of a random process. It means that one does not undertake his *personal judgment* openly, according to which one comprehensive, orderly pattern is real and another one is not, but, according to the Laplacian ideal of objective knowledge, assigns to them—more precisely, assigns to the actual state of the parts of the comprehensive whole—*nonpersonal probability values* by which he can categorize them. This method consequently allows that an illusory scheme might be the consequence of a real, ordering principle because he renders probability value to this logical possibility and, vice versa, allows the possibility that a real, comprehensive pattern might be only the consequence of chance.

This train of thought—as we have seen in the case of Dawkins's Boeing 747 analogy (1.2) and will see again, in detail, in subchapter 4.7—corresponds perfectly to holding that, for the sake of the illusion of objectivity and explicit accuracy, we allow the possibility that the real, meaningful order of life can randomly emerge from meaningless material processes or that the evolution of real, meaningful living beings can occur randomly. However, random structures—as shown in the fake Wales "lettering" of case 3 and the W-scheme of Cassiopeia—have no reality and true meaning.

So, the question of whether a pattern of order is meaningful and real or not cannot be answered by the probability of stellar and pebble movements because our probability statements do not refer to the exact star or pebble movements, which in themselves are entirely deterministic, *but to* existent or non-existent *ordering principles* of comprehensive patterns. As we have seen in cases 2 and 3, the appraisal of an orderly pattern cannot be done by the examination of lower-level, deterministic processes alone: "On these grounds I suggest, quite generally, that the appraisal of order is an act of personal knowledge, exactly as is the assessment of probability to which it is allied."[17]

If the detailed examination of lower-level, deterministic processes cannot determine which scheme is real and which one is only an illusion, then another principle is needed to do the task. Therefore, the recognition of comprehensive, orderly wholes is not only based on personal knowledge, as we have seen at the end of the previous subchapter, but also the appraisal of the reality of different kinds of comprehensive, orderly wholes. In Polanyi's words:

17. Polanyi, *Personal Knowledge*, 36.

Man has the power to establish real patterns in nature, the reality of which is manifested by the fact that their future implications extend indefinitely beyond the experience which they were originally known to control. The appraisal of such order is made with universal intent and conveys indeed a claim to an unlimited range of as yet unspecifiable, true intimations.[18]

Regarding these comprehensive patterns, however, unambiguous statements cannot be formulated, only probability ones. Therefore, in contrast to the Laplacian ideal of objectivity, the possibility of subjective mistakes is *always present* and would be realized if someone made false personal judgments about the examined phenomena. In principle, there is no infallible, critical method; Fisher's one is not infallible either. Nevertheless, if someone is right, then future consequences will confirm his claim in unforeseeable ways—as happened with the theories of Dalton, Copernicus, and Einstein (3.2).

4.4 The Appraisal of the Deepness of an Order

Polanyi states the following concerning how to determine the deepness of an order:

> Any entity—whether an object or determinate process—will be the more clearly set off against its background, the more amply its internal particulars show steadiness and regularity—combined with an amply confirmed absence of any co-variance between these particulars and those of the background.[19]

I am going to use our Wales example once again to clarify the meaning of this statement based on the fact that all recognition of order happens before a distinct background.

In case 2, regarding the randomly scattered pebbles of the Wales example, there is a perfect correspondence between the "pattern" of the scattered pebbles and the background—in consequence of which, there is not and cannot be any recognizable pattern before the background. Every part is moved by the random physical processes in the garden.

In case 1, featuring the Wales lettering arranged by the stationmaster, since parts of the pattern are moved by the stationmaster and parts of the background by the random physical processes in the garden, there is no correspondence between the meaningful pattern and the background at all.

18. Polanyi, *Personal Knowledge*, 37.
19. Polanyi, *Personal Knowledge*, 38.

If the stationmaster stops arranging the pebbles, however, then the movements of the stones are going to disrupt this real pattern too. It is, therefore, a special case of emergence with limited deepness.

In case 3, there is a random pattern—a Wales scheme by the random physical processes of the garden—that is separated from its background to some extent, but we are still inclined to think that, in reality, it has *no meaning* at all. In this case, the parts are also all moved by the lower-level, physical processes in the garden, and this separation of the Wales scheme is only random. It can be seen that it is random (and thus the Wales scheme has no meaning) from the fact that it shows minimal persistence and regularity depending on how much the random shifts of its parts hinder the recognition of the fake pattern and—in the meantime—destroys the separation of the fake pattern from its background. It is, therefore, a vague case of emergence with no real deepness.

I would like to draw our attention to an essential difference between the real Wales lettering and the fake Wales scheme, which already suggests the primary fundament of any emergent phenomena and the main topic of Part Two: Emergence. As we have seen earlier, at the lower material level, both the real Wales lettering and the fake Wales scheme have the same structure that can be mapped out on a sheet of paper. It well illustrates that it is a structure *in space*. The fake Wales scheme is nothing more than a momentary space-structure that has no relationship with higher-level ordering principles. But the real Wales lettering does. However, this significant connection cannot be seen in the space of the sheet of paper, representing only the lower-level, material structure but not the comprehensive existential meaning. Nevertheless, this relationship *also creates a kind of structure*, and this is exactly the reason that the Wales lettering preserves its space-structure (persists in time) in contrast to the random motions of its background. My claim is that this "invisible" structure is, in fact, *in time*, and this is the main difference between the two different types of comprehensive, orderly wholes of case 1 and case 3.

Someone, of course, could use other sheets of paper to map out earlier and future states of pebbles to represent the persistence of the Wales lettering as Laplace's demon does with the whole universe, but it would refer merely to the lower-level, material parts of the lettering by Laplacian knowledge and, in fact, would not represent the real time-structure and existential meaning of the Wales lettering and the relationship between the Wales lettering and the higher-level ordering principles at all. This structure can only be understood ("seen") based on our personal knowledge.

This specific kind of structure is also the reason of the deepness of an order. According to Polanyi:

> We may even grade the intensity of coherent existence on this scale. Owing to its more significant, internal structure, a human being is a more substantial entity than a pebble. The difference can be appreciated by comparing the sciences of anatomy and physiology with the range of interest offered by the structure of a particular type of pebble.[20]

A human being is higher on the scale of coherent existence than a pebble or a primitive prokaryote because it is more developed due to emergence and its long evolutionary history (past). However, this claim can be verified only *on the basis of ordering principles* determining the deepness of this emergence and not on the unambiguous, explicit knowledge of the Laplacian ideal concerning random material parts and processes.

> An ordering principle can be extrinsic, as in the case of a message or any other artefact, or intrinsic, as shown in the ordered coherence of a solid body and in any stable configuration, whether static or dynamic.[21]

Case 1—when the Wales pattern was arranged by the stationmaster—is an example of extrinsic ordering principles (English language and the intention of the stationmaster), but now Polanyi gives an example by a thought experiment for intrinsic ones, too. At the same time, he once more argues for his claim that randomness can never create meaningful patterns because its essence is precisely the fact that it lacks such a pattern.[22] In Polanyi's thought experiment, there are ideal dice on an ideal plane that is moved by *random* Brownian motion of particles.[23]

In experiment 1, according to an extrinsic ordering principle, all dice show one on top. An adequately strong and permanently random Brownian motion is going to dust-up this comprehensive, orderly pattern, and a maximum disorder will be created concerning the faces of the dice.

In experiment 2, according to an extrinsic ordering principle, all dice show one on top, but now, by an intrinsic ordering principle, they are biased in favor of six. First, the random Brownian motion is also going to dust-up the pattern, but then it will release the operation of the intrinsic ordering principle, and at the end of the process, most dice will show six on top in a state of equilibrium.

---

20. Polanyi, *Personal Knowledge*, 38.
21. Polanyi, *Personal Knowledge*, 39.
22. Polanyi, *Personal Knowledge*, 37.
23. Polanyi, *Personal Knowledge*, 39.

In experiment 3, most dice show six on top, and they are biased in favor of it, so actually it is precisely the equilibrium state of experiment 2. Now let's strengthen the random Brownian motion significantly; consequently, this new comprehensive, orderly pattern will also be destroyed, and a maximum disorder will be created again as it was at the end of experiment 1:

> Experiment 2 shows that random impulses may release the operation of forces which tend to produce a stable pattern. Where such a dynamic ordering principle is lacking, as in Experiment 1, the existing order is destroyed in the long run even by the weakest random impulses. But random impulses of a sufficient strength as applied in Experiment 3 will destroy likewise any dynamically stable order.[24]

It follows that a higher-level, comprehensive, orderly pattern is *not in the least* the consequence of lower-level, random material processes which *just release* the operation of ordering principles which are present. At the same time, lower-level, random processes have to go *within certain boundaries*; otherwise, no order will be created. The creation of an orderly pattern has, therefore, two preconditions: (1) an *ordering principle* of that kind of comprehensive pattern and (2) *adequate lower-level, random processes (conditions)*. Without any of them, according to the logic of emergence, there would be no real orderly pattern—only an illusory one, by chance, at best.

So, "man has the power" to recognize and appraise real, orderly phenomena in nature by his natural, tacit skills and personal knowledge. This recognition happens before a distinct (random) background (space), because if there is no random background, then any pattern of order can arise only by chance. Real, comprehensive patterns, however, arise from ordering principles. In normal, earthly conditions, there is quite a steady, material background behind the real, orderly phenomena of life. We have already seen that Newton's mistake—tacitly based on the normal, earthly situation of perception—was that he thought that material processes also happened before (in) an absolute steady (absolute random) background ("space-time") (3.2). Space-time, however, is neither steady nor has its own steady background. These facts suggest that space-time has another type of ordering principle and we need other types of personal, intellectual skills to understand ("see") its real nature and its specific relationship with matter. Similarly, persons (minds) and culture have no steady, material background, but we have to recognize them, appraise them, and understand them in their dynamic background of life. This recognition and understanding will also not be successful in the same way, by the same

24. Polanyi, *Personal Knowledge*, 39–40.

skills and methods as the recognition of the phenomena of matter. These different levels (space-time, matter, life, culture), based on each other, mark the "intensity of coherent existence" due to their own ordering principles and lower-level boundary conditions. Nonetheless, we are only at the beginning of the exploration of this hierarchy of emergent levels and ordering principles and should focus on their most general relationship—randomness—to draw some conclusions.

4.5 Randomness as Emergence

In the previous two subchapters, we have talked about randomness in many different senses. Even in the fourth Nagelian case of randomness, we have seen that the initial velocity and position of planet Mars is random to the principles (laws) of the Newtonian theory of gravity. Naturally, here, in the case of the position of Mars, there are no further higher-level, ordering principles beyond the fundamental principles of Newtonian physics, but we still need to observe, measure, and perfectly explicate an initial position of the planet Mars if we wish to predict its orbit by the help of our lower-level, exact knowledge; therefore, both kinds of knowledge are needed. Planet Mars is a comprehensive, orderly whole just as the Wales scheme is. Neither of them perfectly complies with the Laplacian ideal of objective knowledge. Laplace's demon does not have to measure the different parameters of comprehensive, orderly wholes to make explicit data—it simply "sees" all the fundamental material parts of the universe at once (2.2). Its knowledge, contrary to ours, is uniform and unambiguous—that is, has only one nature.

So, in these cases, this kind of randomness is about the different principles of our *knowledge*. Although our lower-level, physical knowledge does not contain our higher-level, emergent knowledge of comprehensive, orderly phenomena, it could still determine this higher-level knowledge in a denotative/referential sense. This means that by the appropriate methods (e.g., so-called "bridge laws" [5.4]), we can connect the two kinds of knowledge of the two levels to make a proper connection (reduction) between them. Nonetheless, making this connection is so easy and tacit in the case of our Wales example that we are inclined to forget its existence and to think that there is only explicit, physical knowledge.

In the case of the intentionally arranged Wales lettering, however, there are not just two independent (random), determining factors (knowledge) in the existential sense, but—because of the existence of higher-level ordering principles—*in the denotative sense, too*. In consequence, our emergent knowledge of the Wales lettering can*not* be reduced to our explicit knowledge of the physical states of pebbles and their numerically computable movements in the garden because the pebbles are part of a higher-level, emergent system that also determines the state of the stones by its own higher-level, emergent ordering principles.

According to Polanyi, a comprehensive, orderly whole is nothing else but *what cannot be specified based on its parts*.[25] This fact, however, as we can see now, is the consequence of the more fundamental fact that *there is a random relationship* between (1) the emergent phenomenon as a whole and its material parts (case 1) and/or (2) our emergent knowledge concerning the whole and our physical knowledge concerning the lower-level parts (case 3). The first one is the stronger case, necessarily involving the second one ("and"), but the second case can be realized on its own ("or").

So, due to the nature of the actual phenomenon, we can speak of randomness in both the *existential* and the *denotative* sense; *in both senses, the fundamental condition of emergence is therefore but the random relationship between a comprehensive system and its parts*. Consequently, randomness can be regarded *as the most general case of emergence*. In other words, our term "randomness" indicates the different kinds of emergent relationships in one word.

This result concerning the concept of randomness has some consequences for physical systems, too, and these consequences perfectly comply with what we have seen in the case of dice rolling by random Brownian motion in the previous subsection. Polanyi uses heat—or, more precisely, temperature—as an example to show the exact connection between randomness and emergence in physical systems. I would also like to use this example to sum up the preceding discussion, and since heat is the classical example for reduction, we will encounter it several times in the next chapter as well. Polanyi writes:

> The gas can be said to have a definite temperature and a definite pressure only if we assume that its molecules are in random motion; an assumption which is incompatible with our knowing the configuration of molecular motions in the gas. [Since] if we knew exactly the position and velocity of each molecule (within the limits of wave mechanics) we could only predict the behavior of the molecules, but not the comprehensive features defined by randomness.[26]

The molecules of the gas do not move randomly in themselves. It follows from this fact that, in principle, it is possible to conceive such a

---

25. Polanyi, *Personal Knowledge*, 390.
26. Polanyi, *Personal Knowledge*, 391.

lower-level knowledge that specifies the movement of the molecules exactly. This kind of lower-level knowledge is, of course, the Laplacian knowledge of the parts and their behavior. However, this lower-level knowledge cannot describe the comprehensive phenomena of the gas (temperature and pressure) because this kind of comprehensive phenomena is based on the principle that *the molecules of the gas move randomly*. As a matter of fact, this kind of lower-level knowledge cannot even interpret the movements of the molecules as random because their movements in themselves—that is, at the lower-level—are entirely deterministic.

So, the lower-level movements of the molecules can be regarded as random only *in relation to* the higher-level comprehensive systems, but based on this principle, the comprehensive phenomena of the gas (temperature and pressure) can be defined exactly; and their exact correlation too: $pV=NkT$. Nonetheless, this higher-level knowledge is based on such tacit experiences of bodily senses and skills that initially have no connection with the perfectly explicit, Laplacian knowledge of the parts. It means that we speak about the same phenomenon (the movements of the molecules of the gas) from two different points of reference: from a personal one and from a more objective one. Thus, the knowledge concerning the (comprehensive) temperature of a gas—for example, "It is really hot today"—can be regarded as a personal fact, and the knowledge concerning the movements of the molecules of the gas an objective fact (4.2); both of them are true.

In this case, however, as we might already see, the two kinds of knowledge can be connected perfectly if we redefine our higher-level knowledge into an exact form—for example, if we measure the pressure and temperature of the gas with experimental tools based on the principle that the molecules of the gas moves randomly, reducing our redefined, higher-level knowledge to our lower-level one. Consequently, the temperature of the gas will be nothing but the average kinetic energy of the molecules. Nonetheless, this definition presupposes that the molecules of the gas move randomly; thus, in strict Laplacian sense, it is utterly meaningless. It is the reason that Polanyi says that randomness is the most general case of emergence and it is destroyed from any consistent Laplacian point of view:

> I call this a case of emergence, for we can know the randomness of a system, yet cannot know it in terms of a more detailed knowledge of the system. Our knowledge of this emergent quality, randomness, is in fact destroyed by observing the particulars which determine the system below the emergent level.[27]

---

27. Polanyi, *Personal Knowledge*, 391.

With Polanyi's other example, dice rolling in itself is entirely deterministic. If we were in possession of the exact, lower-level knowledge, however, perfectly specifying all of the details of the process, then we could not predict the comprehensive result of the throws since this latter, personal knowledge concerning the overall, comprehensive result is based on the principle that the rolling of dice is random—only in relation to this higher-level knowledge, of course. It follows that the overall, comprehensive result of the throws *cannot be deduced logically* from the particular, random results of individual throws because it is based on our personal probability judgment of the process; it is, therefore, a *tacit integration* of our personal experiences and our evaluation of the comprehensive phenomena of dice—not a formal, logical inference (3.3).

Nonetheless, we are also, of course, able to calculate the overall result of the throws more objectively due to the principles of formal logic, but this overall, deductive result would not be the same at all—unless we ignored the differences by a deceptive substitution. Based on our personal judgment and evaluation of the nature of the process, the overall outcome of the throws is 3.5, but the objective, overall result, based on exact experimentations and deductive calculations would be, after 100 throws, for example, 3.27 (it has been my result just right now) or, after one billion throws, 3.493767592. The objective overall result could be precisely 3.5 *only by chance*. However, *consistent* Laplacian knowledge does not know chance and randomness at all and destroys all kinds of probability judgment. Probability judgments concerning any kind of comprehensive results or phenomena can only be based on personal knowledge.

So, the successful reduction of our higher-level knowledge of the comprehensive phenomena—in our case, temperature—means that there is a well-established connection between our higher-level and lower-level knowledge; referring to the given problem (object), their relation is not random in the denotative sense. This is the reason that the nature of temperature as a comprehensive phenomenon complies with the nature of the comprehensive phenomenon of the fake Wales lettering (case 3) and there is a recognizable, higher-level, comprehensive phenomenon, contrary to the randomly scattered pebbles (case 2). Contrary to the intentionally arranged Wales message (case 1), however, it has no own higher-level, ordering principles; it is only the consequence of lower-lever, random processes and physical laws.

Nonetheless, to speak consistently about a higher-level, comprehensive phenomenon, on the one hand, we have to start from our specific, personal point of view and tacit experiences of the comprehensive phenomena and, on the other, we have to suppose that the behavior of its parts is random compared to higher-levels; otherwise, there is a perfect correspondence between the "two" levels or between the "pattern" and the background. In fact, there is not and cannot be any recognizable comprehensive order on the lower-level or before the background (4.4). But:

> If we trusted ourselves with the capacity of randomizing also several separate parts of a gas, we could also establish differences in temperature and pressure between them and predict that these differences would be equalized by a process of self randomization inherent in a system of particles in random motion.[28]

Randomness is the fundamental nature of material processes. This fact is the basis of the physical principle (second law of thermodynamics) that the entropy (which is the lack of order on the fundamental level) of an isolated system never decreases. In other words: over time, any order of the system is destroyed, and the system moves toward the thermodynamic equilibrium—that is, the state of maximum entropy—until, of course, an ordering principle changes the process, due to, for example, an orderly external energy flow (like sunshine on Earth), and a new order starts to form. However, this fact—and thus the second law of thermodynamics—cannot be interpreted solely on the basis of the ideal Laplacian knowledge of the parts. Consequently, it is not a fundamental law of matter (or the law of fundamental physics) because it expresses the fundamental nature of material processes *only in relation to* any comprehensive, orderly emergent phenomena.

Thus at this point, we can reasonably state that reality has at least two well-distinguishable forms:

1. *Fundamental, random material parts*; properties and behavior of which can be described due to the nature of the Laplacian ideal of knowledge (objective facts);

2. *Comprehensive, orderly emergent wholes*; properties and behavior of which can be described and evaluated based on our personal knowledge (personal facts).

It follows, on the one hand, that material conditions possess (are in relation to) several such comprehensive, orderly phenomena that, from a Laplacian point of reference, have no meaning at all and, on the other, that *all of these comprehensive, orderly phenomena of matter were destroyed due to the fundamental random nature of material processes if there would be no such ordering principles*, for example, the principles of life and evolution or

---

28. Polanyi, *Personal Knowledge*, 391–92.

the principle of simple chemical proportions, *which reverse these destroying processes.*

So, to sum up this subchapter with our original Wales example, in case 2 (the randomly scattered pebbles) and case 3 (the illusory Wales scheme), we have physically-determined, *ontologically one-level* systems the shapes, structures, or other higher-level properties of which—if they have any—we can recognize but these higher-level properties have no real existential meaning. The real and essential meaning of these systems is found only in their physical principles. However, in case 1 (the intentionally arranged Wales lettering), we have an *ontologically multilevel* system with a real and meaningful, comprehensive pattern of order. The typical Polanyian example for case 3 is a *crystal* and for case 1 is a *frog*, which, of course, is not a cultural pattern of order (as the Wales lettering) but rather a biological one.[29]

Naturally, one can question this differentiation and thus the existence of these higher-level systems, but then, if he wants to be consistent, he must also deny the whole emergentist worldview, including the theory of tacit knowledge by which we can even recognize these random systems and ordering principles. At the end, this consistency leads to a worldview in which, for the sake of the objectivist ideal of perfect observational accuracy and systematic precision of science, every phenomenon and system should be explained *by only one kind of principle*—for example, evolution is just by natural selection. Consequently, the reality of such comprehensive, orderly wholes that cannot be explained in this way should be denied.

4.6 Absolute Randomness

We have seen that randomness is the most general case of emergence—at least in its relational form. We have also seen that absolute randomness would be the case when there are no determining factors or conditions (either ontological or epistemological ones), so an event happens without any cause (the fifth Nagelian case of randomness). Following Nagel, Einstein, and Polanyi, however, we have questioned the concept of this kind of randomness as we have challenged the Laplacian ideal of objective knowledge. Nevertheless, it seems that the ruling, Copenhagen interpretation of quantum mechanics speaks about randomness in this sense: some parameters of particles change without any cause. Now, let's consider what the real meaning of absolute randomness is.

In figure 10, due to our main example, there are four different states of pebbles following each other, but we can also think of, of course, any

---

29. Polanyi, *Personal Knowledge*, 394.

particular part of the universe or even the development of the whole universe itself. On what ground could one assert that any of these states are random in an absolute way—that is, that any of these pebble states are formed *without any cause*? Usually, we would suppose that the cause of the pebbles' second state is the first one, the cause of the pebbles' third state is the second one, and so on. Or perhaps the real cause of the third W-scheme is not present in this two-dimensional, Laplacian picture of the universe. Since the concept of absolute randomness involves, of course, an absolute point of reference, we should ask what Laplace's demon could tell us.

Figure 10. Changing pebbles.

As we have seen in chapter 2, Laplace's demon can grasp all the numerical parameters of all the fundamental material parts of the universe at a given moment, and since it is perfectly familiar with the laws of mechanics, it can deduce all the possible past and future states of the universe by these two factors. However, it can do this merely because nothing material hinders it; its point of reference is beyond space and time (2.4). In consequence, since time and the actual moment do not impede its perfect "senses," it can grasp any actual "pebble state" of any time due to its arbitrary (random) "choice" and then calculate all of the others at once; it needs no time to do that. Therefore, in a logical sense, any "pebble state" can follow from any other "pebble state" due to its random "choice"; there is no real time sequence in the "pebble states." We can picture this Laplacian vision with the following: all of the "pebble states" of the universe are mapped out in a four-dimensional, *timeless* space and, in consequence, none of them are the cause of any other because they "exist" in the infinite *present* of the fourth dimension (block universe). For the demon, however, this result is not even in a timeless space dimension—just indexed data ($x_1, x_2, x_3 \ldots$) due to its arbitrary calculations. The point is that without a specific (personal) point of reference, there is no time sequence—that is, a kind of determinate, comprehensive order among the "pebble states"; space in itself has no determinate order without time (6.2). It follows that a personal point of reference, in fact, means that this point of reference *is rooted in a specific space and time*—in *real* space and *real* time. This fact was the reason we stated in chapter 2 that for the demon, without any point of reference, from its absolute view from nowhere, both determinism and indeterminism are meaningless concepts (2.4). Now we can see that it means that the demon knows *neither determinate time order nor random sequences*; the idea of absolute randomness is simply meaningless for it. From the absolute point of view of the demon, the world is neither deterministic nor random. Therefore, based on the Laplacian concept of objective knowledge, we cannot claim that the concept of absolute randomness is well-established.

Human beings, however, due to their specific point of reference, have not only exact, fundamental knowledge about the parts but also personal knowledge about the comprehensive, orderly wholes by which it can be determined which pebble state follows which—due to the flow of real time. For example, based on personal knowledge, we can conclude that frogs develop from tadpoles and not vice versa. Thus if the nature of a phenomenon complies with the Laplacian knowledge of the parts, based on this specific personal knowledge concerning the development of the comprehensive, orderly phenomenon in question, we can interpret the explicit numeric parameters of the Laplacian model—which, in themselves, have no meaning at all (3.4)—and then, on the basis of these two different kinds of knowledge, we can predict any possible past and future states of the given phenomenon. Without any of them, we cannot speak meaningfully about the determinate time sequence of the phenomenon. In consequence, *any determinate time sequence is nothing else but a comprehensive, emergent order at the higher-level*—this is the reason that it cannot be interpreted solely by the ideal Laplacian knowledge of the fundamental parts.

An important question should be asked at this point: what we can tell if our predictions are wrong? Could it be a sign of a kind of absolute randomness? There are several reasons for wrong predictions: (1) our measurement is inadequate and thus our initial data is incorrect; (2) our model (conceptual and explanatory framework) is inadequate; or (3) the nature of the given phenomenon does not comply with the Laplacian ideal of knowledge, thus our whole approach is wrong (we have chosen a wrong conceptual and explanatory framework). Because it is only a methodological question, suppose that our measurement is correct. To conclude, based on this kind of problem, anything to reality is, in fact, a categorical mistake. Also, let's suppose for now that the nature of the given phenomenon complies with the Laplacian ideal of knowledge, so we have chosen a proper approach, including an appropriate methodology for measurement. The question, then, is as follows: is it still possible that our model is right and we have found a phenomenon that is *in principle* unpredictable, so absolutely random?

In a logical sense, yes, but, on the one hand, it would have severe theoretical and philosophical consequences (that I will explicate in a moment) and, on the other, we could never know *for sure* that it is indeed the case since, logically, it *also always remains possible* that we merely do not have enough knowledge to explicate a proper model. Therefore, *on a strictly logical basis, we have no reason* to speak about any determinate unpredictability or absolute randomness. Furthermore, based on our knowledge of the history of science, to claim that we know everything about a phenomenon that can be known and there will be no new discoveries concerning the given phenomenon, its causes, and ordering principles is simply a parody of science and perhaps a denial of meaningful signs of reality for the sake of the unfounded idea of absolute randomness. The ruling Copenhagen interpretation of quantum mechanics still claims that quantum processes are indeterministic in nature.

As we have seen, if we ignore measurement problems, if our model is wrong, there will be two main kinds of possible interpretations of a sign of reality. Perhaps the error is only in the current explication of our model—for example, our mathematical solutions are incorrect or the nature of the given phenomenon does not comply with the Laplacian ideal of knowledge and thus the whole approach is wrong. In the former case, we just have to work further in our original framework; however, the latter one has a specific meaning: the (random) errors in the predictions of our model are the consequence of such comprehensive processes which cannot be interpreted merely by the Laplacian ideal of objective knowledge. It means, as we have seen, that there are at least two different determining factors or principles which are random in relation to each other; therefore, it is not the case of absolute randomness and indeterminacy at all but rather the case of emergence between two levels in the most general sense: *randomness*. With our original Wales example, the stationmaster moves the pebbles in a determinate way due to the principles of English language, but this process appears in the lower-level, Laplacian framework as random prediction errors. The ideal Laplacian framework can work *if and only if* there are no real comprehensive, orderly phenomena beyond the fundamental material level—which, in the case of the whole universe, as we can see now, means that *there is not even time* but merely the four-dimensional space of the block universe (2.4), which enables perfect calculations starting from any arbitrarily chosen "pebble state" to any other "pebble state."

Nonetheless, the severe theoretical and philosophical consequences I mentioned a moment ago will literally go beyond the block universe if someone accepts the concept of absolute randomness since, in the ontological sense—that is, if we want to find a real explanation for the phenomenon of absolute randomness in our universe and not just accept (in a really consistent, positivist way) that certain events happen randomly and without any reason—this kind of event could only be interpreted as the absolute intersection of two independent, causal series (the absolute expansion of the third Nagelian case of randomness). It means that the two causal series cannot have any common past. In consequence, before the intersection, they are *the parts of two different universes*, and this is the reason that these kinds of events happen without any cause. In our world, they literally have no cause. We can and have to explain them with past events of other universes. Based on the concept of absolute randomness, this interpretation of quantum processes necessarily leads to the idea of the *multiverse*; the real, observable universe falls apart, and instead of facing the deficiencies of our model, we theorize an *in principle unobservable* world behind *every* random quantum phenomenon. The other way to deal with the problem in our Laplacian framework is to theorize about unobservable, multidimensional particles (strings).

Based on the relational concept of randomness, however, as we have seen, if there are higher-level, comprehensive objects—for example, frogs, peoples, and machines—then there will be no need to theorize whole unobservable universes (as well as new and also unobservable dimensions) to explain a random event in the lower-level, Laplacian framework. This, of course, does not mean that the causes of quantum processes are human actions (from the perspective of the pebbles, the stationmaster moves the pebbles randomly) but rather suggests that these hidden causes are neither other universes nor tenth and eleventh dimensions of strings; there are random events in the Laplacian framework of modern physics because the so-called material world of the particles do not constitute an exact, single level but rather a complex system of multiple levels (space, time, dark matter, quarks, electrons, and atoms) in exactly the same way as the world itself is a complex system of space-time, matter, life, and culture and where the manifestations of higher-levels seem random in a lower-level framework (as well as the natural processes of a lower-level appear random from the higher-level perspective).

The explanations of these problems in modern physics are, of course, the consequences of the main *philosophical beliefs* of physicists of the twentieth and twenty-first centuries, positivism, materialism, and the Laplacian ideal of objective knowledge. However, based on personal knowledge and the relational concept of randomness as emergence, even indeterminate and unexplained quantum processes can be regarded as meaningful signs of a new reality in the same way that the nearly simple fractions of chemical proportions were the sign of an intrinsic ordering principle (4.3). I mean that they can and should be regarded as the signs of *this* observable universe and *this* observable, three-dimensional space and time. In chapter 6, this approach and this particular understanding of randomness as emergence will lead us to the existential fundaments of matter itself: to space as fundamental, random parts of reality and to time as the fundamental, comprehensive order of reality. Therefore, matter itself is a complex, multileveled manifestation of reality, the nature of which does not perfectly comply with the Laplacian framework.

My conclusion is that the concept of absolute randomness is false. It is based on the *false dichotomy* of determinism versus indeterminism. However, there is no such absolute contradiction because randomness is a relational concept and the most general case of emergence. It means, on the one hand, that comprehensive, emergent phenomena are not indeterministic in themselves at all but cannot be specified based on their parts and, on the other, that any action of higher-lever, ordering principles seems indeterministic in the lower-lever, Laplacian framework. In other words, it seems to "break the causal closure of the physical world," which is the most crucial argument for materialism in philosophy today (5.8). But this breaking is only an illusion of the lower-lever perspective of matter. I will show in detail that the stationmaster as a real, higher-level, emergent actor or any comprehensive, ordering principle never breaks the fundamental principles of physics (5.8; 7.5).

4.7 Emergence and Evolution: The Origin of Personal Knowledge

We have seen in chapter 1 that natural selection is a mechanical explanation accounting for the formation of new species based upon *two* necessary and *fundamental* conditions: the existence of variants and insufficient means for living. When there are insufficient means for living, the variants must compete and a *changing* process starts. This specific mechanism is the Darwinian point of natural selection. Later, the neo-Darwinian theory created some new concepts (such as mutation, genetic drift, migration, species isolation, etc.), but the point of and the fundamental two factors for natural selection *remained the same.*

The theory of natural selection is, of course, the basis of all kinds of Darwinism. From a scientific point of view, the most important difference between Darwinian and neo-Darwinian theories is that the former does not yet include genetics. At the beginning of the twentieth century, it was not clear at all what the relationship between Darwin's theory of natural selection and genetics based on Gregor Mendel's principles was. Darwin's theory, due to observation, merely supposed that there are variations of living beings among which selection works and did not explain the formation of variants. Mendel, at the same time, explicated the principles of heredity entirely independent from the theory of natural selection.

Concerning its methodology, Darwin's work is rather a *historical explanation* by detailed *empirical examinations* based on his personal experiences from his voyage on the Beagle onward (5.5), while genetics is *highly theoretical* and *mathematized*. It is mainly based on R. A. Fischer's statistical methods and dealing with randomness (4.3) that this methodological gap was bridged and the Darwinian mechanism of natural selection was reinterpreted in the framework of genetics. According to Polanyi, by this interpretation, Fischer moved the Darwinian theory in the direction of the Laplacian ideal of objective knowledge, and this process was only continued and strengthened by the neo-Darwinian synthesis.

From a philosophical point of view, the conflicts only multiply. Darwin himself, as we have seen in chapter 1 (and will detail below), *never claimed* that the theory of natural selection could explain the comprehensive phenomena of evolution in nature or that natural selection was the only fundamental mechanism in evolution; however, this is perhaps the most crucial principle of neo-Darwinism. Darwin more modestly argues for the claim that natural selection can explain the formation of new species in wild nature in the same way as artificial selection—that is, breeding livestock can explain the development of new subspecies of dogs, pigeons, sheep, etc.

In most cases, in *Personal Knowledge*, Polanyi speaks plainly about Darwinism. It turns out only from the context which kind or level of Darwinism he refers. Nonetheless, to understand his critique, it is enough to see and always remember the fundamental difference between Darwinism and neo-Darwinism. In consequence, when he harshly argues against explanations by random genetic mutations or states that the theory of natural selection, as a lonely, fundamental mechanism, cannot explain any real comprehensive, evolutionary, orderly phenomena of nature, we will see that he, in fact, does not even contradict Darwin because Darwin himself never claimed these things either. So Polanyi does not debate Darwin at all, merely the neo-Darwinian expansion of his theory.

It follows that if we do not identify Darwinism with neo-Darwinism, then Polanyi could and *should be* regarded as a Darwinian because, in the limited original sense, he completely acknowledges Darwin's theory of natural selection. Moreover, I dare to say that he—and following him, me—is more faithful to the original spirit of Darwin's work because Darwin did not close the questions about, for example, the comprehensive, orderly phenomena of evolution and its ordering principles as neo-Darwinism did (due to the philosophical beliefs of materialism and positivism). Of course,

Darwin was not an emergentist, but he was not a materialist either. I believe that he did not yet know what to think about these fundamental questions and left the door open.

So what is mutation, the most important novelty in neo-Darwinian theory? Mutation is a random process that leads to new variants in a species. It is random but, naturally, as we have seen, only in a *relational sense*. At their lower-level, the *entirely deterministic* physical and chemical processes lead to change in the higher-level, comprehensive biological system of the cell. (A letter is altered by the lower-level erosion processes of the garden in the Wales lettering.) This change cannot be predicted or explained with the help of higher-level biological principles (or, in the case of the Wales lettering, with the principles of English language). So, *in this relationship* and only in this relationship, it is *random*.

This relation, however, is symmetric. The change can lead to a new, comprehensive biological phenomenon at the higher-level of the cell (as the Wales lettering can get a new, comprehensive form by the change of a letter), but it also can*not* be predicted or explained by only the use of the lower-level physical and chemical processes. In itself, a deterministic step of the lower-level processes—that is, a deterministic change in the parts—has no comprehensive pattern of order and meaning but only explicit and numeric parameters according to its lower-level principles. (The new, random form of the lettering—for example, "Whales"—is meaningful only in the context of the higher-level, ordering principles of the English language.) Moreover, there are, of course, several other deterministic steps (physical and chemical processes) at the lower-level that do *not* lead to any changes in the higher, comprehensive level of the cell. (For example, there is a change due to the erosion processes in the background pebbles of the Wales lettering.) Therefore, *they are not called mutations at all*. A deterministic step of the lower-level is a random mutation *only in relation* to the higher-level system.

The concept of mutation *presupposes* the higher-level, comprehensive order and its own ordering principles in relation to which the concept can even be formulated; therefore, mutations are only lower-level, random material processes which cannot be the real source and explanation of higher-level, comprehensive, orderly phenomena, for example, of a new species. To still say that this is the case—as neo-Darwinians tend to do—is a Laplacian fault or deceptive substitution (2.5); this is the more profound reason that, as we have seen in chapter 1, Polanyi says that this neo-Darwinian explanation is merely a "logical muddle":

> We must conclude therefore that the assumption of an accidental formation of the living species is a logical muddle. It

appears to be a piece of equivocation, unconsciously prompted by the urge to avoid facing the problem set to us by the fact that the universe has given birth to these curious beings, including people like ourselves.[30]

Furthermore, mutation is not a new, "additional factor" in the concept of natural selection; it only explains the forming of new variants (first factor), which is, of course, very important—we know more than Darwin himself—but it does *not* change the logical structure of natural selection at all. See the figure.

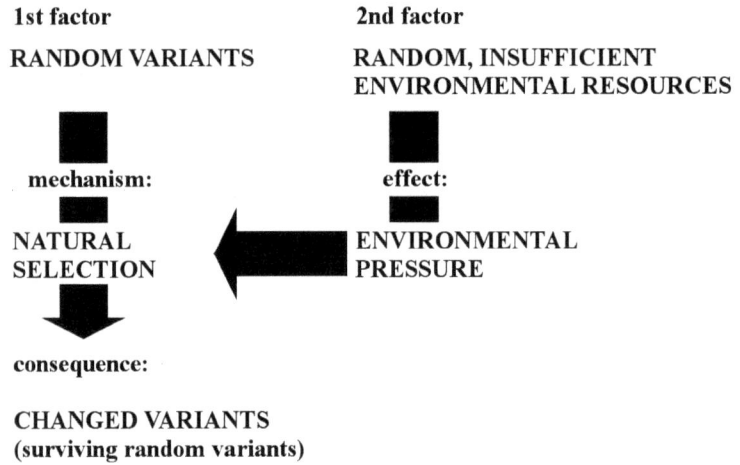

Figure 11. The logical structure of natural selection.

The same is true for genetic drift, migration, etc., which are all important *parts* (objective facts) in the theory of natural selection. We have more and more small pebbles in the Wales lettering due to the scientific inquiry which follows from the Laplacian ideal of objective knowledge, but natural selection itself remains the same: a mechanical explanation based upon *two fundamental* conditions—the existence of variants and insufficient means for living. We still do not know the more important, comprehensive meaning and principles of living beings and their development (personal facts). When a neo-Darwinian thinks that these important, lower-level parts contribute beyond natural selection to explain the comprehensive, developmental process of evolution and the emergence of man, he again commits a Laplacian fault.

30. Polanyi, *Personal Knowledge*, 35.

THE MEANING OF RANDOMNESS

Here, we arrive at a greater problem with neo-Darwinian theory and its vocabulary. Neo-Darwinian theorists maintain evolution and evolutionary development by natural selection, though from natural selection, nothing evolutionary or developmental follows—for *natural selection, by itself, can lead to regression*. As Darwin put it in one place of *The Origin of Species*:

> In some cases, variations or individual differences of a favorable nature may never have arisen for natural selection to act on and accumulate. In no case, probably, has time sufficed for the utmost possible amount of development. In some few cases, there has been what we must call retrogression of organization. But the main cause lies in the fact that under very simple conditions of life, a high organization would be of no service—possibly would be of actual disservice, as being of a more delicate nature, and more liable to be put out of order and injured.[31]

So, a species can lose the magnificent capability of vision if such was its course of adaptation by random forces of environmental pressure. From natural selection, according to its two lower-level random factors, only random change follows (1.2). Darwin knew this and, as we have seen, did not even use the word *evolution* for his theory in 1859.[32]

Neo-Darwinians still speak about evolution and the fact that the neo-Darwinian theory, in reality, denies evolutionary development emerges only in explicit details of the theory. Yet, how could it be the theory of "evolution"? Tacitly, and in a deceptive way, we always substitute the explicit theory with the true meaning of evolution. Since neo-Darwinians also generally believe in evolutionary development and the evolutionary origin of man, only this trifle is excluded from their explicit theory for the sake of explicit accuracy and the Laplacian ideal of objective knowledge.

Remember the last words of Darwin in *The Origin of Species*: "There is grandeur in this view of life, with its several powers, having been originally breathed by the Creator into a few forms or into one; and that, whilst this planet has gone cycling on according to the fixed law of gravity, from so simple a beginning, endless forms, most beautiful and most wonderful, have been, and are being, evolved."[33]

Once again, natural selection presupposes variants (first factor), that is, living beings and life—exactly the same way as the concept of mutation presupposes a higher-level comprehensive order and its ordering principles—thus, the emergence of life cannot be explained by the theory of

---

31. Darwin, *Origin of Species*, 99–100.
32. Sanderson, *Social Evolutionism*, 35.
33. Darwin, *Origin of Species*, 429.

natural selection alone. Darwin is perfectly aware of this fact. Higher-level, comprehensive order cannot be the consequence of lower-level, random material processes. As he perfectly knows, evolutionary development also cannot be explained merely by his theory. He did not commit these Laplacian faults; he is not a neo-Darwinian at all. He knew that we must find other scientific principles—beyond natural selection—to explain the comprehensive, evolutionary development and emergence of life.

However, neo-Darwinians deny that there is a fundamental mechanism or principle other than natural selection in evolution. In this case, then, what originated life? A random event did, with terribly low probability. The image of lightning striking down from the skies into the primordial soup illustrates this answer well; or remember Fred Hoyle's aphorism about the junkyard and the hurricane leaving behind an operational Boeing 747, ready to fly (1.2). In this chapter, we have seen in detail what would mean if, according to the so exact probability calculations, it were possible that the comprehensive, orderly phenomena of life were originated by a lower-level, random material event—it is the case of the fake Wales scheme, arranged by the hurricane, which has no real meaning at all. Or, by the way, the case of random stellar constellations. Are living beings merely illusory, random patterns? Are *we*, human beings, fake, meaningless patterns?

I do not believe that Dawkins or any other neo-Darwinian indeed thinks that we are meaningless, illusory, higher-level patterns, as astrological constellations are. I do believe, however, that Dawkins chooses this option—and then, by a Laplacian magic trick, conceals its real and, in fact, absurd meaning—because he sees only one other option for the origin of life beyond pure chance: *divine design*. Of course, he chooses the "scientific" solution. For him and other neo-Darwinians, according to their materialist convictions and their false conceptual dichotomies, every higher-level, ordering principle of life and evolution is obscure and unscientific. For example, we need only to peruse the works of the great Ernst Mayr, one of the fathers of neo-Darwinian theory.[34] They even have a specific word to stigmatize any theory that dares to propose ordering principles for the consistent explanation of the comprehensive phenomena of life beyond lower-level, random material mechanisms: *vitalism*. They use this term in a stigmatizing sense although originally, even the science of biology itself was established by such vitalist scientists like J.-B. Lamarck (9.2). This materialist stigmatization is the reason that, at one point, Polanyi fiercely complains in *Personal Knowledge*:

---

34. See, for example, Mayr, *What Evolution Is?*; Mayr, *One Long Argument*.

It is obvious, therefore, that the rise of man can be accounted for only by other principles than those known today to physics and chemistry. If this be vitalism, then vitalism is mere common sense, which can be ignored only by a truculently bigoted mechanistic outlook.[35]

Contrary to Dawkins, Mayr, and other neo-Darwinians, Polanyi thinks that only a *magical* hurricane or *divine* lightning can create a real, meaningful pattern of order—the beautiful order of life—but randomness alone cannot. The magic trick in the neo-Darwinian explanation is, of course, the Laplacian faults by which, for a kind of scientific accuracy and exactness, we conceal the real meaning, our real personal conviction in emergent evolution, and neglect to explore the real, higher-level ordering principles of life and evolution. These emergent ordering principles are entirely scientific, however, they are not materialistic. In other words, these emergent ordering principles are unscientific only for someone who thinks that only material principles are scientific. So it is not a question of science at all—who is scientific and who is not, as neo-Darwinians like to picture it—but the *question of fundamental beliefs concerning reality*. Neo-Darwinism is false, not because it is unscientific but because it is based on false philosophical beliefs. It is the reason that it has to use Laplacian faults to cover up its false beliefs.

Before I conclude with our last additional factor in this subchapter, I would like to mention a telling example, emphasizing the difference and how everything so easily becomes "divine design"—that is, unscientific "vitalism"—in the eyes of neo-Darwinians. Moreover, this example comes from a prominent member of the American Polanyi Society, Walter B. Gulick, so, in principle, he is not a neo-Darwinian at all:

> I referred to the vitalistic aspect of his thought because Polanyi describes himself . . . as a vitalist insofar as he thinks a principle beyond the laws of physics and chemistry is what is necessary to explain evolution. My point is neo-Darwinian thought provides all the principled richness necessary to account for evolutionary emergence and does not deserve censure on this point.[36]

So, since the neo-Darwinian theory has every principle that is needed for the explanation of evolutionary emergence, if Polanyi does not think so, then he acknowledges that he is a vitalist, even with these words: "If this be vitalism, then vitalism is mere common sense, which can be ignored only

---

35. Polanyi, *Personal Knowledge*, 390.
36. Gulick, "On the Adequacy of Neo-Darwinism," 59.

by a truculently bigoted mechanistic outlook." He is either a neo-Darwinian or a vitalist; there is no third option. The unquestionable authority of the ruling neo-Darwinian theory is enormous even among the so-called "Polanyian" thinkers. Nonetheless, I wonder whether what Gulick understands under "evolutionary emergence" if he thinks that the neo-Darwinian theory "provides all the principled richness necessary to account for" it. Polanyi's philosophy cannot be understood based on the critical conceptual and explanatory dichotomies.

So, the last additional factor of Darwinian natural selection that I wish to discuss is the most important one. It leads us onto the path toward the real ordering principles of life and evolution. It can transform the original Darwinian meaning of natural selection and will also lead us to a better understanding of Polanyi's critique of neo-Darwinian theory. This factor was called "dynamic species-environmental interaction"[37] by Gulick and concerns not just variants but also the second fundamental factor of natural selection—the insufficient means for living. "There is nothing random or accidental about what traits best allow a species to survive in an environmental niche," says Gulick, and he is right.[38] This is the reason why natural selection is *teleological*. But as randomness is only a relational concept and not something absolute, its counterpart, *teleology, is also only relational* (9.2).

What is an environmental niche? It is a *comprehensive, stable, open orderly system* that contains the evolving species in question. It determines the insufficient means for living and, in consequence, the struggling variants and the species itself. The system—and thus the species in question in it—will change *toward* some form of *stability* or *equilibrium*. Therefore, this change is not random but rather teleological in this relational sense—between the lower-level parts (living beings) and the comprehensive, orderly system. But the most critical questions are: Is this process an evolutionary development or is it only a regression? Which stability means emergence and which implies regression? Which pebble state has a real, meaningful, higher-level pattern of order (and thus higher-level ordering principles) and which does not? Neither the notion of stability in itself nor complexity theory can answer these questions.

There is apparently a connection between complexity and emergence. However, the two notions are far from being the same because complexity theory only gives us a lower-level, explicit, and numeric description of the parts of specific higher-level, comprehensive phenomena (as do genetics and, of course, neo-Darwinian theory) but it does not speak about any of the

---

37. Gulick, "On the Adequacy of Neo-Darwinism," 58.
38. Gulick, "On the Adequacy of Neo-Darwinism," 59.

true meaning, reality, and principles of higher-level comprehensive patterns of order. So, to think that complexity equals emergence is a Laplacian fault because we only speak about explicit equations and numeric parameters hiding the true meaning behind our words based on our fundamental beliefs; in this case, what understandings lie behind of the concept of system, stability, environmental niche, etc.

So, what is an environmental niche? For a neo-Darwinian, it is a complex *material* system—as information and genes are, too. For the sake of perfect, observational accuracy and the systematic precision of science, the neo-Darwinian wants to find more and more accurate and exact descriptions of the parts of the system and its only fundamental ordering principle: natural selection. In Polanyi's eyes, he stares at the pebbles in the garden and forgets the tacit powers by which he, in fact, recognizes the real, meaningful orderly patterns of life: frogs, man, evolution, and the emergence from prokaryotes to man. So, he commits a Laplacian fault.

For Polanyi, an environmental niche is a comprehensive, *emergent* system in the ontological sense, with its own ordering principles. The exact lower-level parts, genes, mutations, natural selection, etc., are significant, but they are insufficient parts of the higher picture to explain the most important questions: What principles determine whether a process in an environmental niche is an evolutionary development or only a regression? What are the emergent, ordering principles of the whole evolutionary system of Earth through which man could develop from the first primitive prokaryotes? This process is not random and, of course, is not a regression but rather an evident evolutionary development; everybody can see this using tacit powers—if not only looking at the explicit details of the lower-level, that is, just at the pebbles and not at the real, meaningful Wales lettering itself.

Polanyi's first, undetailed answer is that: "The *ordering principle* which *originated* life [and sustains evolution] is the *potentiality* of a stable, open system."[39] The stable, open, orderly system of Earth originated life and sustains evolution. The questions are, according to Polanyi: what was the nature of that ordering principle of "potentiality" that enabled this process? What is it now? And, of course, how has this process has been realized in the long course of evolution? I am sure that these are good scientific questions and neo-Darwinians should not refuse to consider them; due to the Laplacian ideal of objective knowledge, their stubborn resistance only hinders science as if the early chemists were insisting on the objective results of complex fractions concerning the structure of chemical compounds. After we

---

39. Polanyi, *Personal Knowledge*, 383–84.

establish the concept of emergence in Part Two, I will give detailed answers to these questions in Part Three: Evolution.

Polanyi and the neo-Darwinians have radically different views on evolution and emergence. This is the consequence of their fundamental philosophical beliefs and commitments. We can see this even in the case of the close connection between the notions of randomness, comprehensive order, and personal knowledge. Polanyi is an emergentist, while neo-Darwinians are materialists. This is the reason they use hard words on each other from time to time. For Polanyi, the neo-Darwinian understanding of evolution and emergence is based on merely "deceptive substitutions," on Laplacian faults. For neo-Darwinians, Polanyi's emergentist view is unscientific, "metaphysical," and even quasi-creationist. Neo-Darwinians feel that Polanyi is the enemy of the Darwinian notion of natural selection, the only scientific theory of evolution, but that is not true. Polanyi entirely believes in natural selection; he merely thinks that it is not enough, that it is only the lower-level, random *condition* of evolution and not the *action* of evolution itself, according to the real, comprehensive, ordering principles of life and evolution:

> Darwinism has diverted attention for a century from the descent of man by investigating the conditions of evolution and overlooking its action. Evolution can be understood only as a feat of emergence.[40]

Neo-Darwinism only focuses on the exact, lower-level, random processes, on the pebbles in the garden, and forgets about the true meaning and principles of higher-level, comprehensive phenomena, which cannot be understood by entirely explicit, Laplacian knowledge alone. However, for Polanyi, lower-level, "random" processes, the random movements of the pebbles in the garden, without a higher-level, emergent ordering principle, cannot lead to real, meaningful patterns of order, life, and man. This Polanyian ontological understanding of emergence and evolution cannot be purged from his philosophy, from his *Personal Knowledge*, because the origin of man, his personal point of reference, and his tacit powers are rooted in his evolutionary emergence: that he is the child of a specific place and time. This is the reason that *emergent evolution is the real foundation of the theory of tacit and personal knowledge*. One must choose between Polanyi and neo-Darwinism, between the emergent meaning of evolution and Laplacian faults. There is no middle ground.

---

40. Polanyi, *Personal Knowledge*, 390.

4.8 Conclusion

By our natural tacit senses, skills, and personal knowledge, we are able to differentiate between random and non-random comprehensive, orderly systems and events. Winning the lottery is random, while the Sun rising in the morning is not. Randomness, however, is not an absolute phenomenon but rather a relation between two different factors or principles—for example, between the lower-level parts and the higher-level, comprehensive order of a system. Solely in the lower-level, conceptual framework, in fact, even the lottery is deterministic; the machine that drowns the numbers works in an entirely deterministic way due to its specific structure and principles. Randomness is, therefore, the more general case of emergence, the sign of a specific relation between different levels of reality.

If a system is random, it will mean that its parts—that is, its lower-level conditions—are entirely determining its comprehensive order. It is case 3 of the fake Wales scheme, where this scheme was originated by a random, lower-level process. In this case, the higher-level, comprehensive order has no existential meaning of its own—that is, in the ontological sense, it does not exist; it is just our subjective impression, due to random circumstances. However, it does not mean that it has no denotative meaning and via reduction, it could not tell anything meaningful about the lower-level processes and principles of the system that shaped it; just think about heat or temperature.

If a system is not random, it will mean that its parts—that is, its lower-level conditions—are merely determining those boundary conditions within which the system, as a comprehensive, orderly whole, works or acts freely according to its higher-level, ordering principles. It is case 1 of the real Wales lettering, intentionally arranged by the stationmaster to greet the arriving passengers. In this case, the higher-level, comprehensive order has its own existential meaning—that is, it has to be regarded as an independent object (which is a consequence of a higher-level ordering principle), but it still partly depends on its lower-level conditions. Nonetheless, the Wales lettering is at the lowest level of emergent hierarchy and cannot even sustain its own comprehensive order. In contrast, a frog is not only able to maintain its own comprehensive order but also can act freely in several different ways.

It is true in both cases, however, that the lower-level, random material processes in themselves are not random at all. Their randomness is only the expression of their fundamental nature in relation to higher-level comprehensive orders: material processes alone can never produce any comprehensive order. On the contrary, random material processes will destroy any such order. In other words, lower-level, random material processes can produce higher-level orders only by chance and only for a short period of time. Real, meaningful higher-level orders are the consequence of higher-level, ordering principles.

So if we recognize a random system—for example, the W-scheme of Cassiopeia—as a meaningful, orderly whole, originated by an ordering principle (as astrology does with constellations), we will commit a severe subjective mistake. A frog could not be a frog if it were created by chance and its higher-level, comprehensive order was entirely determined by its lower-level, random material conditions. It would only be an illusion of our senses, just as the W-scheme of Cassiopeia is only an illusion and not a real, meaningful letter. However, frogs naturally are not just the illusory pattern of our senses, thus, they are also not only originated by lower-level, random material processes.

The neo-Darwinian theory still claims that living beings originated from lower-level, random material processes of mutations and natural selection. This claim, however, as we can see now, is, in fact, the explicit statement that there are no real, meaningful living beings which can act freely but rather only such random, illusory patterns as the W-scheme of Cassiopeia. That is, the explicit statement that there are neither human persons nor personal knowledge by which we can recognize any meaningful, comprehensive, orderly wholes: we are all illusory patterns in the meaningless flows of random material conditions.

However, this cannot be stated honestly—that is, with personal commitment based on real, tacit beliefs. Of course, neo-Darwinians also do not state it honestly just to conceal their real, tacit beliefs behind their explicit expressions of their theory and to conform to the Laplacian ideal of objective knowledge and the ruling philosophies of science today: positivism and materialism. The explicit expressions of their theory become meaningful and useful in practice only by deceptive substitutions. It is not a solution for this problem, however, because this inconsistency in science and the severe tension between the two different systems of fundamental beliefs—that is, belief in evolution and belief in materialism—significantly hinders new scientific discoveries and weakens science itself. Science, therefore, cannot perform its service for society and cannot give us answers to our most crucial questions: who we are, where we have come from, and where we should look for a hopeful future.

Part Two

Emergence

5

Emergence

5.1 Preface

In Part One of this book, I tried to establish the concept of personal knowledge, closely following Michael Polanyi's thoughts. The point of personal knowledge is that the conceptual dichotomy of subjective versus objective is false. Our perspectives are neither merely unfounded, subjective illusions nor is there an objective point of reference, over and above us, determining what truth is. Human knowledge has its own natural foundations; therefore, everything should be understood in a *relational way*, from our personal perspectives—which are rooted in our center, our personal reality, and determined by our evolutionary heritage. Nothing is absolute.

This is true not only for our personal point of view but even the smallest parts of matter and the deepest bottoms of reality. In this sense, we are not unique at all; we are not created in the image of the Laplacian demon, we are the children of the space and time of this universe. Referring to this fact, I mentioned in subchapter 2.4 that in their main philosophical insights, Polanyi and Einstein spoke about the same thing, only at different levels and from different scientific perspectives. In this Part Two, I will unfold the meaning of this claim.

But first, we have to take a closer look at the concept of emergence, which unfolds the different levels of reality for us. Until this point, we have met this concept in contrast to the neo-Darwinian theory and in its more general sense—that is, as a kind of relationship between different levels of order: randomness—so our insight was very different than that of the usual materialist approach today. Our conclusion will be the same, only in a more detailed and established way; but now, we have to investigate the concept from the more familiar point of view of the philosophy of science.

Before we start, consider the words of a prominent theoretical physicist, Lee Smolin, and how he sees the concept of emergence and its significance for science in the twenty-first century:

> Emergence is an important term in a relational world. A property of something made of parts is emergent if it would not make sense when attributed to any of the parts. Rocks are hard, and water flows, but the atoms they're made of are neither solid nor wet. An emergent property will often hold approximately, because it denotes an averaged or high-level description that leaves out much detail.
>
> As science progresses, aspects of nature once considered fundamental are revealed as emergent and approximate. We once thought that solids, liquids, and gases were fundamental states; now we now that these are emergent properties, which can be understood as different ways to arrange the atoms that make up everything. Most of the laws of nature one thought of as fundamental are now understood as emergent and approximate. Temperature is just the average energy of atoms in random motion, so the laws of thermodynamics that refer to temperature are emergent and approximate.
>
> I'm inclined to believe that just about everything we now think is fundamental will also eventually be understood as approximate and emergent: gravity and the laws of Newton and Einstein that govern it, the laws of quantum mechanics, even space itself.[1]

5.2 The Concept and Original Meaning of Emergence

The concept of emergence has become quite popular again in science and the philosophy of science. Countless papers and authors speak about some kind of emergence and try to deal with the problems that arise. The notion of emergence can be found in almost every field of science, from informatics via biology to physics; we can see that, for example, from the words of Smolin. However, these notions seem to be quite different across disciplines.

I believe that the most notable reason for this mottled situation is that the *original meaning* of emergence has faded. We are left feeling that there is a genuine need for the concept of emergence, but we seek back roads and rear entrances instead of the real, foundational meaning. Of course, there are valid reasons for this fading, including two main ones: first, the

---

1. Smolin, *Time Reborn*, xxx–xxxi.

fast rise and *fall* of British Emergentism (as Brian P. McLaughlin put it in his famous and influential paper in 1992);[2] second, the firm *positivist* and *materialist convictions, concepts*, and *methods* of scientists and philosophers today. These reasons are, of course, in close connection with each other, and the latter leads to a concept of emergence that is "metaphysically innocent" and entirely "consistent with materialism" (as Mark A. Bedau formulated it in another well-known and influential paper in 1997).[3]

The first emergentist is often considered to be John Stuart Mill, but the term, in fact, stems from George Henry Lewes's book, *The Problems of Life and Mind*. After the fast fall of the British Emergentists (e.g., Samuel Alexander, Lloyd Morgan, and C. D. Broad), there was a long silence and a few weak and distant voices—for example, those of Polanyi and Roger W. Sperry, a Nobel Prize-winning neurobiologist. Today, perhaps the most prominent figure of emergentism in science is Robert G. B. Reid. We are only talking a lot about emergence but not believing in it.

It is important to emphasize, however, that Mill or Lewes were not emergentists at all; or, to put it differently, if they had been emergentists, then Charles Darwin or even Aristotle would also be one. Mill just used a few terms—most notably, "homeopathic laws" and "heteropathic laws"—which, in their explicit form, are very similar to the emergentist differentiation of non-emergent and emergent relations between levels (especially Broad's "basic laws of nature" and "special laws of nature"). These differentiations, however, are only a small, marginal part of Mill's philosophy, and most importantly, Mill's tacit intention was not at all to be an emergentist by these terms. The same is true for Lewes; instead, in their real tacit intentions, they are positivists and materialists.

Although there are also severe differences between the main works of the British Emergentists, I believe that their fundamental, honest, and *tacit intention* is the same: to *break the false dichotomy of dualism versus materialism with a new concept of reality*. As I mentioned in chapter 1, however, emergentism never became a real, independent philosophical school because—beyond the fact that it was swept right away by the rising power of positivism and materialism—neither Morgan nor Broad could adequately understand and deal with Alexander's starting point: reality, in its fundaments, is *space* and *time*. Both Morgan and Broad started emergence by the chemical level based on the fundamental material level, while Alexander did not even claim that the chemical level is emergent; instead, he focused on life and mind based on the fundamental level of space and time. In spite

---

2. See McLaughlin, "Rise and Fall of British Emergentism."
3. See Bedau, "Weak Emergence."

of the common tacit ground, they could not find a proper *common explicit conceptual and explanatory framework* by which a new and successful philosophical school could have been built. Morgan took a way where the concept of God and his "Activity" and involvement in emergence played a crucial role[4] so it could be understood as a kind of "emergent dualism," while Broad tried to reinterpret emergence in a broader, materialist framework, rejecting "strict materialism" for the sake of an "emergent materialism."[5] I believe this situation can be pictured well with the fact that in nearly seven hundred pages of work, Broad took only three pages to investigate Alexander's theory to respectfully distance himself from his "emergent neutralism."[6] Nonetheless, this unfortunate step, by the way, did not prevent him from fiercely defending the reality of time against Bertrand Russell and John McTaggart's timeless concept of the block universe (2.4).

The reason that they could not find a common conceptual framework is, I believe, the lack of a well-established theory of knowledge on the basis of which they could have satisfactorily interpreted and understood the deep abyss arising between their tacit intentions (toward a genuinely new concept of reality) and the explicit conceptual framework of the Laplacian ideal (which, at that time, due to the fast rise of logical positivism, was regarded as even more fundamental than it is now). Alexander's famous phrase, "natural piety"—to acknowledge certain things without detailed, explicit investigations—was all about this glooming abyss. And, of course, his theory of space and time, as we will see in detail in the next chapter, was also beyond the standard Laplacian approach. Morgan used particular dualistic concepts to simplify and make Alexander's theory more easy to understand in an ordinary philosophical framework—which was, in fact, a huge step backward, leading toward a dead end—while Broad, contrarily, put Alexander aside and, due to the new, positivist spirit of the Laplacian ideal, used highly analytical methods to reconcile ice with fire—which, in a sense, concealed the arising abyss but did not solve the problems; rather, it just laid the foundations for the "emergent materialist" framework in which we tend to speak about emergence today. For example, in his influential 1992 paper, McLaughlin barely pays attention to Alexander; in fact, he deals *only with Broad* under the label of British Emergentism. At one point, he even mentions:

> I am hesistant in my interpretation of Alexander, since, to be frank, I find apparently conflicting passages in his texts and I am

---

4. Morgan, *Emergent Evolution*.
5. Broad, *Mind and its Place in Nature*.
6. Broad, *Mind and its Place in Nature*, 648–50.

uncertain how to resolve the apparent conflicts. I will spare the reader a discussion of these conflicts.[7]

From a consistently emergentist point of view, we will not find such "apparent conflicts" as McLaughlin or Broad did because of their analytical/positivist approach. In a sense, this book, *Personal Reality* is all about making a general conceptual and explanatory framework for emergentism based on Polanyi's concept of personal knowledge. Contemporary works, unfortunately, entirely lack such a framework; for example, the above mentioned Reid bases his claims concerning emergent phenomena on Morgan's simplified, dualistic thoughts, but, at the same time, he leaves out Morgan's dualistic philosophy because such a philosophy cannot stand in science today. In consequence, his claims, unfortunately, become entirely unfounded—even from an emergentist point of view.[8]

So today, after a long silence, the concept of emergence has returned, and it seems to carry two main and significantly differing meanings. First is the old *ontological* or *strong* meaning. This meaning asserts that there are multileveled, comprehensive, orderly wholes (objects), the higher levels of which ontologically *exist*, have existential meaning—that is, they are not material. Second is the new *epistemological* or *weak* meaning. This meaning asserts that the higher levels of orderly wholes *do not exist* ontologically; rather, they are only comprehensive phenomena of matter and have only denotative meaning.

The first, ontological meaning is, of course, the one that was proposed by the British Emergentists. It is important to emphasize once more that in Morgan's or Broad's understanding—and thus, in contemporary interpretations of British Emergentism—emergence starts at the material level, not with space and time. Consequently, in their views, the first level of emergence is that of *chemical phenomena*; therefore, every higher level—over and above the fundamental material level—is ontologically emergent, and there is no place for only epistemological or weak emergence in the lifeless world. In other words, every higher level is emergent both in the weaker epistemological and the stronger ontological sense; therefore, this concept of emergence is not simply contrary to current epistemological concepts of emergence, stating that there are some ontologically emergent phenomena as well, but it is truly a much stronger version of the concept. This fact is one of the main reasons why such a concept is highly problematic. Nonetheless, in a materialist interpretation, the main problem is this: according to "Alexander's

---

7. McLaughlin, "Rise and Fall of British Emergentism," 31.
8. See Reid, *Evolutionary Theory*; Reid, *Biological Emergences*.

dictum,"[9] the higher levels have to be causally effective; otherwise, they cannot be ontologically real. But materialist philosophers think that this active causal effectiveness leads—via so-called overdetermination and downward causation—to the breaking of the causal closure of the lower-level physical world as higher-level persons, for example, voluntarily move their physical bodies.[10] Since, according to them, this violation of the causal closure of the physical world is clearly impossible, higher levels are, therefore, either not real ontologically or they are real, but this is not a new ontological position at all—just the old, well-known, and false dualism. I will detail this materialist approach in subchapter 5.8.

The second, epistemological meaning, however, is also highly problematic. Although, according to Mark A. Bedau, it is "consistent with materialism . . . weak emergence is not just in our minds. . . . Rather, weak emergence is an objective phenomenon that exists in nature."[11] What does it mean for an epistemological higher level to "exist in nature" and "not just in the mind"? Epistemological levels do not exist, ontological levels do. Heat is a comprehensive phenomenon of matter: *we* can experience it, *we* can feel it, but from a consistently Laplacian point of view, it does not exist at all (2.3). The *particles* exist, and heat is only the average kinetic energy of those particles. Also, what does it mean for any emergence to be an "objective phenomenon"? Is it not the fundamental material entities that are objective, e.g., particles due to the nature of ideal Laplacian knowledge? It seems that although Bedau wants to be "metaphysically innocent," he slips quietly into the territory of ontological emergence: "But weak emergence is still rich enough for an ontology of objective, macro-level structures."[12]

In developing the concept of weak emergence, Bedau's aim is to overcome a dilemma between the *complete denial of emergence* (or claiming that it is merely in one's mind) and the position of *strong emergence* of British Emergentism. He, like many other thinkers who start to deal with the problem of emergence today, finds both of these positions to be too extreme in one sense or the other, proposing weak emergence as a middle ground.

It is worth visiting Bedau's argument to see how he is positions his concept of weak emergence. First of all, he distances himself from strong emergence to avoid even the appearance that he wants to break with materialism by his concept. He proposes two main reasons for this. One is the

---

9. Kim, "Downward Causation."

10. See, for example, Kim, *Mind in a Physical World*; Kim, "Making Sense of Emergence"; Kim, "Mental Causation."

11. Bedau, "Is Weak Emergence Just in the Mind?," 457.

12. Bedau, "Downward Causation," 183.

problem of the independent, causal effectiveness of the higher ontological levels we have just seen above. He accepts Jaegwon Kim's argument that the active causal autonomy of the higher levels means that there is *downward causation* and the *violation of the causal closure of the material world* which, according to Bedau's opinion, contradicts the state of science and is hence unacceptable (5.8). In his harsh words: "Although strong emergence is logically possible, it is uncomfortably like magic."[13]

Bedau's other reason is that, in his evaluation, strong emergence appears to have no scientific value. On the possible programs of strong emergence, he quotes Timothy O'Connor, who, in turn, cites Roger W. Sperry and Michael Polanyi. In O'Connor's interpretation, these authors use strong emergence to explain consciousness and the phenomena of life, respectively.[14] Bedau does not find any other possible territories in science for strong emergence and thinks that these many decades-old works give no good argument for the usefulness of strong emergence. On the contrary, he remarks that strong emergence features the symptoms of a degenerative research program, as all of its proponents cite the same, outdated Sperry and Polanyi works but fail to connect it to contemporary research topics or show new results. Bedau thus concludes that, "To judge from the available evidence, strong emergence is one mystery which we don't need."[15] However, Bedau claims that weak emergence—particularly as defined by him—"is metaphysically innocent, consistent with materialism, and scientifically useful."[16]

According to Bedau's argument, contemporary science shows that all higher-level phenomena can be reduced to lower-level material parts. His main idea is that emergence is not the contrary concept of reduction (as it was originally defined by Morgan and Broad) but rather is based on a *particular kind of reduction*—between the (weakly) emergent level and the fundamental level. However, as we will see in detail in the next subchapters, without any further explanation of the concept of reduction as a human knowledge which exists on its own right, the consequence is that it may be tempting to categorize weak emergence as a simple, new kind of theory of epistemological emergence since, according to it, everything is reducible.

So, in contrast to simple epistemological emergence, the distinguishing feature of Bedau's concept of weak emergence is that, according to Bedau's intention, emergence is not just in the mind but "is an objective phenomenon

---

13. Bedau, "Weak Emergence," 377.
14. O'Connor, "Emergent Properties."
15. Bedau, "Weak Emergence," 377.
16. Bedau, "Weak Emergence," 376.

that exists in nature" and thus *can be measured and calculated exactly*.[17] The definition of weak emergence in its newest form is as follows:

> If P is a macro-property of some system S, then P is weakly emergent if and only if P is generatively explainable from all of S's prior micro-facts but only in an incompressible way.[18]

By generative explanation, Bedau means that the macro-property in question can be "exactly and correctly" shown to be produced based on the "micro-causal dynamics" and "earlier micro-states and boundary conditions" of the system in either a discrete or a continuous temporal process. Bedau also points out that this kind of explanation implies that in any given point of time, the macro-property in question is the aggregate or sum of the micro-properties of the system that exists at the same time. This is what he calls *synchronic* reduction of "macro to micro." In other words, there is no emergence of macro-properties over the micro-properties realizing them; rather, emergence occurs *in the process of state changes* in the system. This explanation is easiest to imagine as a computer simulation—although Bedau emphasizes that it *does not have to be* a computer simulation. Bedau states that by iterating over a system's micro-interactions, we are "crawling the micro-causal web." Now, if a system's state in T can be explained without any loss only if we do not skip any in-between states, then the explanation is *incompressible*, and thus we have an example of weakly emergent phenomena.

The most authentic way to illustrate weak emergence is using the example of Game of Life, just as Bedau himself does.[19] Game of Life is a well-known cellular automaton that takes place in an infinite, two-dimensional universe of a regular grid in which each cell is either "dead" or "alive." There are four simple rules of state changes in this universe:

1. Any alive cell with fewer than two alive neighbors dies.
2. Any alive cell with more than three alive neighbors dies.
3. Any alive cell with two or three alive neighbors lives.
4. Any dead cell with exactly three alive neighbor cells will come to life.

Started in certain initial configurations, Game of Life can feature fascinating, ever-changing patterns based only on these four simple rules. But what does it mean for a state in Game of Life to be an instance of weak

---

17. Bedau, "Is Weak Emergence Just in the Mind?"
18. Bedau, "Is Weak Emergence Just in the Mind?," 445.
19. Bedau, "Weak Emergence."

emergence? It means that the state in question cannot be explained *without calculating all the intermediate states*. As was shown above, Bedau proposes that this is an objectively evaluable property of the Game of Life states and other phenomena. Phrasing it in another way, the claim is that there is no more compact explanation to these examples than just *simulating* all of its steps (state changes) from the beginning or "crawling the micro-causal web," which, in this case, is equivalent to playing the Game of Life. To emphasize the objectivity of weak emergence, Bedau even adds that *Laplace's demon would have to do the same*.[20]

Now, perhaps we can feel the spirit of speaking about emergence today. The point of Bedau's concept is that he tries to show an account of emergence that can be as objectively evaluated as fundamental physical particles, so it is not just in the mind—that is, even Laplace's demon itself can "see" it—but it still does not break with materialism.

Nonetheless, it can be said that, in a sense, Bedau's project is very similar to those of the early emergentists: the British Emergentists sought for a middle ground between materialism and dualism, whereas Bedau tries to find a way between strict materialism and strong emergence. In reality, however, Bedau's idea is not new at all because, as we have seen, Broad himself already defined his position as "emergent materialism"—between strict materialism and the kind of strong emergentism that, according to his understanding, was held by Alexander and Morgan. Moreover, Bedau's other main idea that emergence goes along with a special kind of reduction is also not really new because, for example, Broad distanced himself from Alexander just because Alexander claimed that mind and other emergent phenomena in a sense could be reduced.[21] Perhaps we are still where we were a century ago.

Another problem arises if we, contrary to Bedau, accept that epistemologically emergent, comprehensive phenomena of matter are indeed only "in the mind." Then it is indeed not "metaphysically wicked" ontological emergence, but notice that it—at least tacitly—*presupposes the existence of a mind* that experiences the comprehensive emergent phenomena. Perhaps, though, the existence of the mind does not imply dualism but rather only the ontological emergence of the mind.

I dare to hope that this short train of thought has clearly emphasized the severe problems around the notion of emergence in philosophy of science today. I believe that Bedau's struggle with metaphysical innocence and emergence in nature is not accidental but the sign of reality. Epistemological

---

20. Bedau, "Weak Emergence," 379.
21. Broad, *Mind and its Place in Nature*, 639.

and ontological emergence cannot be separated entirely. If someone starts to flirt just "innocently" with the concept of emergence, he will soon be burned with the flame of its original, ontological meaning.

This consequence does not mean, however, that we must return to the philosophy of British Emergentism as interpreted by Morgan or Broad. The ambitious tower of British Emergentism collapsed forever—even before it could have been halfway built—however, this was not because of the original, tacit meaning of emergence, shared by all of them, *but because of the reduction of comprehensive chemical phenomena to quantum mechanics*, as McLaughlin has shown so well.[22] Morgan and Broad were wrong when they thought that chemical levels are ontologically emergent. It was an even more unfortunate mistake when they used the chemical level as a primary example for emergence. The reason for this was that chemical phenomena could be described, measured, and computed quite precisely according to the Laplacian ideal of objective knowledge—as could the patterns of the Game of Life world, by the way. However, not all of them committed these mistakes. Perhaps Morgan and Broad took an unfortunate path when they left behind Samuel Alexander's original concept—it is entirely true that their peculiar, explicated theories of emergence were wrong—this does not mean, however, that their original, tacit intention was also wrong. In this sense, they never left Alexander's original spirit behind. Tacitly, even Bedau flirts with this original intention.

The original, tacit intention of Alexander was that it is possible to conceive of a coherent, *medium* ontological conviction—between dualism and materialist monism. That we are neither created in the image of God nor just a pile of quarks and electrons but rather *real, meaningful, comprehensive, orderly wholes by time*. In fact, this is the true, original meaning of emergence.

In the following, I will investigate this original meaning of emergence and its consequences. I will not examine particular theories in detail (e.g., Morgan, Broad, or Sperry) because it is my firm conviction that this would misdirect the focus toward meaningless, explicit parts. I wish to place emphasis on the meaningful, comprehensive whole—this original, tacit meaning. Nonetheless, I will investigate strong and weak emergences, albeit not to contrast them—they are not rivals but rather the different Janus faces of the *same notion*. On its own, epistemological emergence is not emergence at all, it is *materialism*. There is no "strict materialism" or "emergent materialism"—these are only explicit conceptual beasts that conceal the original, tacit notion; therefore, there is only materialism or

---

22. McLaughlin, "Rise and Fall of British Emergentism."

emergentism. So, I believe that there is no strong emergence and no weak emergence. *There is only one medium emergence,* between dualism and materialist monism, *with two faces.*

5.3 Reduction and Materialism

According to the original meaning of emergence, there are higher levels of comprehensive, orderly wholes that ontologically exist. But what does this mean? To understand, we must first understand the *ontological consequences* of reduction.

1. *Dualism* asserts that there are *two different kinds of reality*, two fundamental *substances*—generally, matter and mind—which are equal in their deepness in reality; their relation is *symmetrical*. There is mind or soul without matter and vice versa.
2. *Materialist* monism asserts that there is only *one kind of reality*, one fundamental *substance*: matter.
3. *Emergentism* asserts that there are *two different kinds of reality*, but only one is fundamental *substance*, matter. The other is not fundamental, it is *emergent*. Thus, their relation is *asymmetrical*. Emergent reality is not self-sufficient but rather is dependent on the fundamental material substance. There are no higher emergent levels without matter, but there is matter on its own. It follows that emergent objects are necessarily multileveled and consist of at least one fundamental and one emergent level of reality.

The question is how can we know that an object is material, emergent, or perhaps has dual substantial nature due to a vital force? In nature, we see trees, houses, machines, frogs, people, and many other *objects. We cannot see the kinds of reality themselves*: we cannot see matter—that is, quarks and electrons, etc.—and we cannot see the emergent levels separately. We cannot see the mind itself.

Of course, a materialist, according to his fundamental beliefs, would say at once that houses, trees, machines, people, etc., are composed of matter, so to see them is like seeing matter. Perhaps, but this is true if and only if we accept materialism *a priori*—only then do we start to see things. However, objects such as houses, trees, frogs, machines, and people are very different phenomena with very different characteristics and behavior in contrast to quarks and electrons. Maybe they are ontologically equal, but *this has yet to be revealed*. So far, *no one* has shown that houses, trees, frogs, people, or even pistons, watermills, or other machines are only composed of matter. Due to the enormous influence of materialism in science and Western culture, we can easily believe it—but *it was only ever revealed at the chemical level* (by the brilliant success of quantum mechanics) that these objects are ontologically equal to the fundamental level of matter. The hydrogen atom, the covalent bond, heat, etc., were reduced to the material level, and not houses, trees, frogs, pistons, and people.

However, this successful reduction of the chemical level was the reason of the fall of British Emergentism because, as we have seen, Morgan's and Broad's particular theories were built upon the conviction that the typical instance of emergence is the emergence of the chemical level. This successful reduction was also the reason that the original meaning of emergence has faded, belief in scientific materialism strengthened significantly during the twentieth century, and now, we can easily believe in the successful reduction of higher levels, trees, frogs, people, etc. But a successful reduction has *never*, in fact, come, and emergence, once again, is an issue—against all kinds of enormous materialist influences in philosophy and science.

The answer to our question of how we can know for sure that an object is material, then, is *the successful reduction* of the higher comprehensive level(s) of that object. At the same time, the goal of reduction is not necessarily the fundamental material level. It is possible to reduce between two higher levels and go no further or even to reduce higher levels to a non-material substance—for example, human notions and acts to mind. In scientific practice, however, these options do not appear because the notion of reduction is *tightly connected* to materialism.

There are two main reasons for this. First, materialists have to reduce the higher levels to show that materialism is true. Second, if someone is a reductionist, why would he stop at a higher level? In principle, what can stop the reduction of levels? The answer, of course, is the fundamental level of material substance. The fundamental is the level that by definition is the last one. In principle, every other level can be reduced. But as we have seen, the end of reduction can be another fundamental level, too. Even so, dualists fight the notion of reduction because, in practice, the question is not the possibility of the reduction of higher levels to the mind but rather the reduction of the mind to matter, according to the viewpoint of materialism and the tight connection of reductionism to materialism.

The notion of reduction, however, is not materialist at all. It cannot be materialist because it is not an ontological conviction about reality; rather, it is only an *intellectual tool* of human knowledge (3.3), useful, for instance, to show the truth or untruth of materialism or to show that dualism is wrong. I will call this specific, intellectual tool of human knowledge an epistemological tool, emphasizing its real nature.

Thus, reduction is an *epistemological tool*, while materialism is an *ontological conviction*—as, of course, emergentism and dualism are, too. It is for this reason that I use the term materialism and not the now-popular "physicalism," which suggests that materialism is like or inseparable from physics and science. But again, physics is an intellectual tool of human knowledge and not an ontological conviction; *they are not in the same category*.

If emergentism is true, physics operates with higher-level, comprehensive, emergent objects without problems (7.4). As a matter of fact, for centuries, physics dealt only with emergent objects; the presupposed fundamental material level of quarks and electrons was discovered in the first half of the twentieth century by quantum mechanics. Physics is *essential* for an emergentist—for example, to answer the biophysical cause of sickle-cell anemia in the ontologically emergent human body. René Descartes, the father of modern dualism, also used mechanical physics without any trouble. Moreover, he was one of the first who worked out a purely mechanical physics, long before Isaac Newton. And the great Newton himself was not a materialist at all. Moreover, in recent years, some eminent physicists argue that physics and emergence cannot be separated—for example, Robert B. Laughlin or Lee Smolin.[23] In the next chapter, we will investigate this problem in more detail and, following the thought of Alexander and Einstein, deal with the problem of space, time, and matter.

Multiple fields provide examples of reduction. In philosophy, the two classic, normative examples are the models of Ernest Nagel and Jaegwon Kim.[24] There are many others, however, and we can find different reduction methods in several scientific fields (such as biology, mathematics, or even technology and informatics, considering Bedau's reduction by "simulation").[25] I will not deal with these different methods here, however, because for our purposes, it is the *consequences* of reduction and not the exact methods that are of interest. It is the consequence of the successful reduction of the chemical level to quantum mechanics and not the concrete method or quantum mechanics itself that allowed for the fall of British Emergentism. No one is interested in specific quantum mechanical equations here.

Moreover, if we define reduction by a concrete method—for example, by Kim's functional reduction model—many other reduction methods

23. See Laughlin, *Different Universe*; Smolin, *Time Reborn*.
24. See Nagel, *Structure of Science*; Kim, "Making Sense of Emergence."
25. Bedau, "Weak Emergence."

would necessarily fall outside the definition. It is a *materialist notion* to think that there is only one valid method of reduction—with the goal, of course, of fundamental material substance. But why would the same method necessarily work for a reduction between two higher levels and between a lower level and the fundamental level? Furthermore, why would the same method work for a dualist reduction of human notions and acts to the mind and for the reduction of the chemical level to matter by quantum mechanical equations? I do not believe that human thoughts and social levels can be reduced to the mind because I am not a dualist; but if I am wrong, and dualism stands, I am pretty sure that the reduction of human notions and social levels to the mind would be something altogether different from the reduction of the chemical level to matter by the equations and operational principles of quantum mechanics.

As for the ontological consequences of reduction, to answer our question of whether an object is material or not, it is entirely *inessential* which particular method of reduction we use. What is essential is the *success* of the reduction, as in the case of the reduction of the chemical level to quantum mechanics. Of course, this does not mean that the success is independent of the particular method—the proper method is the precondition of success—but that the ontological consequences still lie in the outcomes of the success and not in the specific method, which is "only" an epistemological condition. To understand the original meaning of emergence, we must first understand the ontological consequences of reduction.

Thus I do not look here for the proper epistemological tools; I believe *scientists* are responsible for this as it was done by the reduction of chemical levels by quantum mechanics, and I presuppose that if a reduction is possible, a scientist will find the proper epistemological tool at the end. The question for me is the ontological consequence. The task I, as a philosopher, am responsible for, is whether every object is material, whether every object can be reduced to matter—even trees, frogs, and people.

Unfortunately, these two different sides of reduction are often blurred; that is, the investigation of the ontological consequences of reduction on the one hand and the investigation of the particular epistemological tools on the other. Moreover, the debate typically follows materialist intentions and interpretations around the peculiar possibility of reducing important higher-level objects (e.g., qualia, mind, etc.) or, what is worse, it takes place in *a priori* materialist framework, as is the case with biology. Thus, the question of ontological consequences does not arise at all. For example, the classic Paul Oppenheim and Hilary Putnam paper deals with the possibility of reductions of different higher levels in such an *a priori* materialist framework that whether the particular reduction methods are either successful or not, they cannot have any ontological consequences; trees, machines, frogs, and people can or cannot be reduced—it does not matter. Reduction has no real importance or meaning since we already "know" that everything is material *a priori*.[26]

This kind of materialist thinking and the duality of the blurred sides appear in those concepts like eliminative materialism and non-reductive materialism—if materialism could be anything other than eliminative (5.4). The so-called non-reductive materialism is perhaps the most popular philosophical position among academic philosophers today. The term non-reductive reflects the epistemological side, while the term materialism reflects the ontological one. The ontological consequences, however, are still entirely neglected since if they took the result of the epistemological side (the non-reductive, that is, unsuccessful reduction) seriously, then they would not be able to hold the ontological side: materialism. Their position, in fact, literally means *non-materialist materialism*—which makes no sense, of course. It is only a deceptive substitution (2.5); and yet, the most popular philosophical position among academics.

Our ordinary use of language also reflects this duality and can hide the two different sides as well. We often say that we reduced an object or say that we reduced a higher-level description of an object (to a lower-level description of the same). The former reflects the ontological consequences, no matter in which way we have successfully shown that the true nature of the object is material. The latter reflects the epistemological tools by which peculiar method we have connected the higher and lower-level descriptions of the object. In the following, I will definitely separate these two sides to understand the original meaning of emergence.

5.4 Reduction as Emergence

Now, the question is: what is reduction? On the one side, what is the ontological consequence of a successful reduction? On the other, what are we doing when we use the epistemological tool of reduction?

The answer to the latter is the following: *we create an asymmetrical epistemological connection between two descriptions* that refer to different objects—for example:

---

26. Oppenheim and Putnam, "Unity of Science." For a critique of this deficiency, see Rueger and McGivern, "Hierarchies and Levels of Reality."

crystal	←	**description 1** (e.g., chemistry)
		↓ **reduction method**
quarks, electrons, etc.,	←	**description 2** (e.g., quantum mechanics)

Figure 12. The structure of reduction.

Thus, reduction has *three conditions*:

1. It presupposes at least *two different objects*. One of them is higher-level, the other one is lower-level.

2. It presupposes *two descriptions*. One of them refers to the higher-level object, the other to the lower-level one.

3. It presupposes the *reduction method* itself, and we have to perform this *successfully*.

So, then, reduction has *two* sides or faces, just like emergence. One of them—that of the objects—is the *ontological* side. The other—that of the descriptions and reduction method—is the *epistemological* one.

It is important to note that both the descriptions and the reduction method are *human knowledge*. As such, they are not merely meaningful, epistemic references to the objects, but they are *ontological objects* themselves. They do not only have denotative meaning but existential meaning as well (3.4). (In my figures, boldface type means ontological objects.) Consequently, the possibility of reducing them as objects must also be questioned. To think that human knowledge as an object does not have an ontological nature but only epistemic meaning is the *a priori* presumption of materialism—once again, before the act by which they would even try to be reduced, materialism would be confirmed.

It is a typical mistake in the case of the first condition of reduction to speak about only two levels and not about two different ontological objects—for example, to speak about the higher-level of the comprehensive, orderly whole and the lower-level of the parts (as was done by Oppenheim and Putnam).[27] Of course, the source of this mistake is that one of the objects is higher-level and the other one is lower-level, which suggests that, in fact, there are not two different, *independent* objects as dualism holds. But to speak only about the two levels of a part-whole relationship of an object (and not about a higher-level and another different, lower-level object) pre-

---

27. Oppenheim and Putnam, "Unity of Science."

supposes that there is only one object—that is, there cannot be ontological consequences for reduction. It is again the *a priori* presupposition of materialism before the act of successful reduction.

```
           whole      ←    description 1
             ╱              (there is no successful reduction)
object  −  parts     ←    description 2
```

Figure 13. The structure of reduction in the case
of parts-whole relationships.

However, from the fact that a higher-level, comprehensive object is dependent on a lower-level object(s)—for example, the Wales lettering was written in pebbles—it necessarily follows that there is only one real object, and materialism holds if and only if we think in the false dichotomy of materialism versus dualism. Only dualism claims that there are two independent substances.

It is a similar mistake to speak about merely different types of properties—usually higher-level and lower-level properties—and to only call one ontological (e.g., relational base or something similar), which casts a shadow on its ontological meaning.

```
                property type 1   ←   description 1
                    ╱                   (there is no successful reduction)
relational base  −  property type 2  ←  description 2
```

Figure 14. The structure of reduction in the case
of the so-called "relational base."

This camouflage can be deepened by identifying the relational base with the aggregation of lower-level properties, thus making the higher-level properties only a necessary consequence of specific arrangements of lower-level properties. Reduction, then, is merely a necessity; the remaining question is just that of the proper reduction method. If it cannot be found, though, never mind—there would be no ontological consequences anyway (non-reductive materialism).

However, in fact, before the successful reduction, it is not grounded at all that heat is only a comprehensive phenomenon of matter and not the consequence of an enigmatic "fire-object" or another substance, e.g., some form. From Francis Bacon via Galileo Galilei to James Clerk Maxwell and Ludwig Boltzmann, several excellent scientists worked very hard to establish that heat is only a comprehensive phenomenon of matter—the average kinetic energy of the movements of material parts—and should there be no real stake, importance, or meaning in their works?

So, then, what is reduction and what is the ontological consequence of a successful reduction? The answer is the following: *there is only one object— namely, the lower-level one.*

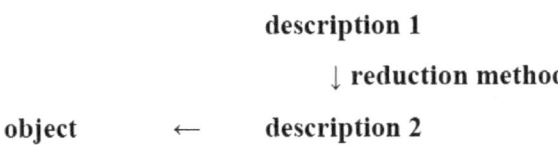

Figure 15. The structure of the successful reduction.

If reduction is successful, it creates an *asymmetrical epistemological connection* between the two descriptions and reveals that in truth, the object of the references of the two descriptions is just *the same*.

This does *not* mean, however, that the two descriptions refer to the one existing object equally and in the same way—that is, that the two different descriptions have exactly the same denotative meaning; not at all. It also does not mean that the two presupposed objects are identical; not in the least. Since reduction is by definition *asymmetric*, it reveals that on its own, the reference of the higher-level description has no meaning—that is, its denotative meaning in itself is simply void. There is no fire-object or other immaterial substance to which it could refer. But reduction by definition also reveals that *via and only via* the reduction method, the higher-level description refers to the same object as the lower-level one refers to; that is, the denotative meaning of the higher-level description is about the same object as that of the lower-level description: heat is only the average kinetic energy of particles, referring merely to the lower-level object(s) and nothing else. After successful reduction, the higher-level description *only via* the reduction method and *via* the lower-level description keeps its reference and real denotative meaning, but via that it *keeps*.

We can*not* say that, therefore, by successful reduction, the higher-level object will be identical with the lower-level one; unfortunately, we often do say that. The phrase "we reduced an object" suggests this, and it is highly misleading. In truth, we *did not reduce* the higher-level object but *only the higher-level description* of the object. The higher-level object was simply *eliminated*. In Nagel's words, reduction is only the "logical relation between certain statements."[28] There is no heat as an independent object. It is only a description that refers to the average kinetic energy of the really-existing particles via a successful reduction method. The former is the *ontological consequence*, and the latter is the *epistemic structure* of a successful reduction.

So, then, by a successful reduction, only *one* object remains which, in accordance with the asymmetric relationship, is the *lower-level* one; at the end, the material substance. *This and nothing else could confirm materialism,* as it has done in the case of heat (by statistical physics) or chemical levels (by quantum mechanics). But there is plenty of work yet for materialists with such objects as trees, frogs, people, pistons, etc. Without such ontological relevance, this work cannot be done, and materialism remains either an attractive or repulsive belief. Many materialists still do not bother themselves with the ontological consequences of reduction; they just "know" that they are right.

It is important to emphasize that the fact that there remains only one object on the ontological side does not mean that the two descriptions can be identified on the epistemological side. The two descriptions *still* contain different conceptions, laws, principles, etc., as well as the reduction method itself, which connects them; thermodynamics and statistical physics or chemistry and quantum mechanics are not the same and cannot be the same. Thus, on the epistemological side, we still have to speak about more and different epistemological tools that is, about different human knowledge. In this sense, heat still exists as a *higher-level, physical* (thermodynamical) *concept* and as *natural human experience*.

So, to sum up: successful reduction is an *ontological statement*, namely the statement that *only one object exists: the lower-level one*.

Now, the question is: what is the ontological consequence of a *failed*, unsuccessful reduction? Before answering, I will reiterate that I will not investigate particular reduction methods—for example, whether Kim's distinguished functional reduction works or does not—but instead I will focus on the ontological consequences. Accordingly, I have so far presupposed that if a reduction is possible, we will find the proper epistemological tool, and I will now examine cases where appropriate methods cannot be found.

---

28. Nagel, *Structure of Science*, 354.

However, it seems that in principle, one can hope forever that the proper method will be found—and a materialist, of course, *has to*. But in reality, the hiatus of the appropriate method will cause increasing doubts, as we have seen in the last decades, as emergentism has started to emerge once again. My goal now, however, is only to shed light on the original meaning of emergence by the analysis of the ontological consequences of reduction.

The answer to the above question is the following: the ontological consequence of a failed, unsuccessful reduction is an *ontological statement*—namely, that *two objects exist.*

On the epistemological side of a reduction, the gap between the two descriptions *remains*. Only a *successful* reduction can bridge that; and without this bridge and the "bridge laws" of a successful reduction method, the two descriptions *remain equal, both of them keeping* their original reference and denotative meaning. This is a kind of epistemological dualism. (The situation of the other, ontological side will be discussed in the next subchapter.)

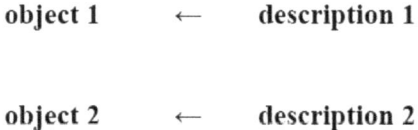

Figure 16. The structure of the unsuccessful reduction.

Contrary to this, the structure of a successful reduction, as we have seen, is this:

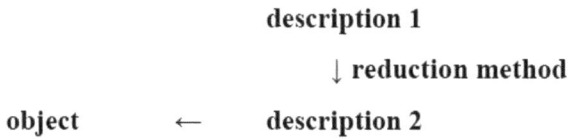

Figure 17. The structure of the successful reduction.

My conclusion is the following: this *asymmetric* relationship on the epistemological side of a successful reduction *corresponds to the concept of emergence*—with the essential difference, of course, that it is not emergence between ontological levels but rather "only" emergence between epistemic descriptions. Therefore, *successful reduction is a kind of epistemological emergence*.

It also follows that reduction and emergence are not each other's enemies but, on the contrary, *they presuppose each other*. A successful reduction *reveals* the asymmetric emergent relationship; and this hidden relationship *makes possible* the successful, revealing reduction—if someone read the hidden signs of reality well (for example, in the case of heat) and successfully did the reduction.

This conclusion can be counterintuitive if and only if we do not clearly distinguish ontological emergence from epistemological (as Morgan, Broad, and the materialists). Materialists *a priori* believe that there is no ontological emergence and thus there cannot be a real difference. It is obviously not emergence, then, because on the ontological side, there is only one object that, in accordance with meaning, cannot be emergent to itself. Human knowledge, "of course," is also not emergent; it has only denotative meaning, so there is indeed no such real difference. On the contrary, for Morgan and Broad, since there is a kind of real difference between the levels, it has to be an ontological difference, too (which, for them, is emergence), and if something is ontologically emergent, then it cannot be reducible. For example, according to Broad, even heat cannot be reducible because it cannot be predicted based only on its lower description—"basic laws of nature" do not contain "special laws of nature"—and if it cannot be reduced, it will have to be emergent (in the ontological sense). His analysis is based on the fact that higher-level human knowledge of comprehensive, orderly phenomena (tacit, natural knowledge from our personal perspectives) is fundamentally different than the lower-level knowledge of the parts (exact physical knowledge from the ideal Laplacian perspective). He clearly sees this fact, but he *has no* proper theory of knowledge to understand and explicate this difference as something only about the existential meaning—that is, about the nature of human knowledge. Therefore, he defines reduction *as predictability* and then drowns the conclusion that heat itself, as an object, has to be emergent.[29]

For the sake of completeness, epistemological materialism would be the case where there are neither higher-level objects nor higher level descriptions of objects, however, this is not a situation we have to deal with; apparently, there are higher-level descriptions. Therefore, we have to deal with *epistemological emergence* and *ontological materialism*, which are just *the same*.

Mark A. Bedau says that weak emergence is "consistent with materialism," but at the same time, it "is not just in our minds. . . . Rather, weak

---

29. Broad, *Mind and its Place in Nature*, 48.

emergence is an objective phenomenon that exists in nature."[30] Now we can understand this paradox. To say that it is "consistent with materialism" means that on the ontological side, there is *only one* material object, which is the case solely *after* a successful reduction. Otherwise, there are two different objects, and then the situation cannot be consistent with materialism.

At the same time, there are *two* different *descriptions* on the epistemological side—the necessary preconditions of any reduction—but they are now connected, *asymmetrically, by* a successful reduction. Without this successful reduction, there is no connection at all; just two different, equal descriptions with their own independent references and denotative meanings—that is, epistemological dualism.

Nevertheless, these descriptions are "only" human knowledge, so are these only in our minds? *No*, because the reduced higher-level description, as we have seen, *has not lost* its reference and denotative meaning, it has *only* been *channeled* in the reduction method to refer to the one real object. We reduced but did *not* eliminate the higher-level description; it still has meaning and relevance for us. According to the two different kinds of human knowledge, we have *personal facts* about the comprehensive order of the object and *objective facts* about the parts of the object (4.2). We eliminated only the higher-level *object*. The higher-level description tells us something about the one real object that cannot be done only by the lower-level description. *This* fact is the reason: "Weak emergence is not just in our minds. . . . Rather, weak emergence . . . exists in nature"—exactly as electrons and quarks are not just in our minds.

However, contrary to Bedau's interpretation, this does not mean an ontological existence for higher levels in any sense; there is no "ontology of objective macro-level structures."[31] On the ontological side, there is only *one* object, one material level which cannot be emergent to itself. This means that there is only one object, but *two asymmetrically connected descriptions refer to it*, each telling us something meaningful and different. So, in this sense and only in this sense—that is, that the epistemologically emergent descriptions can tell us something new about the one and only ontological object—epistemological emergence is not just in our minds but also exists in nature.

Heat, as we have seen (4.5), is a higher-level, physical concept based on natural human experience on the epistemological side, but it has reference and original meaning. This is the reason we can say that a material object possesses a comprehensive phenomenon—that is, a system of fundamental

---

30. Bedau, "Is Weak Emergence Just in the Mind?," 457.
31. Bedau, "Downward Causation," 183.

material parts has some comprehensive, orderly features (for example, pressure and temperature). It is as true as saying that every particle of a material object has well-defined kinetic energy or mass by its fundamental description. Without our natural, personal experience and scientific observations of heat, without the higher-level concepts, laws, etc., and the proper reduction methods, the fundamental description of the particles cannot say anything about heat or other similar, comprehensive phenomena (or any other order of matter).

Bedau is wrong when he thinks that the patterns of Game of Life and his specific reduction by simulation is exactly the same for us human beings and for Laplace's demon.[32] If the knowledge of Bedau's Game of Life demon is all about the exact, numerical definitions of "dead" and "alive" cells and about the four basic rules of Game of Life as the knowledge of Laplace's demon is all about the exact numerical parameters of fundamental particles and about the three basic laws of motion by Newton, then the demon will never even recognize any higher-level Game of Life pattern and never will differentiate between reduced patterns by standard method and reduced emergent patterns by simulation method (2.3). The patterns of Game of Life are interesting to us because we have a specific, personal perspective, but in the ontological sense, they are not objective at all. They can be regarded as objective phenomena only in the epistemological sense because as patterns of a computer program, they can be described and defined very precisely with numerical parameters due to the spirit of the Laplacian ideal of objective knowledge. To put it simply, they are not real, independent objects of reality but rather, due to the ontological consequences of their reduction, a very exact kind of epistemic knowledge by a computer program. But as a materialist, Bedau does not make a clear difference between the ontological and epistemological side; he has no theory of knowledge by which such differentiation can be established in a consistent and well-founded way.

Moreover, Bedau's claim that the phenomena of life is the same as the patterns of Game of Life complies with the claim that we are the same *as the fake Wales scheme* of our example from the previous chapter or the random constellations of astrology, since any pattern of Game of Life is, of course, determined exactly by the lower-level, random motions of the cells and these motions in themselves are, of course, not at all random but perfectly determined by the lower-level rules of the Game of Life world (4.5). In reality, *we* play the game of life, not these lifeless patterns of Game of Life; we will succeed or fail according to our tacit skill and personal choices during the long course of evolutionary emergence—not these illusory, meaningless, and

---

32. Bedau, "Weak Emergence," 379.

random patterns, perfectly determined by lower-level, random processes of an artificial world. Even the name of the game is highly deceptive.

So compared to its fundamental description, heat is a novel and (in an epistemological sense) autonomous, emergent, human, natural experience and higher-level physical knowledge. Fortunately, physics deals perfectly with emergent phenomena. If we do not acknowledge that heat is a reduced albeit still epistemologically emergent phenomenon, it could lead to the questioning of the successful reduction of heat and thus the questioning of one of the most important success of modern science.[33]

It seems to me that Bedau wants to defend weak emergence from reduction, contrasting "standard" reduction to simulation, but it cannot be done and there is no need to do that. Reduced, higher-level, comprehensive, orderly phenomena of matter (or of a simulated logical word) are really exciting—just ask a chemist. On its own, weak emergence is a materialist notion, and to make a distinction between *emergent* and *reduced* higher-level descriptions of phenomena in an ontologically materialist framework is highly problematic. It leads to a reduction-emergence dichotomy, to rivalry on the epistemological side, calling one kind of reduced descriptions emergent and another kind of *also* reduced descriptions non-emergent. It can be even worse to call non-reduced descriptions emergent. In this way, we call higher-level descriptions epistemologically emergent *even* when they have *no* epistemic connection to material descriptions and such higher-level descriptions that *have* definite and clear epistemic connection to the material level we do not call emergent. The basis of this epistemic reduction-emergence dichotomy is, of course, the *a priori* materialist ontological conviction at the other side, which ignores the ontological consequences of reduction and concentrates only on particular reduction methods. However, for emergence, the actual reduction method does not matter; what matters is solely *the success or the failure* of the reduction.

So, to sum up again, we can say that *epistemological emergentism* asserts that *there are two (or more) different kinds of epistemic levels*. However, there is *only one fundamental description*: fundamental physics (e.g., quantum mechanics or string theory). The other(s) is *emergent*. Thus, their relation is *asymmetrical*. The emergent level(s) is not self-sufficient but are necessarily *dependent on* the fundamental level.

This solution, although consistent, can still suggest that emergence as reduction is not an ontological conviction; moreover, it is not the opposite of reduction. Instead, together they lead us to materialism. Nevertheless, this has been only one Janus face of emergence. The other one lies where

---

33. See this argument in Needham, "Reduction and Emergence."

Bedau, as a materialist, does not go. Remember the three conditions of reduction named at the beginning of this section: the objects on the ontological side, the descriptions on the epistemological side, and the reduction method. These latter factors, as we have seen, are not just epistemological tools, as we have interpreted them here, but as human knowledge, they are ontologically existing objects, too. The mind is a *necessary precondition* for epistemological emergence.

5.5 The Two Janus Faces of Emergence

We have seen in the previous subchapter that the ontological consequence of a failed, unsuccessful reduction is an ontological statement—namely, that two objects exist.

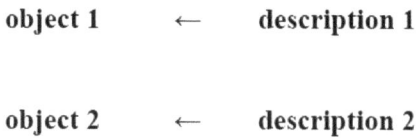

Figure 18. The structure of the unsuccessful reduction.

This conclusion might suggest that we must then accept dualism. But that is not *at all* the case because the two objects can be connected by an emergent relation.

Ontological emergentism asserts that there are at least two different kinds of reality but, contrary to dualism, only one is fundamental substance—matter. The other(s) is/are emergent. This means that the other kind of reality is not entirely independent, eternal, or created but rather evolved from matter. Although it exists, it cannot exist without its material fundament, it *depends on* it. That is, more precisely, there are no two independent objects, just one, multileveled one, which consists of one fundamental and at least one emergent level(s) of reality. Contrary to heat, this higher-level description has its own independent reference and denotative meaning.

Nevertheless, we have seen in the previous subchapter that on the epistemological side, reduction and emergence presuppose each other; otherwise, we have to speak about dualism. Here, the situation is the *same* but not in the same *sense*; this is not the epistemological side. Epistemological emergence and reduction exclude ontological emergence because they mean that the object is material and has only one, fundamental level.

Thus, I assert that *ontological emergence and ontological reduction presuppose each other* as epistemological emergence and epistemological reduction do. Here, a successful reduction also reveals the emergent relationship, and this hidden relationship makes possible the successful, revealing reduction; *otherwise, we would have to speak about dualism.*

However, emergent levels did not exist from the beginning. Once, only matter existed; emergent levels evolved from matter. Why it is surprising, then, that they can be traced back? It is not. It is surprising to call this reduction because the concept of reduction is firmly connected to materialism. But materialism is an ontological conviction and reduction is "only" an epistemological tool. They are not in the same category. Materialism presupposes one kind of reality on the ontological side; therefore, it allows epistemological reduction solely on the epistemological side. This epistemological reduction corresponds to materialism, and ontological reduction corresponds to emergentism.

Dualism	Emergence	Materialism
No reduction	Ontological reduction	Epistemological reduction

Table 3: The relationship between reduction and ontological positions.

It follows that materialism has to deny ontological reduction, so it does. But emergentism *has to call* ontological reduction ontological reduction—and then there remains nothing "mysterious" or "magical" in ontological emergence.

In consequence, there is indeed a severe conflict between emergence and reduction. However, this conflict is neither between epistemological emergence and epistemological reduction—as, according to materialism, we are inclined to think—nor between ontological emergence and reduction; rather, it is *between the reduction and emergence concepts of the different sides.* Epistemological reduction excludes ontological emergence just as ontological reduction excludes epistemological emergence.

Now the question is: what is the essential difference between epistemological and ontological reduction?

```
                    object, higher level  ←    description1
      process of emergence ↑              ←     ↓ reduction method
  beginnings ↑ →     object, lower level  ←    description2
```

Figure 19. The structure of ontological reduction.

First, the reference and denotative meaning of the higher-level description has been channeled in the reduction method only partially and *partially keeps its reference and meaning*. There is a higher level(s) at the ontological side; therefore, a higher-level description(s) has to keep its own reference and meaning. At the same time, there are important *lower-level (random) conditions* for emergent levels without which there is no emergence at all. This partially reduces the reference and denotative meaning of the higher-level description(s)—as we have seen in the case of heat—with the essential difference that here, the reduction is not complete.

Second, the reduction cannot be completed because on the ontological side, there is not just ontological levels but also the *process of emergence itself* (the up arrow of the figure) by which the higher level(s) has/have evolved. Thus, ontological reduction cannot deal *synchronically* with a higher-level description and the lower-level one at the same time. Emergent levels do not and cannot evolve from their actual material foundations (as heat is the actual comprehensive phenomenon of its fundamental material conditions) but rather from the material conditions of the *beginnings* over time. Therefore, ontological reduction has to deal with actual material conditions not only synchronically but also *diachronically*, with the long evolutionary history (past) of the emergent object and the different material conditions of the whole process. This is not an easy task. It means *involving description(s) of the evolutionary process of emergence—from the present to its beginnings—into the reduction method*.

Third, successful ontological reduction asserts that the higher level(s) *did not exist at the beginning* of the process of emergence but rather *at the end*. This corresponds to ontological reduction's diachronic nature, which is missing from epistemological reduction.

Fourth, emergent evolution, by definition of ontological emergence, *cannot be formalized exactly*. It is *indefinable* and leads to *novelty*. Emergent objects are *individual*; they cannot be described as precisely as heat and particles. Naturally, they can be similar (as one frog is similar to another), they can be and have to be categorized, but they cannot be identical because all of them have individual experiences, skills, and (personal) knowledge. Accordingly, they all are connected to one another at different emergent levels that determine their behavior, relations, and existence because, in fact, there are no independent, different processes of emergent evolutions, there is just one single (but highly diversified) emergent evolution on Earth.

Therefore, due to the Laplacian ideal of knowledge, ontological reduction is neither an exact science nor can it be—it is "only" *natural science*; rather, ontological reduction is more an *exhaustive, diachronic description* than a formalized reduction method. It has to deal with different levels of billions of years of an emergent evolutionary process, and each of these levels has its own actual, "material" conditions and the emergent *ordering principles* according to which they will be successful and live or fail and die. Even before all of this, the different emergent levels must be identified. In the end, though, every emergent being and level can be traced back to one fundamental level: to the primordial, material substance and its comprehensive features in the beginning. *This is the real reason we do not believe in dualism* (or vitalism and creationism) and not at the least, the successful epistemological reduction of the chemical level.

So, contrary to Bedau's claim, who, according to his materialist conviction, cannot see any example of ontological emergence in science, there are, in fact, *plenty* examples of ontological emergence and ontological reduction—plenty weak examples. They are weak because natural scientists want to reduce the higher levels of life due to the concepts and conviction of materialism, i.e., the use of epistemological reduction methods and concepts of materialism to explain everything by (and only by) material conditions. Even those who want to break with materialism typically have only materialist epistemic tools to do it because all contemporary science stands on firm materialist grounds.

Nevertheless, this seems to have started to change, albeit slowly. In practice, the reduction (called explanation) of life has always used evolutionary descriptions and models that are diachronic, determine higher levels, understand their principle, and describe their workings, success, failure, etc.—for example, just open *The Origin of Species*. One of the best examples of ontological reduction is Lynn Margulis's explanation of the origin of eukaryotic cells,[34] and one of my favorite attempts at ontologically reducing the human mind is Merlin Donald's *Origin of the Modern Mind*, which we will see in detail in chapter 10. And this very book is also, of course, the ontological reduction of our personal reality from our actual, moral, and political crisis, back to the beginning of time, focusing on the most

---

34. Margulis, *Origin of Eukaryotic Cells*.

important philosophical and scientific principles of our lives. Only the "official" interpretations say that there is nothing more than what materialism and the "right method" of science allow us, but epistemological reduction, in reality, has *never* shown that. If epistemological reduction also fails in the future and materialism goes on denying ontological reduction, then this will only strengthen dualism and creationism. Yet materialists have to deny ontological reduction and try to reach epistemological reduction. Fortunately, biologists resist this—but do not dare to think that they are not materialist. Still, I believe it would be beneficial to interpret and create these models, descriptions, and explanations on their own natural grounds, to call the existing practice of fractional ontological reduction to ontological reduction and build it up, and to use emergent interpretations, suppose and seek real emergent principles, and handle material conditions in their rightful places. If materialism is wrong, this can really inspire biology—and, I believe, the social sciences—on evolutionary grounds. In Part Three and Part Four, I will explain and argue this claim in detail.

At first glance, epistemological emergentism as an independent and "metaphysically innocent" theory seems to be richer because it assumes higher-level, comprehensive, epistemologically emergent phenomena; but as we have seen, without the existence of human knowledge—which is the precondition of any higher-level, comprehensive phenomena—it is only controversial materialism. *Epistemological emergence has to be one Janus face of emergence; the other is ontological emergence. Together, they are the one proper medium ontological conviction between dualism and materialist monism.*

Now we see that the ontological reduction of higher levels can reveal that a higher-level object has neither dual substantial nor vital nature. Disbelief in dualism and vitalism comes not because of the successful epistemological reduction of the chemical level or heat *but because of successful evolutionary explanations—that is, ontological reductions of life.* Charles Darwin shook dualism and creationism, not Bacon, Maxwell, or quantum mechanics.

Nonetheless, the ontological reduction of biological and cultural life is not complete, and by exact criteria, due to the Laplacian ideal of objective knowledge, it never will be, because it is not exact science. Therefore, the belief in dualism will remain with us for a long time, if not forever. As we demand exact criteria for completeness, we also see that, oddly enough, such *materialist notions* as the denial of ontological reductions *can strengthen the belief in dualism and creationism.* The reason for this is the wrong materialism versus dualism dichotomy, which can only be transcended by the original notion of emergentism.

5.6 Polanyi's Understanding of Emergence

In the first half of this chapter, I argued that the concept of medium emergence is the proper ontological theory of emergence. Now, to avoid any doubt, because this book is based on *Personal Knowledge*, I have to show that Michael Polanyi's understanding of emergence complies with this concept. The point of his personalism is not his well-known, fierce anti-reductionism but rather his frequently ignored anti-materialism—because reduction is not an ontological conviction but rather an epistemological method, which can be used to support personalism against materialism, too.

Let me shortly sum up what we have seen until now. At the same time, I'm going to place our conclusions in a broader context and show the central claim of the next subchapter through Polanyi's words about the logical impossibility of materialism. In this subchapter, we will also take another step toward the emergentist understanding of evolution.

Originally, emergence was a medium ontological position between dualism and materialist monism. According to dualism, there are two different kinds of reality—generally described as mind and matter or soul and body—which are independent, fundamental substances. This is the ontological conviction of the European Christian tradition. According to materialism, there is only one kind of reality and one fundamental substance: matter. This is the ontological conviction of modern (especially twentieth and twenty-first-century) European science. Consequently, there is a fatal conflict in Western civilization at the level of our fundamental beliefs that has already erupted to the surface a few times during the last two and a half centuries (12.3, 12.4).

Adherents of emergentism accept the dualist concept that there are two different kinds of reality. However, they hold that only one of them is fundamental, while the other is emergent—that is, emergentists also accept the materialist concept that there is only one fundamental substance, matter. It follows that emergent realities are dependent on fundamental matter and have to evolve from it, so they do: *man is the achievement of emergent evolution.*

Dualism	Emergentism	Materialism
Mind	Emergent realities	
independence	↓ *dependence*	
Matter	Matter	Matter

Table 4: The three ontological positions concerning the relationship between different kinds of realities.

This is the ontological conviction of Michael Polanyi and the root of his personalism. We are neither eternal souls nor just complex systems of matter but rather real, emerged persons in our bodies.

Since the emergent kind of reality is real, it cannot be reduced to fundamental matter. Nevertheless, because it is not an independent, substantial reality but rather a dependent, evolved one, it can and has to be reduced to fundamental matter.

In the first case, we are speaking about reduction in the *synchronic* sense. This method corresponds to the Newtonian concept of the reversibility of time and the Laplacian knowledge-ideal of objectivism and exact sciences. Time is not a real, independent factor but rather a special dimension of space; therefore, every higher-level phenomenon can be reduced at the moment, that is, synchronically. This means that there are no higher-level phenomena in the ontological sense; every higher-level phenomenon is only an *epistemic* phenomenon. Reduction in the synchronic sense means *ontological elimination*. Since epistemic, higher-level phenomena are dependent on fundamental matter, they are *emergent*, and because they are only epistemic phenomena, they are emergent in the epistemological or weak sense. The theory of weak or epistemological emergence is a *materialist theory*.

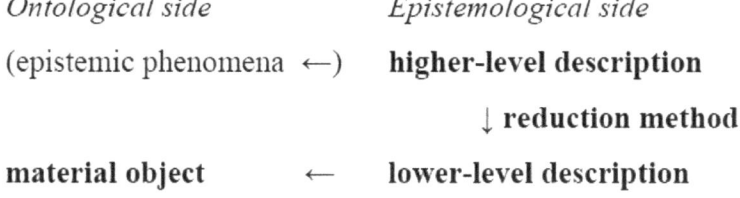

Figure 20. The structure of epistemological emergence.

In the second case, we are speaking about reduction in a *diachronic* sense. According to the views of Henri Bergson, Samuel Alexander, and Michael Polanyi, time is irreversible and a real, independent factor; therefore, we cannot reduce every higher-level phenomenon at the moment without taking account of this independent factor. This means that higher-level phenomena exist in the *ontological sense* and thus cannot be reduced synchronically. However, they can and have to be reduced in a diachronic sense because they are dependent on fundamental matter and evolved from it over time. Reduction in the diachronic sense means *ontological emergence*. Now, at the end, we can see why a theory about the reality of time is so crucial for a consistent theory of emergence. We will deal with this problem further in the next chapter.

According to the theory of strong emergence, highly influenced by C. D. Broad, *every* higher-level phenomenon is emergent in the ontological sense and, therefore, cannot be reduced synchronically. Broad's main example of this kind of emergence was chemical phenomena. Thus, the chief difference between the theories of strong and weak emergences is their relationship to *synchronic reduction*. The former asserts that *no* higher-level phenomena can be reduced in this way, while the latter asserts that *everyone* can.

Medium emergence is not just a medium ontological conviction between dualism and materialist monism but *also* a medium ontological position between strong and weak emergences. Its adherents acknowledge that many higher-level phenomena can be reduced synchronically, but, at the same time, reserve that many cannot. The former has been demonstrated by the exact sciences in the cases of physical and chemical higher-level phenomena such as heat, covalent bonds, etc. The reason for the latter is twofold. First, *no one has ever shown* that biological and cultural higher-level phenomena can be reduced synchronically; moreover, the evolutionary explanations of those phenomena are clearly *diachronic* and do not correspond to the knowledge-ideal of objectivism and exact sciences. Second, it simply can*not* be done because it is *logically impossible*; doing so would lead to the denial of our own knowledge or even the denial of our own existence. In Polanyi's words:

> If, then, it is not words that have meaning but the speaker or listener who means something by them, let me declare accordingly my true position as the author of what I have written so far as well as of what is still to follow. I must admit now that I did not start the present reconsideration of my beliefs with a clean slate of unbelief. Far from it. I started as a person intellectually fashioned by a particular idiom, acquired through my affiliation to a civilization that prevailed in the places where I had grown up at this particular period of history. This has been the matrix of all my intellectual efforts. Within it, I was to find my problem and seek the terms for its solution. All my amendments to these original terms will remain embedded in the system of my previous beliefs. Worse still, I cannot precisely say what these beliefs are. I can say nothing precisely. The words I have spoken and am yet to speak mean nothing: it is only I who mean something by them. And, as a rule, I do not focally know what I mean, and though I could explore my meaning up to a point, I believe

that my words (descriptive words) must mean more than I shall ever know, if they are to mean anything at all. This prospect may sound deplorable, but a program that accepts it may at least claim to be self-consistent, while any philosophy that sets up strictness of meaning as its ideal is self-contradictory. For if the active participation of the philosopher in meaning what he says is regarded by it as a defect which precludes the achievement of objective validity, it must reject itself by these standards.[35]

Polanyi says of the (cultural) emergence of persons that only a person can understand anything—even in the case of the most precise assertions—and, if in accordance with an objectivist program, "the active participation of the philosopher in meaning" is left out, then the existence of the person will be denied. Of course, nobody can deny his own existence; to do so is logically self-contradictory, thus, the objectivist program is self-destructive. In the next subchapter, I will show that the synchronic reduction of persons corresponds to this train of thought, and since it cannot be achieved, materialism must therefore be invalid. Before doing so, however, I will first demonstrate that Polanyi's concept of personal knowledge corresponds to the concept of medium emergence.

Polanyi starts "The Rise of Man," the thirteenth and final chapter of his *Personal Knowledge*, with the following:

> (1) Living beings can be known only in terms of success or failure. They comprise ascending levels of successful existing and behaving.
>
> (2) We can know a successful system only by understanding it as a whole while being subsidiarily aware of its particulars; and we cannot meaningfully study these particulars except with a bearing on the whole....
>
> (3) Therefore, to interpret systems that can succeed or fail in the more detached terms, by which we know systems to which no distinction of success or failure applies, is logically impossible....
>
> (4) Accordingly, it is as meaningless to represent life in terms of physics and chemistry as it would be to interpret a grandfather clock or a Shakespeare sonnet in terms of physics and chemistry.... Lower levels do not lack a bearing on higher levels; they define the conditions of their success and account for their

---

35. Polanyi, *Personal Knowledge*, 252–53.

failures, but they cannot account for their success, for they cannot even define it. . . .

We must face the fact that life has actually arisen from inanimate matter, and that human beings . . . have evolved from tiny creatures resembling the parental zygote in which each of us had his individual origin. I shall meet this situation by re-establishing within the logic of achievement, the conception of emergence first postulated by Lloyd Morgan and Samuel Alexander.[36]

Firstly, Polanyi states that the *neutral* terms of physics and chemistry cannot represent life which, according to the logic of achievement (8.6), can be known only in the *normative* terms of *success* and *failure*; only success leads to evolutionary emergence, failure leads to extinction. However, these concepts can be understood only at the level of the comprehensive, orderly system and not by the exact terms referring to the lower-level, random parts. It follows that we cannot give full and explicit descriptions of the higher-level comprehensive, orderly phenomena of life because we have to use our tacit powers to appraise successful achievements and failures and express them in the normative terms of biology (9.6): the lower-level mechanism of natural selection in itself cannot tell which actions of living beings are a success and which are a failure (9.7). This means that higher-level descriptions of life cannot be reduced to lower-level physical and chemical descriptions. However, it does not follow from this fact that life is entirely beyond matter; on the contrary, life depends on matter because lower levels define the conditions of higher levels and "account for their failures." Life is dependent on lower levels because it has arisen from inanimate matter during the long course of evolution. This means that life is an emergent phenomenon in the ontological sense.

I would like to emphasize that this is not just my conclusion; in his next sentence, Polanyi himself defines his ontological standpoint as a kind of concept of emergence: "Re-establishing within the logic of achievement, the conception of emergence first postulated by Lloyd Morgan and Samuel Alexander." It is astonishing how many of Polanyi's interpreters have missed or overlooked this critical fact and its consequences. Polanyi refers to Lloyd Morgan and Samuel Alexander, two of the three great British emergentists.

However, it might *say even more* that he left out the third, C. D. Broad, who is undoubtedly the most important of the three for the Anglo-Saxon analytical tradition. In contrast, I consider Alexander to be the most important of the three. The main difference between them, briefly stated, is that

---

36. Polanyi, *Personal Knowledge*, 381–82.

Broad's leading example of emergence, as we have seen, was the *chemical phenomena*, while Alexander illustrated his paradigm with *life*; he did not judge the chemical phenomena to be emergent in the ontological sense at all, he only maintained that it is a question of further scientific investigations.[37] We know that science—or, more precisely, quantum mechanics—had shown in a very short period of time that he was perfectly right.

With Broad's terms, Alexander holds an "emergent neutralist" position between dualism and materialist monism, while Broad himself tries to create a new "emergent materialist" position in the hemisphere of materialism. Similarly, concerning the nature of knowledge, Broad tries to define everything exactly, including higher-level, emergent phenomena, while Alexander always emphasizes that certain essential and meaningful features of life and mind have to be acknowledged with "natural piety."

So, Polanyi says that he is re-establishing Alexander's and Morgan's concept of emergence *within the logic of achievement*. His point is that he regards living beings as active knowers who evolve as they try to solve the problems they have to face while they act toward their goals. *These achievements* by living beings are the *driving force* of evolution, not some vital principle or merely the mechanical and neutral notion of natural selection (9.7).

This understanding of evolution is once again positioned between two well-known concepts: vitalism and neo-Darwinism. The former is a kind of dualist theory of evolution, while the latter is a materialist one; between them is the emergentist theory of evolution. This is the reason Polanyi attacks neo-Darwinism so fiercely; as a materialist theory, neo-Darwinism reduces life to inanimate matter. A detailed analysis of these differences and Polanyi's understanding of evolution will be, of course, the foundation of Part Three: Evolution of this book.

Living beings can act and solve problems because they have the knowledge to do so, and this knowledge is *tacit* because—other than man—living beings cannot articulate their knowledge into explicit assertions. This means that for Polanyi, *every living being has a kind of personhood* because personhood is the precondition of having any (tacit or explicit) knowledge at all. In his next subchapter, Polanyi writes about emergent evolution in the following way:

> The next stage on the way toward *personhood* was reached by the protozoa. The appearance of a nucleus within a bed of protoplasm indicates an increased complexity of internal organization, underlying an external behavior of immensely augmented self-control. Protozoa move about of their own accord and

37. Alexander, *Space, Time, and Deity*, 2:61.

engage in a variety of deliberate purposive activities. A floating amoeba emits exploratory pseudopodia in all directions, which will catch food or else attach themselves to solid ground and then drag the whole mass of protoplasm with the nucleus in it toward this foothold. All these manoeuvres are coordinated: the amoeba hunts for food. Thus it grows fatter until it reaches the size at which its *personal life* ends by fission.

A further great step was achieved by the aggregation of protozoan-like creatures to multicellular organisms. This enabled animals to evolve a more complex physiology based on sexual reproduction, a manner of propagation which greatly strengthened their *personhood*.[38]

Let us recall that the title of his book is *Personal Knowledge*. Polanyi makes an effort at many places in his text to make clear that he means to use the term "person" very broadly, denoting even the simplest life forms with it. Thus, for him, Alexander's concept of emergence "re-established within the logic of achievement" means the *emergence of persons* during the long course of evolution. There are no divine eternal souls, nor is mind just a complex pile of random material processes; instead, there are emerging persons.

> The inarticulate mental capacities developed in our body by the process of evolution become then the tacit coefficients of articulate thought. By the forming and assimilation of an articulate framework, these tacit powers kindle a multitude of new intellectual passions.[39]

Our knowledge is tacit and personal because of our evolutionary emergence as persons, and this is the reason we cannot represent the tacit achievements of living beings by the neutral and explicit terms of physics and chemistry; this is the reason we cannot reduce life.

In a subchapter entitled "The Logic of Emergence," Polanyi makes clear that he has taken Samuel Alexander's side and not C. D. Broad's:

> The first thing to observe here is that, strictly speaking, it is not the emerged higher form of being, but our knowledge of it, that is unspecifiable in terms of its lower level particulars. We cannot speak of emergence, therefore, except in conjunction with a corresponding progression from a lower to a higher conceptual level. And we realize then that conceptual progression may not always be existential, but that it becomes so by degrees.

38. Polanyi, *Personal Knowledge*, 387. Emphasis added.
39. Polanyi, *Personal Knowledge*, 389.

For example: pour a handful of shot into a flat-bottomed saucepan, and you will find the grains forming a regular pattern. Crystals owe their symmetrical shapes to a similar principle: molecules of identical sizes and shapes tend to form regular aggregates in the same way as grains of shot in a saucepan. Is this the emergence of a new comprehensive feature? It is arguable that we could know the complete topography of the atoms in a crystal, without seeing that they form a regular pattern. There is, indeed, always a noticeable logical gap between a topography and a pattern derived from it, and to this extent, no pattern is specifiable in terms of its topography. Yet since in the case of a crystal we can easily pass from the pattern to the topography and back again, the conception of such a pattern is in fact not destroyed by a knowledge of its topographic particulars. I would acknowledge, therefore, in this case, two distinguishable conceptual levels but not two separate levels of existence.[40]

I believe Polanyi clearly differentiates between the ontological and epistemological sides of reduction which, as we have seen, is highly neglected by mainstream analytical and materialist approaches. According to this differentiation, he asserts that there are two kinds of emergence. One of them is when there are two "conceptual" levels but only one "existential," which corresponds to my understanding of epistemological emergence.

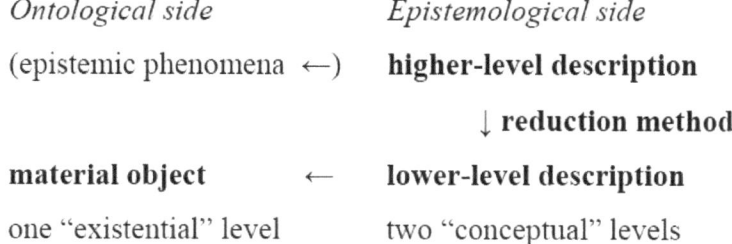

Figure 21. Polanyi's understanding of the structure of "conceptual"/epistemological emergence.

The other kind of emergence is, of course, the ontological one—about which we have been speaking throughout this subchapter in the cases of life and evolution—when there are two "conceptual" and two "existential" levels. The reason that there is no strict boundary (for example, by synchronic

---

40. Polanyi, *Personal Knowledge*, 393–94.

reduction) and conceptual emergence becomes existential "by degrees" is that there is no absolute point of reference, no Laplacian ideal of objective knowledge; instead, we have to appraise the successful evolutionary achievements of living beings by our tacit powers from our own, personal point of reference of our particular place and time (center).

So, we have seen that for Polanyi, emergence is not defined by synchronic reduction—as it would be for theorists of strong and weak emergence—but rather by the logic of evolutionary achievements. He does not assert that every higher-level, comprehensive phenomenon can be reduced, as it is suggested by the theory of Bedau's weak emergence, nor does he assert that no higher-level, comprehensive phenomena can be reduced, as the theory of Broad's strong emergence suggests, but he still clearly claims that life is ontologically emergent. Therefore, Polanyi's concept of emergence *corresponds entirely to* my theory of medium emergence.

5.7 A Short Reductionist Argument against Materialism

If Polanyi's emergentist ontology—which I believe is the foundation of his whole theory of tacit and personal knowledge—is true, then materialism has to be false. But is materialism indeed wrong?

In subchapter 5.4, I demonstrated in detail that reduction and emergence are not rival concepts; this is only a materialist interpretation. In an ontological sense, emergent levels can be reduced (diachronically) to primordial matter, leaving nothing "mysterious" or "magical" in them; diachronic/ontological reduction is only natural science. But now, the question is how can we know that an object—a rock, a machine, a frog, or a person—is material? The answer is, of course, that it has to be *synchronically*/epistemologically and *successfully* reduced to fundamental material conditions. More precisely, if a higher-level description of an object cannot be reduced in this way, it will mean that it has original reference and meaning and the object is multileveled and not material. (In this subchapter, I will not argue against dualism by simply denying it, so, in this case, I have supposed that non-material objects are multileveled, emergent ones.) But if a higher-level description of an object can be successfully reduced in this synchronic way, then there will be no higher-level object; there are no higher levels at all but rather only the fundamental material substance.

Dualism	Emergence	Materialism
No reduction	Ontological reduction	Epistemological reduction

Table 5: The relationship between reduction and ontological positions.

Let us put aside our prior convictions for a minute and investigate the objects surrounding us. What does materialism assert? It asserts that there is only one kind of reality, one fundamental substance: matter. That is, every higher-level description of objects can be and *has* to be reduced synchronically. There cannot be any exception; otherwise, materialism cannot stand. So, then, why do we have to believe in materialism? It is a radical ontological claim, and so far, very few higher-level descriptions have been reduced synchronically (e.g., heat, the hydrogen atom, etc.). Furthermore, these examples are from the *same* field—exact sciences. There are numerous descriptions of higher-level objects, and there are many *fields* besides the exact sciences. Even so, materialism may be true, but if we believe in it, we do *not* believe in it because we have accomplished this empirical examination, describing higher-level objects precisely and reducing all higher-level descriptions synchronically. We can be sure in merely one claim about materialism that it is a *terribly bold metaphysical program*.

What does (medium) emergentism assert? It asserts that there are two different kinds of reality: one is the fundamental substance—matter—and the other is the emergent levels that depend on it (which are the achievements of emergent evolution). That is, there are those higher-level descriptions of objects that can be reduced synchronically and there are those that cannot. The former implies epistemological emergence and the latter ontological emergence.

So, then, what is the reason for disbelieving in emergence? For emergentism, unlike materialism, it is sufficient that only one higher-level description of an object—or, more precisely, only one kind of higher-level description of objects—proves to be epistemologically irreducible, e.g., knowledge or the mind. In comparison to materialism, emergentism is a *far more moderate* ontological claim and, *as a matter of fact, it corresponds to our experience and the actual state of science* insofar as it seems that there are both reducible and irreducible higher-level descriptions of objects.

If materialism seems far more believable than emergentism—and this is the case for most scientists and philosophers—the reason for it seeming so is certainly not due to the bright success of its empirical investigations and synchronic reductions of higher-level descriptions of objects. It is rather the false dualism versus materialism dichotomy, used by both materialists and dualists, which undermines the concept of emergentism. We have seen several examples of such argumentation (5.3), primarily in the case of reduction, where these theorists skillfully and cleverly discredit the achievements of diachronic reductions, for example.

One final question regarding the possibility of the synchronic reduction of one specific object of this subchapter—that is, the possibility of the synchronic reduction of reduction itself. As we have seen in subchapter 5.4, reduction has three conditions, at least two different objects (though one of them can perhaps be eliminated), two descriptions of them, and the reduction method itself. On the ontological side are the objects, while on the epistemological side, we have the two descriptions and the reduction method that refers to them. The descriptions and the reduction method are not only meaningful, epistemic references to the objects, however, they are also ontological objects in themselves. *Reduction is a human epistemological tool—that is, knowledge—which has to exist and be wielded skillfully and successfully; otherwise, no reduction will ever be possible.* Thus, if someone believes in materialism, similarly to every other object, he will have to synchronically reduce reduction itself too.

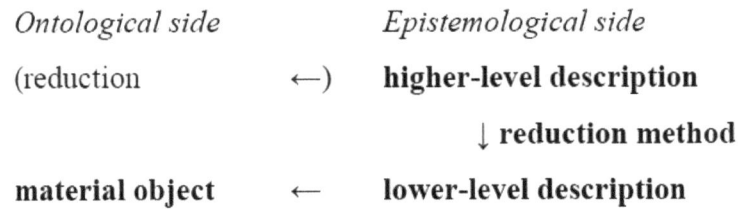

Figure 22. The structure of the (synchronic/epistemological) reduction of reduction.

As we have seen, a successful synchronic reduction is an ontological statement—namely, that *only one object exists: the lower-level one*. In this case, it is the material substance (in bold on the ontological side of the chart above). But the other, higher-level object does *not* exist. In this case, it is the reduction itself which, in fact, is not there. Therefore, in this case, a successful synchronic reduction asserts that *there has been no reduction at all*.

However, the existence of reduction as an object on the ontological side is the *precondition* of a successful synchronic reduction; *otherwise, it cannot be realized*. Now we are not speaking about two different things—a higher-level object and reduction as knowledge, as it would be in every other case—but rather about the same thing: reduction. Therefore, reduction as an object is necessarily on the epistemological side, too. It was always there; it has to be there. But now, after a successful reduction, "it is no longer there"; and if "it is no longer there," then the consequence is the following:

Ontological side		Epistemological side
reduction	←	**higher-level description**
		(there is no successful reduction)
material object	←	**lower-level description**

Figure 23. The consequence of the (synchronic/epistemological) reduction of reduction.

The synchronic reduction of reduction is therefore necessarily *unenforceable* and *self-eliminating*. It cannot be turned against itself. It cannot be successful.

> For if the active participation of the philosopher in meaning what he says is regarded by it as a defect which precludes the achievement of objective validity, it must reject itself by these standards.[41]

It follows that there is *at least one* higher-level description of an object that *cannot be reduced synchronically*. However, materialism asserts that *every* higher-level description of an object can be and has to be reduced synchronically. Therefore, materialism is not and *cannot be valid*.

More precisely, according to this argument, there is more than one higher-level description of an object that cannot be reduced synchronically, because if we believe in emergentism, then reduction—as a form of human knowledge—will be the achievement of emergent evolution, which is a single, comprehensive, orderly process. Thus, all of the antecedents of human knowledge have to exist and have to be emergent, too. I will not argue for this in detail at this point, only in Part Three: Evolution. I would merely like to note that, according to this view, one kind of higher-level description of objects is irreducible synchronically—namely, higher-level descriptions of knowledge, from the knowledge of the first primitive prokaryotes to the highest intellectual levels of human knowledge. A living being—a frog, for example—is ontologically emergent in comparison to something like heat because the frog

---

41. Polanyi, *Personal Knowledge*, 252–53.

has the knowledge to be successful in achieving its goals—that is, in preserving itself, moving, eating, learning, and storing knowledge about the world. It is not just a comprehensive, orderly structure in space (like heat) but also a comprehensive, orderly phenomenon of emergent evolution *in time* (4.6, 7.7). It cannot be reduced synchronically because its knowledge is tacit and personal, and thus cannot be formulated in the neutral and explicit terms of the synchronic reduction of exact sciences.

So, then, reduction itself is an *ontologically emergent object* that cannot be reduced synchronically. In point of fact, *this is the reason* that, according to the logic of achievement, its essence and *real existential meaning* are the consequence of its *success* or *failure* and not its lower lever random "material" conditions—that is, the particular reduction methods (the pebbles in the lettering). And now it should be clear why materialists are inclined to think that this is not so and focus on only its conditions.

5.8 The Main Contra-Arguments of Materialism

In the eyes of materialists, of course, the argument of the previous subchapter does not work. The main reason for this, as I discussed in detail in subchapter 5.3, is that materialists do not distinguish the two (epistemological and ontological) sides of reduction; thus, it has no real ontological consequences. But how could it have? For materialists, it is *evident* that everything is material. The only question is the particular *synchronic* method of reduction—that is, only the condition for its success or failure, not the success or failure (consequences) itself. Thus, if a description of reduction and human knowledge has not been—and, in fact, cannot be—reduced successfully, then nothing will happen, and materialism remains valid (at most in the deceptive label of non-reductive materialism).

A fundamental belief—in this case, I should rather say dogma—can repel every doubt, argument, and logic, especially if it is concealed behind skepticism, the critical method of doubt, and the exactness of the Laplacian ideal of objective knowledge. We have to humbly acknowledge that we have unprovable, acritical beliefs, and then, we have to face even our deepest fundamental beliefs honestly and ground them on the most essential principles of philosophy and science: truth and speaking the truth. This is the only way to prevent our fundamental beliefs from hardening into the sacred stone of our actual conceptual and explanatory systems and social and scientific institutions.

For example, the great Jaegwon Kim himself concedes that human knowledge—in his words, "consciousness" and "qualia"—cannot be reduced, and yet he still wants to defend a kind of materialism.[42] The reason he neglects elementary logic is the materialists' false conceptual and explanatory dichotomy between monism and dualism. Kim sees dualism as the only other real possibility besides materialist monism, and he finds dualism even less attractive. Of course, he knows about emergentism, but epistemological emergentism is, in fact, materialism, and Kim finds ontological emergentism impossible.[43] The main reasons for this skepticism are (1) the concept of physicalism, (2) the notorious notion of downward causation, and (3) the breaking of the causal closure of the physical world, which is usually regarded by most philosophers as the most obvious "fact" or "evidence" supporting materialism.[44]

(1) In subchapter 5.3, I have already argued in detail that the now-popular term "physicalism" is a *deceptive substitution* for materialism; it suggests that materialism is similar to and inseparable from physics. However, physics is an epistemological tool and not an ontological conviction; they are not in the same category. Therefore, arguing with physicalism is simply an *argument from authority* that works because of only one reason: materialism rules most of the scientific institutions of the Western world today. In reality, however, materialists do not consider it to be a genuinely different ontological position from materialism. Nevertheless, the rationale for using the term "physicalism" is this: at the beginning of the twentieth century, physics has started to follow a different ontology than that of the earlier, Newtonian paradigm. However, this argument is highly problematic for several reasons.

First of all, Newton was not a materialist at all but rather a dualist who sometimes even in the case of physical questions allowed himself to use the concept of God.[45] Second, if emergentism is true, then physics will operate with higher-level, emergent objects unproblematically (5.3). Third, it is not evident at all that theories as varied as Einstein's general theory of relativity, Bohr's and Heisenberg's quantum mechanics, or string theories follow the same ontology; on the contrary, just think about some of their famous claims concerning reality (e.g., the "curvatures" of space-time, indeterminism, ten-dimensional, tiny strings, etc.). Fourth,

42. Kim, *Physicalism, or Something Near Enough.*

43. See, for example, Kim, *Mind in a Physical World,* "Making Sense of Emergence"; Kim, "Mental Causation."

44. See, for example, Montero and Papineau, "Naturalism and Physicalism."

45. See, for example, his first letter to the publisher of *Principia* in Turnbull, *Correspondence of Isaac Newton,* 3:1688–94.

materialists themselves do not take this distinction seriously, but only if it supports—or, rather deceptively, *seems* to support—their position and agenda in certain debates and institutional situations against non-materialist positions. If they took seriously the notion that twentieth-century physics implies a genuinely new ontology due to the actual results and concepts of Einsteinian relativity theory, Bohrian quantum mechanics (Copenhagen interpretation), and string theories, then there would be cutthroat debates between "Bohrians," "Einstenians," and "string theorians" in mainstream journals and conferences about the right ontology. In reality, however, there is not even a vague sign of such serious debates; they all accept the old, well-known thesis that everything is material.

We, however, will take the results, concepts, and philosophical consequences of twentieth-century physics seriously, and thus we will see that twentieth-century physics, in fact, confirms the principles of emergentism rather than those of materialism; to put it simply: it is perfectly true that the results of twentieth-century physics imply a new ontology, and this is exactly the reason that they do not imply physicalism—that is, the old ontology under a new label—but rather emergentism, the indeed new ontology. I will formulate this complicated argument in the next chapter with the help of Alexander's theory of space-time and Einstein's theory of relativity. In consequence, materialism follows from neither Newtonian nor twentieth-century physics but is, in fact, the consequence of the Laplacian ideal of objective knowledge (2.3), the Galilean and positivist practical approach to science (6.2), and—especially—the broader cultural processes in the background (12.3, 12.4).

(2) The concepts of downward causation and the breaking of the causal closure of the physical world are tightly connected. Higher-level comprehensive realities act in order to achieve their goals ("Alexander's dictum") and do so by moving their bodies, which are fundamentally composed of matter. Thus, for example, when a frog catches a fly or a working piston moves a car, they create top-bottom effects (downward causation), which interfere with the regular causal chain at the fundamental material level (breaking of the causal closure of the physical world). This is the materialist understanding of what happens when a frog catches a fly or a piston moves a car. However, this is just the materialist understanding, not what happens in reality. I will be able to establish my argument in detail after the next two chapters (7.5), but after my claim of the previous subchapter, I first have to shed light on the fundamental problems of these main materialist contra-arguments.

Consider, for example, a piston that transforms the energy of exploding petrol into rotary motion or a mill that does the same with the energy of flowing water. In both cases, lower-level processes do not go on freely, according to their lower-level principles—as the autumn wind blows the leaves freely/randomly on the street—since the specific structures of the piston and the mill, according to higher-level principles of engineering, govern (control) and harness lower-level, physical processes in several distinct steps in order to move a car or to grind wheat.

Nevertheless, a machine can control and harness lower-level processes *only via* its material *parts,* in full accordance with the fundamental laws and principles of physics. The fixed walls of a piston, while controlling and harnessing the flow and explosions of petrol, *do nothing* to contradict the fundamental laws and principles of physics. Higher-level, comprehensive, emergent structures (boundary conditions) are not independent vital forces or Cartesian substances. Higher-level, emergent structures do not work on their own—that is, against their material conditions—but, on the contrary, they rely on their material conditions and operate in accordance with them. A piston is such a comprehensive, emergent structure, shaped into its material fundaments by man according to higher-level ordering principles. The interaction between the piston as a higher-level, comprehensive, emergent structure and the controlled and harnessed lower-level, physical-chemical processes inside the piston can be understood only at the lower-level. This is necessary since the fundamental physical processes, in accordance with their nature, *exist only* at the fundamental lower-level and thus *can interact only* at that level. It follows that a higher-level, emergent structure can control and harness the lower-level, physical-chemical processes in its body only via its own material conditions.

So, higher-level, emergent structures do not violate the fundamental physical laws and principles of nature. The materialist understanding of the process is, of course, the contrary, but they already neglect several essential facts at the beginning: engineering is engineering because it has its own ordering principles compared to physics; pistons (and any other comprehensive, orderly whole, of course) cannot be specified based only on their material parts; and they cannot be constructed based solely on physical and chemical principles and laws, so they are not material at all. This means that, in spite of the deceptive language, in the materialist understanding of the process, there is, in fact, no piston at all (elimination of the higher-level object at the ontological side), which therefore does not and cannot control the lower-level processes; the term "piston," in fact, refers only to a complex material system which affects other material processes in exactly the same way as the autumn wind blows the colorful leaves on the street.

The materialist understanding of downward causation and the breaking of the causal closure of the physical world, of course, stems from their fundamental beliefs, according to which, *both* the higher and the lower levels are working *mechanically*, and thus the higher levels would necessarily break the lower causal chains. However, higher emergent levels are emergent precisely because their nature is different from that of the fundamental material level—that is, they are emergent because *they do not act mechanically but, essentially, differently*. In Polanyi's view, they act according to the logic of achievement; they use their bodies to control and harness lower-level processes for the sake of a goal—which is not done by real, material process (like the autumn wind that blows randomly). According to the logic of achievement, the lower levels also do not have an effect on the higher levels mechanically but rather merely determine those *material conditions* in which higher, emergent levels can act. No one can create a piston from air or water. Iron or aluminum makes it possible; however, it is not the physical and chemical properties of iron or aluminum that determine the shape and function of the piston but instead the higher-level, ordering principles of engineering, according to which an engineer can create a piston from iron—or, more precisely, *in* iron—among the specific material conditions of iron.

Thus, materialists are correct in assuming the existence of a kind of downward causation; it must exist, otherwise higher, emergent levels could not act and could not be real ("Alexander's dictum"). However, the breaking of the causal closure of the physical world does not follow from the fact of downward causation; this is merely the materialist (mis)understanding of downward causation as a mechanical process.

(3) Similarly, the concept of the causal closure of the physical world is also only a materialist understanding of the universe. So, contrary to their claim, it is not a fact or evidence based on science but rather a *principle* based on the concept of materialism. Materialists regard it as a fact—or, at least, a well-established, scientific hypothesis, which cannot be doubted rationally—because the behavior of textbook physical processes (e.g., the behavior of billiard balls on the table) can be perfectly described by the laws of Newtonian mechanics—that is, in these cases, there is no higher-level factor that distracts the deterministic/mechanical behavior of the billiard balls. This is indeed a fact. Materialists, however—due to their materialist conviction, of course—extend the scope of this fact to all phenomena because, in their view, all phenomena of the world have exactly the same material nature and behave exactly the same way in this regard as billiard balls. They simply neglect the fact that, for example, my behavior concerning when I am going to press the next key and which key I will press cannot be described in this mechanical way. In reality, my behavior is guided by the principles of English language and my intention to communicate my thoughts with you. They, of course, also neglect the fact that the overwhelming majority

of the objects—for example, frogs, pistons, watermills, etc.—also cannot be described in this mechanical way. So, the only facts that matter in their view are the facts of physical textbooks. This is the way that, due to the materialist convictions, a narrow-scope, physical principle becomes rationally indisputable evidence, "based on science," against the overwhelming number of facts of real life.

At this point, I could also mention the ruling, Copenhagen interpretations of quantum mechanics, which strongly questions the deterministic nature of physical processes and thus the concept of the causal closure of the physical world, too. So, this materialist interpretation neglects not just real life facts but also quantum mechanical textbooks. But, as I detailed in subchapter 4.6, since I do not believe in the false determinism versus indeterminism dichotomy (and here, I like to base my argument on philosophical principles), I would not do that.

My claim is that the concept of the causal closure of the physical world is merely a part of the materialist belief system. In an emergentist worldview, the causal closure of the physical—or more precisely, the material—world simply does not exist because the world is, of course, *not merely material at all*. Matter is only *one aspect* of reality; therefore, it cannot constitute a closed world in itself. So, to accept the concept of the causal closure of the physical world, one first has to accept materialism itself.

The main problem with the concept of the causal closure of the physical world is, therefore, that materialists mix up two essentially different concepts: one epistemological, the other ontological. This severe philosophical problem is camouflaged by the fact that they speak about the causal closure of the physical—and not about the causal closure of the material—world, as the causal closure of a *human epistemological tool* called physics and the causal closure of the *ontological reality* (which we call the world) would be exactly the same. However, to think that the world is causally closed and to use a causally closed physics are two radically different things: only materialists regard them as identical.

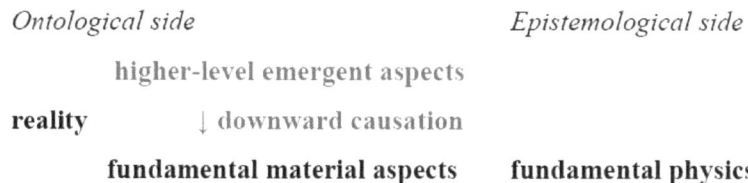

Figure 24: The structure of the materialist understanding of the causal closure of the physical world and downward causation.

If someone, according to a materialist conviction, identifies the causally closed system of physics with a coherent system of reality, and this is the whole world for him (black letterings), then he will necessarily find that higher-level emergent aspects of reality—if they would exist (gray lettering)—break the causal closure of the lower, physical level. Since higher levels, according to the logic of emergence, are, on the one hand, causally effective and, on the other, have to act through their fundamentally physical bodies, they necessarily break (by downward causation) the causally closed system of (physical) reality. This conclusion is the reason that, according to the materialist argument, such levels do not and cannot exist. However, to conclude from the causally closed system of our actual physics—that is, from a characteristic of an epistemological tool to an ontological claim—that emergentism cannot be true, is a severe category mistake.

Thus, the argument is actually the following: Materialism is true. Physics is a causally closed system. Therefore, reality is physical and a causally closed system (the causal closure of the physical world). To be real, emergent levels have to be causally effective (Alexander's dictum). Since emergent levels are dependent on the physical level, to be causally effective, an emergent level has to have an effect on the physical level (downward causation). However, such causation would create new effects beyond the physical world, thereby disrupting the causal closure of the physical world. Therefore, emergent levels do not and cannot exist, and materialism is true. In short: materialism is true because materialism is true. And facts about the synchronic reduction of objects, of course, do not matter.

As I said earlier, fundamental beliefs can repel every doubt, argument, and logic if they are not based on respect for truth and speaking the truth but are confined into rigid conceptual and institutional frameworks; this is the reason we have to examine this unfortunate process in science and philosophy in detail. In the case of the fundamental belief of materialism, this will lead us to the broader territory of culture, to the cultural history of the Western world, and today to relativism and Marxism (Part Four: Personal Reality). Because, as we can see now, the arguments for materialism and the belief in materialism—via the false dichotomy of dualism versus materialism—do not come from the territory of science at all.

5.9 Conclusion

At the beginning of the twentieth century, British Emergentism rose and fell over a very short period of time, and the original meaning of emergence faded away. Today, the concept of emergence is here again, but it is severely influenced by materialist concepts and methods. A weak or epistemological understanding of emergence has arisen, and the possibility of an ontological or strong emergence is questioned.

However, in contrast to materialist interpretations, reduction is, in fact, not the opposite of emergence, and the ontological consequence of a successful standard (epistemological or synchronic) reduction used in exact sciences is the elimination of the higher-level comprehensive object. At the same time, very few scientific descriptions of higher-level objects have been reduced in this way so far; this is not the reason at all why we believe in materialism but rather the false materialism versus dualism dichotomy, which forces us to choose the former.

Reduction has three preconditions, two different objects on the ontological side and the reduction method itself on the epistemological side—but as human knowledge, the reduction method is an ontological object, too. Therefore, the epistemological reduction of the description of reduction and human knowledge is unenforceable and self-eliminating. Materialism—as well as an independent, materialist theory of epistemological or weak emergence—does not and cannot stand.

However, the fact that we cannot reduce everything in this way does not lead us back to dualism because there is an emergentist concept of reduction, too—namely, the ontological or diachronic reduction of natural sciences. Ontological reduction can trace the emergent levels of life back in time to the primordial, material substance and its comprehensive, epistemologically emergent features of the beginning.

Therefore, emergence necessarily has two faces: one epistemological, looking into the material world, and one ontological, which is the comprehensive, emergent levels of life and evolution itself. I believe this is the proper medium ontological conviction between dualism and materialist monism.

I also believe that this theory of emergence perfectly complies with Michael Polanyi's theory of personal knowledge because this particular theory of emergence faces the fact that emergence is but life and the arising knowledge of living beings which cannot be categorized by the concept of synchronic reduction due to the Laplacian ideal of objective knowledge.

Nonetheless, a crucial question should be asked: what is the real nature of ontological reduction? What does it mean to be diachronic contrary to synchronic? The short answer is that the standard synchronic reduction of exact sciences complies with the *nature of space*, while the ontological or diachronic reduction of natural sciences complies with the *nature of time*. So, the real question is what the nature of time is—the existence of which is denied by the exact sciences due to the Laplacian ideal of objective knowledge, where time is only a fourth, space-like dimension. Fortunately, we do not have to start to answer this fundamental question on our own because Samuel Alexander, the father of emergentism, started everything with this question in his book, *Space, Time, and Deity*.

6

Space, Time, and Matter

6.1 Preface

Personal knowledge is based on the fact that there is no objective point of reference; the Laplacian beast is only a phantasmagoria. Every person sees the world from his own personal center, anchored in his own body in a particular space and time. Personal reality is based on the fact that we are neither eternal souls nor just piles of quarks and electrons but rather comprehensive, orderly wholes by evolution. However, without the reality of time, the concept of evolution loses its real existential meaning, and nothing will stop the (synchronic) reductionist program of positivism and physicalism.

Laplace's vision is based on the Newtonian concept of absolute space-time, while the victory of positivism in science was the consequence of Albert Einstein's theory of relativity and the rise of quantum mechanics at the beginning of the twentieth century. Einstein's theory eliminated Newton's concept of absolute space-time. Nevertheless, it still did not stab the Laplacian beast to death; moreover, it even more strongly questioned the reality of time because, in general relativity, space-time has become only a mathematical abstraction by four-dimensional Gauss coordinates.

So, in a sense, Einstein's theory perfectly complies with the main philosophical point of personal knowledge: there is no objective point of reference over and above the universe (space-time), everybody sees the world from his own relative space and time; however, in another sense, it questions even the main ontological fundament of emergentism and personal reality, that is, the reality of time.

At the end of his introduction to *Time Reborn* (and after the paragraphs we have seen in the Preface of the previous chapter), eminent theoretical physicist Lee Smolin concludes:

Time will turn out to be the only aspect of our everyday experience that is fundamental. The fact that it is always some moment in our perception, and that we experience that moment as one of a flow of moments, is not an illusion. It is the best clue we have to fundamental reality.[1]

If in his earlier work, *The Trouble with Physics*, Smolin criticized the direction that twentieth-century physics had taken—especially string theories—then in *Time Reborn*, he proposes to solve the problems of modern physics by acknowledging a fundamental fact: *time is real*.

Although coming from a theoretical physicist, the claim is clearly a *philosophical* one. He does not question, for example, the validity of the Lorentz-transformation in special relativity or the importance and truth of the equivalence principle in general relativity but rather their ruling understanding, due to the positivist philosophy of sciences, which denies the reality of time.

Modern physics began with Albert Einstein's theory of special relativity. Einstein, largely under the influence of positivist philosopher Ernst Mach, was already inclined to integrate a positivist philosophical understanding into his ideas of physics. However, it remains unclear if it is possible to give another non-positivist philosophical understanding to the theory of special relativity and, more generally, to modern physics. Can an understanding that is, according to Smolin's claim, based on the concept of the reality of time be integrated into modern physics?

My answer is affirmative: it is possible—based on Samuel Alexander's theory of space and time. It will solve the contradiction that, in a sense, Einstein's theory perfectly complies with the main philosophical point of personal knowledge, and in another one, it questions the main ontological fundament of emergentism and personal reality. The former fact comes from Einstein's physical theory—more precisely, from the main *philosophical basis* of Einstein's theory, that is, from his interpretation of the *Galilean principle of relativity*—and the latter from the positivist *philosophical understanding* of his theory.

6.2 Alexander's Concept of Space-Time

As we have seen in the previous chapters, emergentism was established by Samuel Alexander with his *Space, Time, and Deity*, but it never became a truly independent philosophical school. First of all, it was swept away by the

---

1. Smolin, *Time Reborn*, xxxi.

rising power of positivism and materialism, and neither of the two major followers of Alexander could acknowledge his starting point: *that reality, in its fundaments, is space and time.* Lloyd Morgan took a path that could easily be understood as a new kind of dualism, whereas C. D. Broad, in turn, took one that could be interpreted as a kind of so-called non-reductive materialism or physicalism. Since today's understanding of the concept of emergence is based on Broad's terminology, the term emergent refers merely to *complex material systems* in space (emergence in the epistemological sense) and not to comprehensive, orderly wholes, which are genuinely new and ontologically different from its composite parts due to the reality of time (emergence in the ontological sense).

Smolin tries to reach a concept of the reality of time, but due to the positivist spirit of our era, he, unfortunately, uses Broad's terminology. However, if he is correct that time is the only fundamental entity in the universe, then matter itself should be emergent compared to time, and elementary particles of matter, in accordance with meaning, are not complex material systems but rather genuinely new comprehensive, orderly wholes in/of space-time. After all, to maintain the thesis of the reality of time requires the abandonment of both materialism and positivism as well as the Broadian terminology for the sake of an Alexanderian one. According to Alexander, emergence starts on the level of space and time, and thus the material level is the first real emergent level of reality. *Matter is but the emergence of time.* Matter has genuinely new, comprehensive material qualities compared to time because in matter, time emerges in a genuinely new form: *physical time.*

In Aristotelian physics, form and matter cannot be separated. Primary matter without any form can be conceived only theoretically and does not exist in itself. Likewise, primary forms without matter can also be conceived of only theoretically and do not exist in themselves. Consequently, primary matter that does not exist in itself and is not completed by anything is nothing but *space*, which underscores the close relationship of the concepts of space and matter in Aristotelian physics. However, when non-existent primary forms, logically speaking, complete non-existent space, matter comes into being—more precisely, four material elements that comply with the four primary forms: earth, water, air, and fire. In itself, matter is inert, in its own natural space around the *center of the universe*, and any active movement or change in time is the consequence of teleological actions of forms. Put differently, there are no inert movements of matter, for matter in itself is necessarily at rest. Matter is organized into complex objects by different forms at each level of reality: the world is hierarchical, and the thinking man is at the top.

The concept of modern dualism proposed by René Descartes shows surprising similarities to Aristotelian physics until a certain point. Primary, non-existent matter is also space itself, with the sole primary quality of extension. However, primary forms that complete space are not based on *natural human experience* any more than Aristotle's earth, water, air, or fire, but rather on *geometry*. They are entirely theoretical; therefore, it follows that matter possesses some clearly definable, exact primary qualities—shape, size, and weight—and has a *particle nature*. The universe *has no definite center*, material particles interact only mechanically, and any complex object is the consequence of those mechanical processes. Matter in itself is also inert, but due to mechanical interactions, it is in a state of constant vortical motion. Since no vacuum between particles exists, they constantly drag each other. However, man is entirely different from other complexes because he possesses a soul that has no extension, but its primary property is thinking, according to which man alone is capable of teleological actions.

Then, in the eighteenth century, Newtonian physics, based on Galilei's findings and his principle of relativity, overthrew the Cartesian physics on the continent, too. In Newtonian physics, space and matter are sharply *separated*. Matter is composed of such particles which can be regarded as *point-like* masses; thus, it does not possess any definite primary qualities anymore—solely *mass*. Space, in turn, is an *absolute* background, entirely independent of matter. There is also no definite center of the universe; every particle can be regarded as its own center, its own *inertial frame of reference*, if it is not accelerating, of course, due to some external effect—that is, it is in rest or in uniform motion, in a straight line. These latter two states (rest and uniform motion), according to the Galilean principle of relativity, are the *same physical states*; it is only a question of our actual point of view which body can be regarded to be at rest or in uniform motion. Both weight and inertia are the consequences of mass, which leaves only the well-known question of whether they are one or two different masses. However, in the consistent Cartesian or even Aristotelian sense, matter is not entirely inert because point-like masses create *gravitational forces* that "spread through" space with no time. Thus, matter creates active—or, in a narrow sense, teleological—movements in itself. It follows that bodies accelerating due to gravity cannot be regarded as inertial frames of reference. Nevertheless, *there is an absolute frame of reference*: space-time—which, in this sense, perfectly *complies* with the Aristotelian notion of the center of the universe.

Notice that in this classical interpretation, the Galilean principle of relativity constitutes merely the practical treatment of mechanical processes. In itself—that is, without any mechanical setting to another rigid body (e.g., Earth's surface)—no material body is at rest or in uniform motion in space, because the scope of gravitational forces is infinite and they spread throughout space without time. The sole exception is the chosen frame of reference, which, in the actual model, is the center of the universe—although that is not reality but merely our practical modeling. Thus, in Newtonian physics, one real frame of reference exists: *absolute space-time*. Contrary to Aristotelian and Cartesian philosophy, the Newtonian paradigm tells us *nothing* about man and his specific characteristics (like thinking, intuition, knowledge, etc.). According to modern understandings, it is, of course, not necessary for physics, but for the complete description of the world, *it is*. It means that for practical reasons, Newton—and before him Galilei—gave up the full description of the world for better modeling some mechanical processes of matter. For practical purposes, as we can see, they even ignored the fact that, in reality, no mass-point is at rest or in uniform motion in itself because the scope of gravitational forces is infinite. Therefore, classical physics is *per definition* not the complete description of the universe. In Galilei's and Newton's hands, philosophy shrank into natural philosophy (physics), which is entirely alright but, contrary to positivists and materialists, we must not forget this fact. Here, we can also see that the later, consistent positivist approach of Ernst Mach and Rudolf Carnap is already embedded in the classical physics of Galilei and Newton in an embryonic form: the primary goal is not the complete philosophical understanding of the world at all but rather to find practical solutions for certain fundamental mechanical/physical problems in exact conceptual frameworks and ignore any other kind of experience and (personal) fact. This practical approach was the cradle of the Laplacian beast. Newton, however, was still a dualist.

In Newtonian physics, there is not only matter but also an absolute, non-material space-time. However, since both space and time are modeled by a *four-dimensional, Cartesian coordinate system*, this poses a few consequences. First, time is not a reality independent from space but rather a reversible fourth dimension of space-time. Second, Newtonian space-time *does not reflect the natural, empirical properties of real space and time at all* but rather only the properties of a four-dimensional, rigid material body, by which space-time can be exactly specified and, in practice, the different time and space distances between mass-points can be measured by mechanical instruments. Third, space-time is thus an absolute and precisely definable, four-dimensional lack of matter—that is, a vacuum—among mass-points: a four-dimensional matrix of exact data. Classical physics is not based on experience (as the followers of Galilei and Newton always like to emphasize, especially in contrast to "dogmatic" Aristotelian physics) but rather on practical solutions, mathematical abstractions, and instrumentally generalized observations. Einstein's problem comes from this fact, too.

In a sense, Alexander's starting point for his emergentist theory of space and time is also this fact that Galilei and Newton utterly abstracted from some of our natural personal experiences—namely, (1) time is not reversible; (2) neither time, nor space is absolute; (3) time is not space-like (i.e., it is not the fourth dimension of space); and (4) space is not matter-like (i.e., space-time is not a vacuum). Therefore, Alexander's theory is based on such natural, empirical evidence (personal facts) due to which, on the one hand, space-time possesses fundamentally different qualities than matter, and, on the other, time also possesses fundamentally different qualities than those of space.

According to Alexander, time is (1) *successive*. It is a continuous whole, and instants of time following each other are based and built on each other. Time is also (2) *irreversible*. It has a definite direction, and instants of time have a comprehensive order of past, present, and future. Lastly, time is (3) *transitive*. It preserves its previously acquired properties, and instants of time transmit those properties to subsequent instants.[2] Altogether, on the one hand, time is *active*: new instants of time are constantly emerging one after another. On the other one, time has a *comprehensive, orderly structure*.

By contrast, space is (1) not successive. It is not a continuous whole, and points of space are independent of each other and do not build or derive from each other in any sense. Space is also (2) not irreversible. It has no definite direction, and points of space have no comprehensive order. Lastly, space is (3) not transitive. It does not preserve its previously acquired properties, and points of space do not transmit their properties to adjacent points. Accordingly, space in itself *has no comprehensive, orderly structure*, and in themselves, all points of space are entirely separate from each other—that is, there is no comprehensive relationship among them (for example, a dimension). Between any two points of space exists an infinite number of other points; and if points of space are entirely separable from each other—even with an infinite number of other points—then they will not constitute any real, continuous space. Therefore, space in itself neither exists nor is substantial but rather is only a *theoretical abstraction*. In that sense, Alexander's concept of space complies perfectly with Aristotelian and Cartesian concepts of primary matter, for only Newton ascribed absolute reality to vacant space to be able to objectively define the mechanical motions of mass-points.

Although time, in contrast to space, has definite comprehensive, orderly qualities, similarly to Aristotle's primary forms, it cannot be regarded as an entity in itself because *it has no own space (dimension)* where it could

---

2. Alexander, *Space, Time, and Deity*, 1:50–52.

actively manifest itself. Precisely as a point of space has neither extension nor any comprehensive relationship with other points, so it cannot be regarded as a real entity but rather only as a mathematical abstraction. Therefore, time can actively manifest itself *only in space*—or, more precisely, in the independent points of space. As a matter of fact, according to Alexander, since points of space have neither comprehensive structure nor dimensions, the creation of three comprehensive, orderly dimensions of space is the consequence of the manifestation of time in points of space. These manifestations connect the independent points of space and create real, dimensional space-time—which is, actually, the most fundamental way that time manifests itself in points of space. Moreover, space has three dimensions because of the modes of that fundamental manifestation of time in points of space: the three independent dimensions are the consequences of the three separate qualities of time.[3]

Yet, the point of the concept is that, in itself, neither space nor time can be regarded as a real entity. *Only space-time as a comprehensive, orderly whole exists.* In itself, neither independent points of space nor instants of time have any dimension. Only time manifests itself in points of space in three dimensions. Therefore, space-time—as a comprehensive, orderly whole and as a real entity—is *three-dimensional.* The four-dimensional model of space-time is only a mathematical abstraction. Space and time, as Aristotle's and Descartes's primary matter and forms, respectively, can only be separated theoretically.

However, such thinking does not mean that space and time have the same ontological status since, as shown, only time possesses comprehensive, orderly qualities, only time actively manifests in points of space, and only time creates the dimensions of space-time—and not vice versa. Since space does not exist in itself, it cannot determine any active manifestations of instances of time; however, since time does not exist in itself, it also cannot determine any passive conditions—that is, the points of space of its manifestation: they are in a *random relationship* to each other. Space is, in fact, the lower-level precondition of any higher-level comprehensive, orderly manifestation (existence) of time. Space is, therefore, the *possibility-condition* of time in which the latter can manifest and create genuinely new aspects (comprehensive orders) of reality: in this basic case, space-time itself. Consequently, time and space have an *emergent relationship.* Three-dimensional space-time is composed of points of space but, due to time, has comprehensive, orderly qualities that no composite parts have.

3. Alexander, *Space, Time, and Deity,* 1:52–56.

So, different aspects of reality (e.g., one dimension of space-time) come into being, as instances of time actively manifest in points of space in genuinely new ways. As mentioned, the relationship between Alexander's time and space is very similar to that of Aristotle's or Descartes's primary forms and primary matter, respectively. However, Aristotle's or Descartes's distinction is a purely *logical* one, between eternal substances, whereas Alexander speaks of *active processes* by time—as instances of time manifest in points of space and genuinely new aspects of reality emerge. Therefore, space-time is *motion* itself. Space-time is not an eternal substance of form or matter, as it is in Aristotle's and Descartes's theories, but rather the possibility-condition of every further higher-level, comprehensive order that emerges from it due to time—the same way that space-time emerges at the lower-level just as instances of time manifest in points of space. Physically speaking, space-time is not vacuum—that is, an utter lack of matter between material objects—because it is *never empty*. In space-time, according to the emergent nature of time, there is always some activity, some motion, and, to use a physical term, some energy. Therefore, new material (higher-level) aspects of reality always emerge. Physically speaking, there is always the possibility, however remote, that a particle—more precisely, a quantum—will emerge from even the seemingly most vacant parts of space-time.

Reality—in other words, the history of the universe—of course, starts with the first aspect of reality, which, as demonstrated, is the first active manifestation of time in a point of space. Since the extension of that state of the universe is zero—that is, a singularity back in time—but this state is in active motion, its density and temperature are both infinite, mathematically speaking. Thus, according to the emergent nature of time, (1) time manifests itself in three different dimensions at the level of space-time, and (2) genuinely new material forms of manifestations of time emerge at the higher material level.

(1) The former means that the universe expands. I cannot argue yet but, at first, probably way faster than the speed of light, which in physics is called cosmological inflation. This phenomenon is the consequence of the simplest form of manifestation of time in space when time manifests itself only in one dimension—after, of course, a dimension has emerged in the most fundamental way, which can expand. Time at once manifests in the other two dimensions as well, but those manifestations are—at least in this aspect—independent of each other. Everything happens in one concrete, separate dimension, or, put differently, time is not absolute. Thus, if starting from a point of space, time manifests in different dimensions, then it will be no longer the same time; or, if it remains the same time, then it will be a higher-level, emergent manifestation of time (our second case).

So, in this simplest case, only a point-instant emerges, which, due to the active nature of time, *is in motion*. Since time has no own dimension, that point-instant moves *in space*—that is, manifests itself in more and more points of space, continuously creating a dimension of space-time, which explains why space-time expands. Accordingly, the future of that point-instant is in the direction of its movement, its past is behind it, and its present is its center—that is, *its time overlaps with the straight dimension of its manifestation*. Physically speaking, the result is the straight world-line of a point-instant in three-dimensional space. Thus, the center of the point-instant (or its present) moves constantly in space and therefore, due to the nature of time, has a *definite speed*.

According to Alexander's argument, the universe, in an absolute sense, has no size, because space-time is not absolute and because there is no objective point of reference outside the universe. However, from every point-instant as a point of reference, according to its relative time (i.e., date) and space (i.e., place), the universe has a definite size. Consequently, the space at the point of which time first manifested is the *same space* as the space of all points of space, now or at any time. Different points of space and sizes are possible only due to the constant manifestations of time, whereas space itself remains the same. Without time, there is no difference in the size of a point of space and infinite points of space.

The activity of the first manifestation of time has naturally decreased as time has progressed as well as partly changed in nature (our second case), yet it is still present everywhere. The reason for that dynamic result is twofold. First, (the present) space itself is exactly the same as the space of the first manifestation of time, so this kind of manifestation can be still present everywhere. Second, since there are far more points of space in space-time now, where time can manifest itself in this simplest form, the activity of such manifestation has strongly decreased. Therefore, if the former factor that it is still present everywhere is more important than its decreased activity, then the universe will not only expand but it will also expand at an accelerating rate. In physical terms, those two factors determine the value of Einstein's cosmological constant.

(2) The latter forms of the manifestation of time mean that time manifests itself in points of space in more than one dimension, yet it remains the same. As a consequence, *matter emerges from space-time*. I will be able to detail this process in subchapter 6.6, after the examination of Einstein's theory of general relativity that explains it, but the point of the process can be shown in a simpler case first. In this case, time manifest itself in two dimensions and remains the same, which means that time does not move in two dimensions as two separated point-instants but rather moves around a

center as one point-instant. In other words, time manifests in two dimensions *within a specific radius*. As such, the center of the entity is *at rest in space*, contrary to the former case, in which the center of the point-instant moves in space along a straight dimension. Hence, I call the former type of entities *open* and the latter type *closed*.

Contrary to the case of one-dimensional point-instants, the futures and pasts of closed-type entities are not bound to a definite direction of a dimension of space-time along which the entities move, but their futures and pasts can be found at once in both directions of both dimensions of space-time. Therefore, due to their new kind of emergence, in a sense, their time *separates* from space-time itself. In other words, a two-dimensional space-time continuum, due to the specific, multidimensional form of manifestations of time therein, has independent and permanent *physical time* bound to its center and exists from its emergence until its disintegration. *This* physical time can be abstracted from the normal dimensions of space-time, or, mathematically speaking, can be regarded as an independent dimension; however, in reality, it is only a new kind of manifestation of time in a definite space-time continuum. By contrast, one-dimensional point-instants have only present at a certain point of space and the same present all along their space dimension. That is, they are *at rest in time*. If an entity has physical time, then it possesses *material qualities* as well. It is not merely space-time, but also emergent matter.

Conversely, two-dimensional entities have only one material quality—namely, mass or, more precisely, inertial mass—and as we will see in subchapter 6.6, physical time and mass are actually *the same*. Whereas the former is the description from the point of view of the level of space-time, the latter is the description from the level of matter. The result is an entity with only one material quality—mass—which thus participates solely in gravitational interaction. That is, it is dark for electromagnetism. It is *dark*, and it is *matter*.

So, due to the different kinds of manifestation of time in points of space, the universe expands, and genuinely new forms of material entities emerge from space-time. Although Alexander regards the identification and categorization of those entities as the task of physics, he adds that light and similar entities are likely in another category of material entities than atom-like entities in the nucleus and that perhaps electron-like entities are yet another category.[4] According to the Standard Model of elementary particles of modern physics, there are bosons ("interactions," like light) and fermions ("material particles"), which have quite different properties. Among

---

4. Alexander, *Space, Time, and Deity*, 2:53–54.

fermions, there are also two fundamental categories with different type of particles: quarks (composite entities of the nucleus) and leptons, like the electron. These results of modern physics are typical examples for positivism for why the term physicalism is much more precise than the traditional term of materialism. Nevertheless, these remarkable results in physics were predicted by Alexander, based on his theory of space-time, way before the birth of quantum mechanics and the Standard Model. Although this chapter addresses the understanding of Einstein's theory of relativity—and not the Standard Model—briefly showing the explanatory power of Alexander's emergentist concept of space and time in that case, too, is worthwhile. Alexander's light- and electron-type entities can be obtained assuming that time manifests itself in three dimensions yet remains the same, which can occur in two fundamental ways.

The first requires two dimensions to be closed and one to be open, which is possible by adding the above one- and two-dimensional entities. The resultant entity—a three-dimensional space-time continuum—from a certain dimension appears as a closed particle with an inert center and, from another dimension, as an open wave of space-time with a moving center. In this case, this idea is not a conceptual contradiction that needs to be accepted for practical reasons (as in the case of quantum mechanics) but rather a clear reality deduced from Alexander's principles. The entity has no mass or physical time in its open dimension, but it moves in a straight line at a specific speed that, as we will see, is the same from any inertial frame of reference. The vectorial radius of the time that manifests around the center of the entity in two dimensions is $\sqrt{2}/2\pi$. If that radius is multiplied by the Planck constant (h), then the result is the value of the spin (S) of light; and in this case, we speak about real spinning, not a mass-point's strange, conceptually problematic quality.

The second way requires all three dimensions to be closed. That entity has an inert center and well-definable mass and physical time from every dimension, although the lifetime of a concrete entity cannot be exactly defined due to the emergent nature of time. The vectorial radius of the time that manifests around the center of the entity in three dimensions is $\sqrt{3}/4\pi$. If that radius is multiplied by the Planck constant (h), then the result is the value of the spin (S) of the electron. Although it is clearly a particle from every dimension if it moves at a rapid speed, it appears as a de Broglie-Bohm-type concept of the quantum, in which a wave follows a mass-point. Those waves are, of course, the effects of the time of the entity in space-time.

The nucleus has a far more complicated structure and cannot be regarded as an elementary particle—even in the case of the hydrogen atom. More strangely, the quarks of a proton or neutron cannot be separated and observed separately. Although I do not know how the nucleus can be explained based on Alexander's theory, according to the Standard Model, a proton is composed of two up quarks, one down quark, and three gluons, where the rest masses of the particles are (in MeV/c^2) 2.3, 4.8, and 0, which total 9.4. The rest mass of the proton is still 938 MeV/c^2. If the proton is an emergent, comprehensive space-time continuum of moving quarks and gluons in a specific system of space-time, then the results will be unsurprising. Various experiments have shown that colliding photons with sufficiently high energy (E = hf, in which E is energy, h is the Planck constant, and f is frequency) can create an electron and a positron (i.e., the anti-particle of the electron), which suggests that at a lower-level, photons and electrons are composed of the same "material" and not point-like elementary particles at all. Both mass and energy are the material consequence of the specific closed and open manifestation of time in space in those particles. However, the π-s in spins (S) already cast doubt on that theory of elementary particles of point-masses.

There are several other examples of my argument detailed in the following subchapters on the case of Einstein's theory of relativity, but at this point, it is already possible to claim that quantum mechanics and modern physics did not refute Alexander's emergentism as McLaughlin claimed. To me, it seems exactly the opposite.

6.3 Einstein's Theory of Special Relativity

According to Einstein's argument, the theory of special relativity was born from the apparent contradiction between (1) the Galilean principle of relativity and (2) the law of propagation of light.[5]

(1) *The Galilean principle of relativity*: As we have seen in the previous subchapter, the point of this principle is, on the one hand, that Galilei rejected the Aristotelian notion of the center of the universe, which is the absolute resting point of reference (center) of all movements in Aristotelian physics. In this sense, the principle of relativity is the expansion of Copernicus's revelation that the Earth is not at the center of the universe with Galilei's own notion that all celestial objects and motions have the same nature as earthly objects and motions have. Consequently, there is no distinguished center in the universe (even at the center of the Sun) determining all movements, but, for example, falling objects on Earth fall toward the center of the Earth the same way as falling objects on Mars fall toward the center of the Mars, etc. On the other hand, Galilei claimed that rest

---

5. Einstein, *Relativity*, 17–20.

and uniform motion in a straight line are physically *equivalent*, contrary to the Aristotelian notion that rest (in reference to the center of the universe) is distinguished compared to any movement. It follows that in Galilean physics, every resting or uniformly moving object can be an inertial frame of reference. So, for example, if a resting object is hit by another one in Aristotelian physics, the object will shortly lose the gained momentum and be at rest again, but in Galilean physics, it will uniformly move due to the gained momentum. The reason that it will still halt again is not that rest and uniform motion are different physical states, but that in earthly conditions, there is always some friction; that friction is the real cause of the loss of momentum. It also follows that none of the resting or uniformly moving objects are distinguished compared one to another—that is, it is only due to the chosen frame of reference which object is at rest and which is in uniform motion or which object is in slow and which is in fast uniform motion. However, this also means that the same laws have to apply to both resting and uniformly moving objects at different speeds. With Einstein's example, since the same laws apply to both the train, which is in v_1 uniform motion compared to the track, and to a man, who is in v_2 uniform motion on the train compared to the train (because, for example, he is walking toward the front of his railway carriage), we can get the speed of the uniform motion of the man compared to the track (v_x) by the simple addition of the velocities of the first two motions (that is, $v_x = v_1 + v_1$), which is called Galilei-transformation in physics. Therefore, due to the principle of relativity, the different speeds of uniform motions *could sum up approaching infinity*. By contrast, in Aristotelian physics, the speeds of different objects do not sum up because there is only one frame of reference.

(2) *The law of propagation of light* is the consequence of the results of optics and electrodynamics in the nineteenth century. It says that light, compared to all inertial frames of reference, propagates in a vacuum at the same *constant, finite speed of c*. This means that the speed of light is distinguished among other uniform motions. With Einstein's example, the speed of the uniformly moving light is the same compared both to the resting track and to the uniformly moving train, which *contradicts* the Galilean principle of relativity. The speed of light is not relative; it is *absolute*. In a sense, the law of propagation of light is a return to Aristotelian physics because there is a distinguished point of reference (a "center"), according to which every resting and uniformly moving object can be compared in an absolute way. This is exactly the reason that it contradicts the Galilean principle of relativity, according to which every state of rest and uniform motion is relative compared one to another. It is worth noting that from this absolute "center" of

the speed of light, *every* inertial frame of reference is at rest, which, actually, is quite telling (has existential meaning).

We have seen in subchapter 3.2 that the aim of the famous Michelson and Morley experiments was to define the speed of Earth compared *to the ether*—that is, to a *continuous, material medium* which fills up the space. At that time, contrary to Newton's earlier, corpuscular concept, where particles of light propagate in vacuum, light was considered to be a *wave* that spreads through the absolutely motionless *ether*. Thus, in a sense, this motionless ether can be identified with Newton's absolute space (or, as a matter of fact, with Aristotle's center of the universe), compared to which the absolute motions of different objects can be defined—among them, of course, the absolute motion of Earth, too. On the basis of this concept, however, the results were significantly less than they expected, which, according to the traditional, positivist history of science, led to the rejection of the concept of ether and Einstein's theory of special relativity.

As we have also seen, however, Hendrik A. Lorentz's dynamical ether theory—thanks, for example, to the introduction of the so-called *Lorentz-transformation*—explained the results of the experiments just as correctly as Einstein's theory of special relativity did. Therefore, the rejection of the concept of ether and the wave concept of light was not based merely on the experimental results. Furthermore, it happened despite the fact that it led to such severe problems (e.g., that light is *both a particle and a wave* at the same time, which is a definite conceptual contradiction, and that light is such a wave that it has no medium through which it could spread). Nonetheless, Einstein's argument, in fact, is neither based on the results of the famous Michelson-Morley experiments at all (as he acknowledged that to Polanyi) nor, of course, on these conceptual contradictions but rather on other theoretical considerations concerning the apparent contradiction between the law of propagation of light and the Galilean principle of relativity, which was way too much concern for Einstein:

> The epoch-making theoretical investigations of H. A. Lorentz on the electrodynamical and optical phenomena connected with moving bodies show that experience in this domain leads conclusively to a theory of electro magnetic phenomena, of which the law of the constancy of the velocity of light in vacuo is a necessary consequence. Prominent theoretical physicists were, therefore, more inclined to reject the [Galilean] principle of relativity, in spite of the fact that no empirical data had been found which were contradictory to this principle.
>
> At this juncture, the theory of relativity entered the arena. As a result of an analysis of the physical conceptions of time

and space, it became evident that *in reality, there is not the least incompatibility between the principle of relativity and the law of propagation of light,* and that by systematically holding fast to both these laws, a logically rigid theory could be arrived at. This theory has been called the special theory of relativity to distinguish it from the extended theory.[6]

Mathematically, Einstein's solution is straightforward: he replaced the Galilei-transformation with the Lorentz-transformation. Lorentz introduced this transformation into his dynamical ether theory to explain the contraction of electrons at high velocity, which, according to him, is the drag effect of ether on propagating electrons—that is, a real and absolute phenomenon due to the nature of ether. The contraction of objects, as Einstein himself acknowledges, thus explains the negative results of the Michelson-Morley experiments. Contrary to the Galilei-transformation, in the case of the Lorentz-transformation, the speeds of uniformly moving objects sum up in a way that the value of the sum never exceeds the speed of light in vacuum. In other words, thanks to the Lorentz-transformation, it is indifferent if the train moves compared to the track at speed v, the light will move both compared to the track (i.e., to the chosen inertial frame of reference) and the moving train at speed c.

The real (philosophical or metaphysical) question is: in Einstein's understanding, what is the meaning of "an analysis of the physical conceptions of time and space" from which "it became evident that *in reality, there is not the least incompatibility between the principle of relativity and the law of propagation of light*"? Einstein, on a purely theoretical basis, shows that, contrary to Newton's concept, distances of space and periods of time are *relative*—that is, the behavior of measuring-rods and clocks at different speeds of uniform motion will change. It means that although light, in fact, makes a smaller distance compared to the moving train than to the track, from the train, it still does not seem that light moves slower by speed v (due to the Galilei-transformation) because the moving clock on the train (due to the Lorentz-transformation) will *go slower* just as much that the speed of light will still seem exactly c, contrary to the factually shorter distance traveled by the light beam.

The main point of Einstein's argument is that *the concept of simultaneity is relative* and the Newtonian concept of absolute time is therefore *unfounded*. He once again uses the example of the train and the track. Suppose that lightning strikes down on the track at two different points, A and B. On what basis can one state that the lightning struck down at A and B at

---

6. Einstein, *Relativity*, 27–28.

the same time? Einstein's answer is this: if the light of the lightning arrives at the same time to an observer who is at point M, exactly halfway between A and B on the track. However, there is a problem. Suppose that when the lightning strikes, there is a very long, uniformly-moving train on the track with another observer on board. When this happens, the observer on the train is at point M', which coincides with point M on the track. But because the train is moving at speed v, the observer on the train would not observe that the lightning struck A and B at the same time since the light of the lightning (toward which the train is going) would reach him earlier. Both of the observers would observe simultaneous events only if the speed of the light were infinite—which it is not:

> Events which are simultaneous with reference to the embankment are not simultaneous with respect to the train, and vice versa (relativity of simultaneity). Every reference-body (co-ordinate system) has its own particular time; unless we are told the reference-body to which the statement of time refers, there is no meaning in a statement of the time of an event.
>
> Now before the advent of the theory of relativity, it had always tacitly been assumed in physics that the statement of time had an absolute significance, i.e., that it is independent of the state of motion of the body of reference. But we have just seen that this assumption is incompatible with the most natural definition of simultaneity; if we discard this assumption, then the conflict between the law of the propagation of light in vacuo and the principle of relativity . . . disappears.[7]

Einstein definitely rejects the Newtonian concept of absolute space and time: "Every reference-body (co-ordinate system) has its own particular time." At the same time, however, he claims that "there is no meaning in a statement of the time of an event . . . unless we are told the reference-body to which the statement of time refers." In what sense does an object have "its own particular time" if it is utterly meaningless without another "reference-body to which the statement of time refers"?

This problem appears in the theory of special relativity in the following way. Suppose that there are two twins, and one of them is on a spaceship and the other is on Earth. The spaceship uniformly moves compared to Earth at speed v. Regard the two objects as each other's inertial frame of reference. It follows, according to the theory of special relativity, that time goes slower on the spaceship that moves at speed v, and one can calculate the exact value

---

7. Einstein, *Relativity*, 26–27.

of the time of the spaceship by the Lorentz-transformation $t_{spaceship} = \frac{t_{Earth} - \frac{vx}{c^2}}{\sqrt{1 - \frac{v^2}{c^2}}}$, that is, $t_{spaceship} < t_{Earth}$. To put this into its famous form: the twin on the spaceship is aging slower. But since, according to the Galilean principle of relativity, there is no absolute frame of reference (center of the universe, Newtonian absolute space-time, ether, etc.), the following statement, according to Einstein's theory of special relativity, is also entirely correct: the Earth uniformly moves at speed v compared to the spaceship; therefore, time goes slower on Earth, which can be calculated by the Lorentz-transformation $t_{Earth} = \frac{t_{spaceship} - \frac{vx}{c^2}}{\sqrt{1 - \frac{v^2}{c^2}}}$, that is, $t_{Earth} < t_{spaceship}$. So the twin on Earth is aging slower. Now, who is aging slower? Which statement is true?

The perhaps surprising answer is *neither of them*. Despite Einstein's deceptive wording ("every reference-body (co-ordinate system) has its own particular time"), the theory of special relativity *tells us nothing about real times*—that is, what is the time of an object *in the metaphysical sense*. It merely defines by the Lorentz-transformation the *seeming* time of an object (e.g., the spaceship) from an optional (random) inertial frame of reference (e.g., from Earth) for the reason that neither the Galilean principle of relativity nor the law of the propagation of light should be violated. The same is true for the change of mass; the famous equivalence of which with energy ($E=mc^2$) is also the consequence of special relativity. Close to the speed of light, the mass of the spaceship significantly increases, but compared to the spaceship—which, according to the Galilean principle of relativity, is a perfectly equivalent statement—the Earth goes nearly at the speed of light, and therefore it has significantly increased mass. These are not real values in the metaphysical sense, however, since the Earth's mass would never increase because of a fast spaceship far away; these are merely *mathematical calculations* which were introduced by Einstein *in the explicit framework* of physics to solve the apparent contradiction between the law of propagation of light and the Galilean principle of relativity.

In a mathematical sense and from a positivist point of view that rejects real philosophical (metaphysical) questions concerning reality, he correctly resolved the contradiction. The real consequence of this solution, however, is not that he replaced Newton's absolute concept of time with a relative one, where every object has "its own particular time"; rather, he entirely banished time from physics.[8] The same is true for space. After Einstein, as shown in detail in subchapter 6.5, space-time is but arithmetical data of a

---

8. For Smolin's account, see Smolin, *Time Reborn*, 54–75.

four-dimensional matrix calculated from an optional frame of reference. The following metaphysical questions, in turn, remained unanswered:

1. What is time—that is, what is the real meaning that every object has "its own particular time"?
2. What is space?
3. Why does light have absolute speed?
4. How can an entity be both particle and wave at the same time?
5. How can a wave propagate without any medium?
6. And, of course, why do we have an entirely different personal experience of time in real life than what Einstein describes in his theory?

From a positivist point of view, the answers to these questions are not necessary at all; it is entirely enough that our calculations solve certain (mathematically and/or experimentally) well-defined problems in our exact conceptual framework of science.

6.4 Understanding Special Relativity

As we have seen in subchapter 6.2, Alexander's emergentist theory of space and time is based on experience, not on mathematical abstractions of rigid, material bodies. His goal is not to solve specific practical and mathematical problems in certain very exact, conceptual frameworks but rather to understand the nature of space and time. It follows that, according to him, space and time are neither material nor explicit mathematical data, created by mechanical (material) instruments, but rather the fundaments of reality, an emergent relationship from which every higher-level aspect of reality emerges. Since space-time is emergent and not material, it cannot be measured by mechanical instruments. Space-time in itself has no size (that is a material quality), only the vacuum (distance or lack of matter) between material bodies can be accurately measured. This means that there is no absolute space-time; every manifestation of space-time has to be regarded as its own center which behaves according to the nature of its own center, and every manifestation of space-time has its own particular relationship with every other manifestation of space-time. As a matter of fact, as it will soon be clear, this is the emergentist understanding and real, existential meaning of the Galilean principle of relativity.

We have also seen that the manifestation of time in points of space has two main types: time can manifest itself in an open or closed way in a dimension. Suppose that there are two closed type entities (A and B) on a given axis (X). Following Galilei and Einstein, let's neglect any gravitational effect for now. How will these entities behave in space-time? Since there is neither absolute space-time nor an absolute point of view (inertial frame of reference or an absolute center of the universe), this question can be answered only in relation to different points or instants of space-time. Naturally, both the centers of A and B occupy a point of space-time, and since both centers are at rest in space, this means that compared to the points of space-time occupied by their centers, both A and B are at rest as well. Compared to each other, in turn, they are either at rest or in uniform motion at the given speed of v. As Galilei rightly observed, if, on the one hand, there is no absolute point of reference and, on the other, the gravitational effects are neglected, then the principle of relativity applies.

Now, let's suppose that there is an open type entity (C) on the axis (X) as well, which is open in the dimension of axis X. How will this open type entity behave in space-time at a given moment compared to a certain point of space-time? (1) First, for point of reference, choose the space-time-point that is occupied by the center of C. Since this entity is open, its center is not at rest in space but rather, due to the nature of time, moves in its open dimension uniformly—that is, on axis X at given speed v_c. (2) Now, for point of reference, choose the space-time-point that is occupied by the center of A. Since the center of A in itself is at rest, the speed of C compared to both A and to the space-time-point that is occupied by the center of A is exactly the same (v_c) as it is compared to the point of space-time occupied by its own center. The same is true, of course, for B, too, because B is the same closed type entity as A. (3) Now, choose for point of reference the point of space-time that is occupied by the center of B in the special case when B uniformly moves at speed v on axis X compared to the resting A. What is the speed of C in this case? Notice that Einstein's question referring to the track ("A"), the uniformly moving train ("B"), and the speed of light ("C") is entirely equivalent to this example. The answer is that the speed of C is still v_c since *B*—and not our point of reference—moves uniformly at the speed of v. Points of space-time do not change their space-time relations to different types of material entities just by themselves, but if gravitational effects are not neglected (as we will see in subchapter 6.6) the situation will utterly change, of course. (4) Finally, if we ask the question: independently of A, what is the speed of C compared to the point of space-time that is occupied by the center of B? We are backing to our former question because B in itself is necessarily at rest compared to the space-time-point that is occupied by its own center, so the speed of C is still v_c both to this space-time-point and to the center of B.

Einstein cannot state that the speed of C is v_c—that is, of course, c compared to the point of space-time occupied by C's own center, because for him, space-time is not an independent reality and cannot be the point of reference: in the theory of special relativity, no material entity has any speed in itself. If there were only one material entity in the universe, it would be utterly meaningless to ask what its speed is. This is the reason that Einstein *has to separately and in an absolute way postulate* that the speed of light (in a vacuum) is constant (c) from any frame of reference.

By contrast, from Alexander's emergentist theory of space-time, it follows that, on the one hand, there are closed (electron) type entities, which are at rest in space and, on the other, there are open (light) type entities, which move in space uniformly. The former ones have their own physical time and move in time (exist at a certain place), the latter ones (in their open dimension) have no physical time—that is, they are at rest in time (do not exist at a particular place). If there were only one closed, material entity in the whole universe, the speed of that entity would be zero, and if there were only one open entity, its speed would be c. It follows, as was shown, that open type entities, compared to closed type entities, move at speed c, regardless of which closed type entity is the chosen frame of reference.

The reason that this assertion can be deduced from Alexander's concept of space-time is that, according to the theory, space-time is not just a vacuum or exact mathematical data in physical models (conceptual frameworks) but rather the *source of any movement* in space-time. Space-time is the manifestation of time in points of space—which is movement itself. At the higher material level, this can happen in two fundamental ways, as time manifests in closed and open type entities. So, contrary to Einstein's theory of special relativity, based on Alexander's theory of space-time, the constant speed of light from any inertial frame of reference—that is, the law of propagation of light—is not an independent postulate but rather *the consequence of the nature of space-time*; more precisely, it is the result of one fundamental way, as time manifests in points of space and matter emerges. Instead of a postulate, we have an explanation, based on real ordering principles.

Nonetheless, Einstein's starting problem is still unanswered—that is, what is the reason behind the apparent contradiction of the law of propagation of light and the Galilean principle of relativity? As we have seen, for Einstein, it is a mathematical problem: he took over the Lorentz-transformation from Lorentz's dynamical ether theory, so the different speeds of closed type entities do not sum up to infinity anymore. (1) Why does Einstein's mathematical solution work, and (2) what can be said based on Alexander's philosophical principles? One thing is certain: the mathematical formula has to be the same because it was verified countless times; moreover, for most of the physicists, its truth—thanks to its scientific beauty—was obvious even before any verification (3.2).

(1) First, as we have seen in subchapter 6.2, in the case of the Newtonian paradigm, the concepts of space-time and matter were entirely separated for the very first time: there is absolute space-time, modeled by a four-dimensional Cartesian coordinate system, and there are point-masses. Galilei's *philosophical* starting point that, contrary to the Aristotelian notion of the center of the universe, there is no absolute, inertial frame of reference is true. However, Galilei's other, *practical* solution for applying his principle of relativity—that is, to neglect every gravitational effect (or, in Einstein's words, "A body removed sufficiently far from other bodies continues in a state of rest or of uniform motion in a straight line"[9])—can*not* work if someone wants to speak about *real* (in a metaphysical sense, existing) movements in space-time since *in reality, if there is matter, there are always gravitational effects, too.* Galilei also neglected every other kind of movement (beside some mechanical ones), primarily the movements of living beings, when he supposed that all earthly objects and their movements and all celestial objects and their movements have the same nature. He was right in his intention since he formulated his claim against Aristotle, who thought that celestial objects were different in nature; however, Galilei's brave notion still turned out to be a mistake since the nature of light and its movement do not comply with the nature and movements of "ordinary" matter, and at the beginning of the twentieth century, this mistake questioned even the practical/mathematical application of his own relativity principle. As Einstein mentioned, at that time, physicists were ready to reject the principle itself.

Therefore, the Galilean principle of relativity in its actual physical form is not about real movements in real space-time—especially not about the nature of these real movements—but rather a principle for *practical/mathematical treatment of some mechanical issues*; mainly in earthly conditions where (1) there is a vast, rigid, material body (the surface of Earth) as the "absolute" background ("space-time") of material objects; (2) there are only closed type entities at low speed; (3) the gravitational effects can be neglected (or modeled as the strange material force of Newton); and (4) there are also no electromagnetic effects. Newton generalized Galilei's findings in his well-known paradigm, but the unexpected results of optics and electrodynamics in the nineteenth century showed that the nature of light does not comply with his paradigm. This is the reason that the *real* movements of light in space-time contradict the Galilean principle of relativity. Not in its main philosophical core, since it is perfectly true that there is no absolute, inertial frame of

---

9. Einstein, *Relativity*, 11.

reference (Aristotelian center of the universe) but *in its actual mathematical/ physical form*. This was the reason that I said (6.2) that classical physics is not based on experience—in this case, concerning space-time and light—but rather on practical solutions, mathematical abstractions, and instrumentally generalized observations. Einstein, however, at least tacitly, recognized that in the deeper philosophical sense, the contradiction is just apparent; which means that in the metaphysical sense, there is no real contradiction. Galilei's relativity principle does not have to be rejected because of the law of propagation of light. So, Einstein, contrary to other physicists of his era, recognized the point of the problem and found the mathematical solution by replacing the Galilei-transformation with the Lorentzian one. But since his solution is still purely mathematical, it is not surprising that it does not give answers to the questions of the philosophical side of the problem, primarily to the question of why the speed of light is absolute.

(2) Second, as we have seen in subchapter 6.2, in the case of closed type entities, physical time can be represented mathematically as an independent dimension, which I will call time axis—although, in reality, it is just a new kind of multidimensional manifestation of time in a closed space-time continuum bound to a resting center. This fact is the reason that closed type entities can be modeled due to the Newtonian paradigm (at least at slow speeds, of course), where time as an independent time axis is the fourth dimension of a four-dimensional abstract space time. It follows that these kinds of entities, due to the actual state of their time axis, can freely have different speeds (see the next paragraph). However, open type of entities—like light—resist the Galilean principle of relativity and this kind of modeling because they have no time axis at all (but only in their open dimension, of course). In other words, in the mathematical sense, the "time axis" of these kinds of entities overlaps their open space-dimension; therefore, in their open dimension, they have a definite, constant speed of c. Mathematically speaking, it follows that the natural state of closed type entities is that their time axis is *perpendicular* to space-dimensions, which means that they are at rest in space, while the natural state of open type entities is that without an independent time axis, they are bound to their open space-dimension and uniformly move in space with a constant speed of c, and this fact cannot be changed. All of this is the consequence of the fact that time manifests itself in points of space in different forms in the center of these entities.

Now, let's ask: what is the situation with the time axis of a closed type entity (B) that uniformly moves at speed v in dimension X compared to another closed type entity (A) that is at rest? The answer is that the time axis of B will seem to be *leaning toward* the time axis of A—that is, will not be perpendicular to dimension X—which merely means that B moves in space compared to A. The reason for this phenomenon is that in Alexander's theory of space and time, every movement is the consequence of different manifestations of time in points of space; therefore, if B is not at rest anymore, that means that the time of B not just manifests itself in the space-time continuum around the center of B but in dimension X, too, due to its movement in space. Mathematically, it means that the time of B is divided between the time axis of B (physical time) and dimension X due to the speed of B in dimension X. Do not forget that we are still at the understanding of Einstein's special relativity, so we still do not consider gravitational effects and there are only relative movements in different inertial frame of reference; thus, this conclusion is also true for A compared to B. Actually, we try to count the time of B from the point of view of A.

Both the time (t) of A and B is $\frac{1}{c}$ at rest, which means that the time which manifests in A or in B covers a unit of distance at their time axis due to the well-known correlation of $v = \frac{s}{t}$. Now, however, it was supposed that B has a speed of v compared to A—that is, the time of B (t) is divided between its time axis and dimension X. This means that the measured physical time of B compared to A (t_B) at a given point of space x_B will be as much less as the time of B (t) manifests as the movement of B in dimension X (t_x)—that is, $t_B = t - t_x$, due to the covered unit of distance $t_x = \frac{s_x}{c}$ and $s_x = vt$, t_x is $\frac{vt}{c}$—that is, $t_B = t - \frac{vt}{c}$. This formula can be written in its more well-known form, $t' = t - \frac{vx}{c^2}$, because, as we have seen, $t = \frac{1}{c}$ and x—more exactly, x_B—is the exact space-coordinate of the time axis and center of B on dimension X compared to A, where the physical time of B manifests itself in the mathematical sense at the given moment of our examination. Nonetheless, this calculation is not yet complete since the time axis of B is leaning toward A. Consequently, due to the above calculation, the measured physical time of B at point x_B from A will not only be less but also more because due to this leaning, the unit of distance according to which it has to be measured will be less. Mathematically, this shortening of the unit of distance can be calculated by applying the Pythagorean Theorem: $\sqrt{1^2 - s_x^2}$ —that is, since $s_x = vt$ and $t = \frac{1}{c}$, it is $\sqrt{1 - \frac{v^2}{c^2}}$ in its well-known form. Therefore, the exact ratio by which the measured physical time of B will be more is $\frac{1}{\sqrt{1 - \frac{v^2}{c^2}}}$. Finally, if we merge the two formulas, we will get the well-known formula of the Lorentz-transformation, concerning measured times in uniformly moving systems: $t' = \frac{t - \frac{vx}{c^2}}{\sqrt{1 - \frac{v^2}{c^2}}}$.

So, contrary to Einstein, there is no need to postulate that the speed of light (and, actually, the speed of other open entities) is constant from every inertial frame of reference and, after that, deduce the equations of the Lorentz-transformation from this postulate—those can be deduced directly from Alexander's emergentist theory of space and time. It follows, of course, that the apparent (mathematical) contradiction between the law of propagation of light and the Galilean principle of relativity—on which Einstein's whole theory of special relativity is based—can be solved in the mathematical sense, too. The fact that the Lorentz-transformation can be deduced from Alexander's theory of space and time is, of course, the simple consequence of the other fact that the law of propagation of light already follows from his theory. Thus, the Lorentz-transformation is, in fact, the mathematical expression of the relation of two different kinds of movement—that is, the consequence of those phenomena as time manifests itself in two fundamentally different ways in points of space: mathematically speaking, perpendicularly or parallel to the dimension of uniform motion in question.

Moreover, on the basis of Alexander's emergentist theory of space and time, more can be stated than by Einstein himself since, in this emergentist framework, there are speeds and movements of different entities not just in relation to each other as an inertial frame of reference, in terms of four-dimensional coordinates abstracted from an infinite, four-dimensional rigid material body, but *also in relation to emergent space-time*. As it was emphasized at the end of the previous subchapter, special relativity cannot answer the question factually of which object goes closer to the speed of light—the spaceship or the Earth. Thus, the time of which object goes slower and the mass of which object has become much more: it is all the question of an *arbitrarily chosen* frame of reference. Einstein's calculations are based on a simple postulate without a real philosophical (metaphysical) explanation. More exactly, his philosophical explanation, according to the logic of positivism, is that there is no need for real metaphysical explanations: time is not real.

Nonetheless, based on Alexander's theory, we have already spoken about real times so far since, in itself, every closed type entity is at rest. This is not only the consequence of a well-chosen frame of reference but also the natural state of these types of entities in space-time—that is, *in reference to* space-time. Therefore, if we still neglect gravitational effects, there will be no moving, closed type entity until, due to some material effect, the first one will start to move. And if that material effect is permanent, the movement, of course, will be acceleration, and after the end of the effect, the closed type entity will go on in uniform motion because the physical time (in the time axis) of that entity will preserve its former quality (that is, its angle to a dimension of space-time) due to the transitiveness of time. The point is, the reason that the time of the spaceship will, in fact, go slower and its mass will be more is that the *spaceship has changed* its speed compared to the point of space-time occupied by the center of Earth due to real material effects, *not* the Earth compared to the point of space-time occupied by the center of the spaceship. Time is real and not reversible. The history of an object determines its actual position and behavior in space-time because time is not just irreversible but also transitive and thus preserves its acquired qualities—which, in this case, of course, is the emergentist understanding of the Galilean notion of preservation of momentum.

Lorentz was right when he thought that there are real effects on closed type entities due to the medium in which they move (in a sense, it is the simple application of Newton's third action-reaction law), so he introduced the Lorentz-transformation to explain the contraction of electrons. But he was wrong when he thought that this medium was an absolute, continuous material (ether), the ultimate resting inertial frame of reference. Space-time is not some ether which could be used as an *absolute*, four-dimensional, rigid, *material frame of reference* but rather an *emergent reality*. This means that although there are (in the Aristotelian sense) natural movements in space-time (resting closed type and uniformly moving, open type entities), there is still no absolute frame of reference (Aristotelian center of the universe) in reference to which these natural movements have to be understood. The philosophical core of the Galilean principle of relativity that there is no such distinguished center is true. Einstein recognized this fact and rejected both Newton's concept of absolute space-time and the concept of ether, both of which questioned the validity of the Galilean principle of relativity. He recognized a real rationality in nature and found a mathematical solution to the problem that came from the nature and constant speed of light, but he could not formulate the real, existential meaning of his discovery (3.2). However, to better understand the meaning of the philosophical core of the Galilean principle of relativity that every entity has its own center in space-time, it is time to go into the territory of Einstein's theory of general relativity. But before that, for the sake of completeness, let's answer the questions we left unanswered at the end of the previous subchapter:

1. What is time?—Time is the composite part of emergent comprehensive material entities.

2. What is space?—Space is the necessary possibility-condition in the points of which time can manifest itself.

3. Why does light have absolute speed?—The speed of light is not absolute (the consequence of a postulate), it is only the consequence of one kind of natural manifestation of time in points of space.

4. How can an entity be both particle and wave at the same time?—Thus that time manifests in two dimensions in a closed and in one dominant dimension in an open way.

5. How could a wave propagate without any medium?—Naturally, not at all; the medium in which light propagates is the emergent space-time itself.

6. Why do we have entirely different personal experiences about time in real life than as Einstein describes in his theory?—First, because modern physics is not the complete description of the world; rather, it is based on mathematical abstractions and practical considerations. Second, because measured physical time is neither biological/physiological time nor time itself.

6.5 Einstein's Theory of General Relativity

The reason that Einstein called his former theory special relativity is that it is not valid in accelerating systems of reference—only in those that are at rest or uniformly moving. Nonetheless, for Einstein, it is necessary that all systems of reference are equivalent for the formulation of the general laws of nature; in short, this is the "general principle of relativity."[10] However, in accelerating systems, the mechanical behavior of bodies is changed; therefore, they cannot be regarded as equivalent to resting or uniformly moving systems (at least in classical mechanics). Einstein uses his train example once again: there are different forces and thus different behaviors of bodies in a resting or uniformly moving and in an accelerating or braking carriage; every passenger can feel the difference.[11] With another, perhaps more expressive example: to describe the motions of stars, the surface of Earth cannot be chosen to be the frame of reference because due to the daily rotation (acceleration) of the Earth, the results will be entirely unrealistic—as it is happened, by the way, before modern science. Consequently, for the description of nature, resting or uniformly moving systems have to be regarded as distinguished systems of reference. However, there is no real explanation for this phenomenon in classical mechanics. According to Einstein, it is an untenable situation which has to be eliminated: this was

10. Einstein, *Relativity*, 61.
11. Einstein, *Relativity*, 62.

the main motivation for him to work out the theory of general relativity. According to him, this problem of classical mechanics was already clear for Newton himself and he "attempted to invalidate it, but without success."[12] However, Ernst Mach, the most important positivist philosopher of the late nineteenth century, "recognized it most clearly of all" and claimed that "mechanics must be placed on a new basis."[13] Mach's claim was successfully achieved, according to Einstein, by the theory of general relativity.

The results of optics and electrodynamics in the nineteenth century not only played a significant role in the formulation of special relativity but also in the development of general relativity since these results led to the introduction of the concept of the *gravitational field*. Consequently, there is no directly and immediately acting gravitational force (e.g., between the Earth and the Moon) as was initially conceived by Newton; rather, the mass of the Earth creates a particular gravitational field around its mass-center and, in reality, this field determines the movement of the Moon. It follows that the gravitational field can neither be identified with real space nor with Newton's absolute space; it is but a *mathematical abstraction* from the laws of Newton: it can be used very successfully in practice, but there is, in fact, no answer what its real metaphysical basis is—that is, what the real medium of gravitational effects is. Moreover, contrary to the electric and magnetic fields, it has an extraordinary quality: its effect on the movement of objects does not depend on the mass of these objects and what their actual physical states are. With the famous experiment of Galilei, gravitational acceleration, contrary to other accelerations, does not depend on the fact that the ball rolling down a slope is lead or wood.

Mathematically, Newton's formulas treat this strange—and, in a philosophical sense, very problematic—situation in the following way: normal (inertial) acceleration (a), which is always the consequence of a direct material effect, is directly proportional to the accelerating force (F) and inversely proportional to the mass of the accelerated object (m)—that is, $a = \frac{F}{m}$. However, gravitational acceleration (a_g) between distant objects is directly proportional to the mass of the accelerating object (M) that creates the gravitational field and inversely proportional to the squares of the distance which is between the centers of the two objects (r^2)—that is, $a_g = G\frac{M}{r^2}$, where G is the gravitational constant and the mass of the accelerated object has no role in the acceleration. Notice the vital role of the centers of the objects in the latter case. Nonetheless, now the question is: what is the reason that gravitational acceleration has these strange qualities? (1) There is no real medium in which

---

12. Einstein, *Relativity*, 72.
13. Einstein, *Relativity*, 72–73.

the gravitational effect propagates; (2) the mass of the accelerated object does not matter; and (3) the decrease of the gravitational force is proportional to the squares of the distance of the centers of the objects, why not only to the distance? By contrast, the reason why the acceleration is directly proportional to our accelerating efforts and inversely proportional to the mass of the object ($a=F/m$) is quite clear when we are accelerating a body with our own hands; as well as why the centers has no role at all in the process. However, Einstein does not search for the answers to these essential philosophical questions; he just wants to extend his theory of special relativity to accelerating systems. Nonetheless, I will answer these questions in the next subchapter based on Alexander's theory of space-time.

It is well-known that the basis of the theory of general relativity is the so-called *equivalence principle*. As Smolin puts it:

> This is why Einstein was a genius of the first order. Not because of the mathematical complexities of the eventual realization of general relativity . . . but because of how he succeeded in changing our perspective about one of the simplest aspects of our experience.[14]

That is, there is no such Newtonian gravitational force which pulls us down, but we experience as the chair as a counterforce *pushes us up*. The typical example of the equivalence principle is the falling elevator: there is the same physical state of weightlessness both in space and in a falling elevator. According to the Newtonian paradigm, however, in the first case, there is no gravitational effect which pulls us down, but in the latter one, it is exactly the case: the lift falls because of the gravitational force or field of the Earth. Einstein himself uses the following example:

Imagine a "spacious chest" in space in which there is an observer. This is our frame of reference. Suppose that there is a rope, outside, at the "top" of the chest, by which some alien "beings" are uniformly accelerating the chest with g—which is the value of the gravitational acceleration on the surface of Earth—compared to another chest (B), which is at rest, beside chest A, in space. It follows that if the observer in chest A does not know that the chest is in space, then he will probably think that the chest is on the surface of the Earth because, due to the acceleration, he does not experience any weightlessness and cannot detect any difference—even between the accelerations of falling lead and wooden balls.[15] This means, according to Einstein, that the two *understandings*—(1) that from the point of reference

---

14. Smolin, *Time Reborn*, 67.
15. Einstein, *Relativity*, 66–67.

of chest B, chest A *is accelerating* and (2) that from the point of reference of chest A, chest A *is at rest in a gravitational field*—can be regarded as physically *equivalent* to each other.

> We have thus good grounds for extending the [Galilean] principle of relativity to include bodies of reference which are accelerated with respect to each other, and, as a result, we have gained a powerful argument for a generalized postulate of relativity.
>
> We must note carefully that the possibility of this mode of interpretation rests on the fundamental property of the gravitational field of giving all bodies the same acceleration.[16]

There is still no explanation for this strange fundamental property of gravitation that the mass of accelerated objects does not matter; even so, this is the basis that the Galilean principle of relativity can be generalized—that is, can be extended from resting or uniformly moving systems onto accelerating ones; otherwise, the observer in chest A could detect with his instruments that, in reality, he is not in a resting gravitational field, where heavier balls fall faster, for example, but in an accelerating system (chest), where lead and wooden balls "fall" in the same way. This means that the same object can be regarded as resting (or uniformly moving) from certain frames of reference and as accelerating from certain other frames of reference, but the two physical descriptions are still equivalent to each other. Precisely the same way as Galilei identified resting and uniformly moving systems with each other against the Aristotelian notion that rest (in reference to the center of the universe) is distinguished compared to any movement.

At this point, we should ask which frame of reference is the real one: is chest A accelerating or is it at rest in a gravitational field? As we have seen in the previous subchapters, the theory of special relativity cannot say which system's time goes slower in the metaphysical sense because it can only state anything about the different properties of a system *in reference to other systems*. In consequence, if someone randomly chooses another frame of reference, the formerly uniformly moving system will halt and the resting system starts to move (and vice versa), and since, according to the Galilean principle of relativity, rest and uniform motion are equivalent physical states, there is no real basis to decide which system is, in fact, moving and which system is at rest. In the case of Einstein's chest A, at least at first glance, the situation is the same: from the frame of reference of chest B, the observer in chest A is accelerating, but from the other frame of reference of chest A, he is at rest in a gravitational field. Vice versa, however, the situation, contrary to special relativity, is *not the same* at all since, despite the fact that chest B is accelerating

16. Einstein, *Relativity*, 68.

at exactly the same rate in reference to chest A as chest A is accelerating to chest B, it still cannot be stated that, from another frame of reference, there is a gravitational field present in the resting chest B.

Gravitation is a more tricky phenomenon than any uniform motion. What is the reason for this difference? The reason is that the starting point of Einstein's whole thought experiment was that chest A is, *in fact*, accelerating, thanks to the alien beings who pull it with the rope. This is not true at all for chest B, which is pulled by nobody. So, one can, of course, choose his preferred frame of reference, but it will not change the empirical fact that, in the case of chest A, *there is a real, material effect causing acceleration*, while, in the case of chest B, *there is none*. Therefore, the observer in chest A could merely *think* that he is at rest in the gravitational field of the Earth because he *does not know* that he, in reality, is accelerating in space. For example, he does not know this fact because there is no window in the walls of the chest and he, of course, does not remember that he was kidnapped by aliens. So Einstein ignores a *real fact* (chest A is accelerating) just to show that in a *mathematical*—and thus, actually, in a kind of practical—*sense* acceleration and rest (more precisely, an accelerating system of reference, and such a system of reference that is at rest, but there is a gravitational field present, and the gravitational acceleration of this field exactly complies with the inertial acceleration of the former system of reference) can be *regarded* as equivalent physical states. Moreover, although Einstein's whole train of thought is *based on* this real fact, he ignores it. In the case of the inverse acceleration of chest B, his argument would not be correct. This means that, in Einstein's understanding, the equivalence principle is a *mathematical correlation*, not a metaphysical one. So, in this sense, he perfectly follows Galilei and classical physics, searching only for practical solutions in a definite, exact conceptual framework (6.2). Nonetheless, Einstein himself says the following about this problem:

> I must warn the reader against a misconception suggested by these considerations. A gravitational field exists for the man in the chest despite the fact that there was no such field for the co-ordinate system first chosen. Now we might easily suppose that the existence of a gravitational field is always only an apparent one. We might also think that, regardless of the kind of gravitational field which may be present, we could always choose another reference-body such that no gravitational field exists with reference to it. This is by no means true for all gravitational fields but only for those of quite special form. It is, for

instance, impossible to choose a body of reference such that, as judged from it, the gravitational field of the earth (in its entirety) vanishes.[17]

So, according to Einstein, the gravitational field in chest A still exists. His reasoning is that it is not always possible to choose such a frame of reference in reference to which there is no gravitational field in the system in question—that is, in reference to which the system is only accelerating—and his example is the Earth. Therefore, contrary to the theory of special relativity, where everything is only the question of the well-chosen frame of reference, in the theory of general relativity, there are such distinguished systems of reference with gravitational fields like Earth in the case of which there are no such other accelerating systems of reference in reference to which the gravitational field of the distinguished systems (the gravitational field of the Earth, for example) vanishes (at least entirely). The reason for Einstein's last statement is that—contrary, for example, to chest A, which, in reference to chest B, is accelerating in only one direction of one dimension, so, from the point of view of chest B, its gravitational field could easily vanish into acceleration—there is no such frame of reference in reference to which the gravitational field of the Earth could disappear—that is, could be transformed, in the mathematical sense, into acceleration—because in that case, the Earth would have to accelerate in all directions of all three dimensions, according to the particular nature of the gravitational filed of the Earth, and this is just impossible.

Einstein's argument, however, is wrong on several points. (1) First, the reason that there are gravitational systems in reference to which such frames of reference from the point of view of which the given gravitational fields can be transformed into accelerations cannot be found does not change the fact at all that, for example, chest A is not such a system; so its gravitational field can easily be transformed. (2) Moreover, it is perfectly known that in the case of chest A, such a system of reference is not even needed because in reality, there is no gravitational field present in chest A—it is dragged by alien beings in acceleration. (3) Finally, contrary to Einstein's most profound conviction, as we will see in detail in the next subchapter, such a frame of reference can be given from the point of view of which the gravitational field of the Earth vanishes into acceleration entirely. Actually, contrary to Einstein's mathematical understanding, this is the *real existential meaning* of the equivalence principle.

However, to do this in a coherent way, we have to leave behind the practical/mathematical solutions that ignore real facts as well as the exact

17. Einstein, *Relativity*, 69.

conceptual frameworks of modern physics that strangle our options due to the beliefs of positivism and materialism and, once again, base our approach on experience, personal facts, and philosophical principles. We have to leave behind the ruling positivist approach, which does not want to allow real philosophical (metaphysical) explanations into science—even for Einstein himself. This positivist approach is the reason that after the exact mathematical definition of the equivalence principle, he struggles with the answer concerning which point of reference is real and which is only a mathematical abstraction. Nonetheless, Einstein's primary goal, as it was shown, is not to answer fundamental philosophical questions concerning the nature of different aspects of reality but rather to fulfill Ernst Mach's claim and, with the expansion of his theory of special relativity, to formulate a broader conceptual framework in physics—which now also includes accelerating systems of reference. His main recognition is that in a mathematical (and practical) sense, accelerating and resting systems with gravitational fields present can be regarded as equivalent. The so famous curved spacetime is the consequence of this recognition.

Suppose that a body C uniformly moves compared to the resting chest B. However, if we choose chest A for frame of reference—which, compared to chest B, is accelerating—then compared to chest A, C will probably be accelerating in a curved path. The only case where this path will not be curved is one where the movements of A and B are on the same line. There is, of course, nothing surprising in this yet, it is simple classical mechanics. However, according to the equivalence principle, the curved accelerating movement of body C can be regarded as the gravitational effect of the gravitational field present in chest A. According to Einstein: "In general, rays of light are propagated curvilinearly in gravitational fields."[18]

Although he does not detail it at all, it is easy to see Einstein's conclusion. Let's take the Earth, for example, for frame of reference. The Earth is at rest, and since the velocity of Earth is negligible compared to the speed of light, for the sake of simplicity, let's consider the Earth to be at rest compared to the path of light as well. If the Earth were a classical Galilean system of reference—that is, if it had no gravitational field—then the light would go beside the Earth in a straight line. But since, in reality, it has a gravitational field (which complies with the point of view of chest A, according to which, chest A is at rest with a gravitational field), and in a mathematical sense, this gravitational field is equivalent to an accelerating movement toward the path of the light beam (which, in turn, complies with the point of view of chest B,

---

18. Einstein, *Relativity*, 75.

according to which, chest A is accelerating), it follows that the light beam will go by the Earth on a path which is curved toward the Earth.

As we have seen, Einstein, according to positivist philosophy, did not base his considerations on real metaphysical (ordering) principles concerning reality—moreover, he started his whole train of thought neglecting actual empirical facts—but rather on a mathematical equivalence: we can model both resting and accelerating systems with the same mathematical apparatus in the same exact conceptual framework. This means that he does not want to say that if there is a gravitational field present, then there will necessarily be a real acceleration and vice versa—that is, he does not want to say that the Earth is, *in fact*, accelerating in every direction at the same time. But if this is the case, and the Earth is, in reality, at rest and not accelerating toward the light beam—as chest A would do—then in order for the light to go by the Earth on a curved path, Einstein has to suppose that *the space is curved* around the Earth; this is the reason that the light goes on a curved path. So, in a sense, light still goes in a straight line, but the meaning of the straight line is changed. Finally, the well-known conclusion follows that the gravitational field is nothing else but the curvature of space-time caused by the mass of material objects. My question is: whether it is well-established to conclude a real property of space-time from a mathematical equivalence based on neglecting real facts?

Einstein explains his reasoning in detail with another example. Suppose that there is a disc in uniform, rotary motion and there are, once again, two observers. Observer A is at the edge of the disc, while observer B is outside of the disc. Thus, due to the rotary motion of the disc, observer A is continuously accelerating, but B is at rest. It follows that observer A—at the edge of the disc—experiences a force which acts outwards, in a radial direction. Observer B understands this force as an effect of inertia—that is, as a centrifugal force. Observer A, however, according to the theory of general relativity, can regard himself as a resting system of reference, which means that he understands the centrifugal force acting on him due to the rotary motion of the disc as an effect of a gravitational field. Then, observer A starts to detect the properties of the space-time continuum of the disc with his clocks and measuring-rods. The questions are, of course, what will be the results at the edge of disc (A) and at the center of it (A')? *From the point of view of B*, both himself (B) and the center of the disc (A') is at rest, but the edge of the disc (A) moves perpendicular to the radius of the disc with the given speed of v. It follows, according to the theory of special relativity, that the clocks at the edge of the disc will go slower than the clock at the center of it and the measuring-rods will be shorter in the perpendicular direction to the radius compared to the measuring-rod at the center—that is, space-time is not "straight." Einstein's conclusion is this:

> It is obvious that the same effect would be noted by an observer whom we will imagine sitting alongside his clock at the center of the circular disc. Thus on our circular disc, or, to make the case more general, in every gravitational field, a clock will go more quickly or less quickly, according to the position in which the clock is situated (at rest). For this reason, it is not possible to obtain a reasonable definition of time with the aid of clocks which are arranged at rest with respect to the body of reference.[19]

The question is why should observer A' (who is, of course, observer A at the center of the disc) get the same results as observer B if the starting point of Einstein's whole reasoning was that the disc is *at rest* from the point of view of A (and thus of A'), contrary to the point of view of B, from which it moves? This *literally* means that from the point of view of observer A, *there is no difference* between the speeds of the center of the disc (observer A') and the edge of it (observer A); therefore, *there will be no differences* in measured times and distances. The answer is that Einstein still assumes, according to the theory of general relativity, that acceleration and rest with a gravitational field can be regarded as equivalent. So, as it was shown in the case of his former example of chest A, Einstein (1) firstly neglects the real, empirical fact that the disc is moving (spinning due to some material effect) to be able to assume that it is at rest and that, from the point of view of observer A, there is a gravitational field present in it. (2) Then, from the point of view of B, he neglects his former neglecting and, according to his theory of special relativity, based on the fact that the disk is moving, he claims that clocks and measuring-rods will give different results at the center (observer A') and the edge (observer A) of the disc. (3) Finally, he once more neglects the empirical fact that the disc is moving, concluding that the clocks and measuring-rods give different results due to their exact coordinates on the disc because of the gravitational field present in the resting disc; the space-time of the disc is therefore curved.

Notice that, as we have seen in the former subchapters, according to the theory of special relativity, there are measured times and distances merely in reference to a particular point of view—that is, only in a mathematical and not in a real, metaphysical sense. Also, notice that Einstein does not measure space-time itself but rather the different space and time distances *on the disc*, a rigid, material body, and he assigns certain, exact x, y, z, and t coordinates to the points and instants of this rigid, material body. Therefore,

19. Einstein, *Relativity*, 81.

these coordinates describe certain abstract properties of a material body, not the properties of space-time itself. Nonetheless, according to Einstein, the consequence of the phenomenon that the clocks and measuring-rods at different coordinates behave differently is the following:

> This proves that the propositions of Euclidean geometry cannot hold exactly on the rotating disc, nor in general in a gravitational field, at least if we attribute the length i to the rod in all positions and in every orientation. Hence the idea of a straight line also loses its meaning.[20]

The mathematical solution of this problem is, of course, to replace the "straight," Cartesian coordinates of Euclidean space with its more general, "curved" form—called Gaussian coordinates—which can treat these kinds of curved "spaces" as in the case of the surface of the rotating disc. The reason I wrote "space" in quotation marks is, on the one hand—as Einstein himself also emphasizes—in this mathematical treatment, it becomes utterly meaningless to differentiate time coordinates from the space ones and, on the other, that, as we have just seen, this is not the understanding of real space and real time at all but rather *the mathematical treatment of an abstract, four-dimensional continuum based on a rigid, material body,* the dimensions of which physicists often just mark as x_1, x_2, x_3, x_4. In Einstein's words:

> We refer the four-dimensional space-time continuum in an arbitrary manner to Gauss co-ordinates. We assign to every point of the continuum (event) four numbers, x_1, x_2, x_3, x_4 (co-ordinates), which have not the least direct physical significance, but only serve the purpose of numbering the points of the continuum in a definite but arbitrary manner. This arrangement does not even need to be of such a kind that we must regard x_1, x_2, x_3, as 'space' co-ordinates and x_4 as a 'time' co-ordinate.[21]

The coordinates are arbitrary and have no physical significance (existential meaning) because, according to positivism—or, in this case, more precisely, a physicalist metaphysical conviction—*neither space nor time is real.* The coordinates are perfectly exact parts of a perfectly exact conceptual framework but not real at all. Therefore, "space" is only the lack of matter between points of masses and "time" is only the fourth dimension of this vacuum accurately defined by four-dimensional Gauss coordinates.

> Let us consider, for instance, a material point with any kind of motion. If this point had only a momentary existence without

20. Einstein, *Relativity*, 82.
21. Einstein, *Relativity*, 94.

> duration, then it would be described in space-time by a single system of values x_1, x_2, x_3, x_4. Thus, its permanent existence must be characterized by an infinitely large number of such systems of values, the co-ordinate values of which are so close together as to give continuity; corresponding to the material point, we thus have a (uni-dimensional) line in the four-dimensional continuum. In the same way, any such lines in our continuum correspond to many points in motion. The only statements having regard to these points which can claim a physical existence are in reality the statements about their encounters. In our mathematical treatment, such an encounter is expressed in the fact that the two lines which represent the motions of the points in question have a particular system of co-ordinate values, x_1, x_2, x_3, x_4 in common. After mature consideration, the reader will doubtless admit that in reality, such encounters constitute the only actual evidence of a time-space nature with which we meet in physical statements.[22]

This remains from Newton's absolute space-time after the generalization of the Galilean principle of relativity to accelerating systems of reference by Einstein. So, perhaps it is not well-established to conclude a real property from a mathematical equivalence, but this fact has no consequence on Einstein's argument because he does not make any statement concerning the real properties of real space-time. Nonetheless, the point of his claim is that *the system of these Gauss coordinates ("point-instants") has to be the new general body of reference.*

> The Gauss co-ordinate system has to take the place of the body of reference. The following statement corresponds to the fundamental idea of the general principle of relativity: "*All Gaussian co-ordinate systems are essentially equivalent for the formulation of the general laws of nature.*"[23]

6.6 Understanding General Relativity

In the mathematical or positivist sense, Einstein's theory of relativity is one of the most successful theories in physics, and it is also one of the two fundamental pillars of modern physics beyond doubt. However, in the traditional philosophical or metaphysical sense, it gives few answers to our most important questions; moreover, Einstein's argumentation, as we have seen,

22. Einstein, *Relativity*, 94–95.
23. Einstein, *Relativity*, 97.

can be questioned at several points. Nonetheless, the point of his theory is that the Galilean principle of relativity can be generalized to accelerating systems of reference by the equivalence of accelerating and resting systems with gravitational fields—where the systems of Gauss coordinates become the new general frame of reference instead of the Newtonian absolute space-time or the Lorentzian absolute ether. In the mathematical sense, the equivalence is perfectly working in this exact conceptual framework, although, in reality, Einstein could not identify accelerating systems with resting ones with gravitational fields. He always just neglected the real, factual differences—for example, that it is perfectly known that in reality, there is no gravitational field in chest A, but it is accelerating due to a material effect. As a matter of fact, in the case of Earth, he did not even try the real identification—after the case of chest A (or, in the case of observer A and A' of the rotating disc), he fell into severe problems of reasoning. Why does Einstein feel the need to fall into traps of those problematic arguments concerning the reality of the equivalence when, in the mathematical and in the practical senses, his theory works perfectly?

The answer follows from the next question: how could Einstein's theory work perfectly in the mathematical sense if, in reality, resting systems with gravitational fields and accelerating systems were different? The answer is: in no way. Therefore, if it still works perfectly, then resting systems with gravitational fields will *have to be entirely identical* with accelerating systems in reality—that is, *in the metaphysical sense, too*—even in the peculiar case of Earth. This conclusion, of course, is such a philosophical statement that is utterly needless in a consistently positivist approach. As it could be seen, Einstein fundamentally follows a positivist approach—probably primarily due to the influence of Ernst Mach—but at this point—probably because of the above reasoning—he still feels the need for a more profound metaphysical argument. It is well-known that in the case of quantum mechanics, Einstein could never entirely accept the mainstream positivist approach of Niels Bohr and his followers.

As we have seen in the previous subchapter, the point of Einstein's argument about the metaphysical identification of accelerating and resting systems with gravitational fields—that is, in chest A, trailed by aliens and similar systems, the gravitational field is not just apparent but real—is that there are such resting systems of reference, like the Earth, in reference to which there are no such other systems of reference from the point of view of which the given gravitational fields can be transformed into accelerations (at least not entirely). However, the real situation is exactly the opposite in both the case of chest A (inertial accelerations) and in the case of the Earth (gravitational accelerations).

First, if we want to speak about real metaphysical identity, we cannot neglect but *have to face* actual, empirical facts—namely, there is no gravitational field at all in chest A and those similar systems of reference which are accelerating due to a visible, *material* effect. These *inertially* accelerating systems can be modeled as they would be resting systems with gravitational fields present only because of two reasons: (1) at the deeper level, rest and (gravitational) acceleration are, in fact, exactly the same (in the metaphysical sense), and (2) the real factual differences are neglected. For example, in the real gravitational field of the Earth, the intensity of the gravitational effect changes by distance, but this is not true at all in the case of chest A. In fact, with really precise instruments, the observer in the chest could detect that he is not in a gravitational field because the intensity of the "gravitational field" of the chest would be exactly the same at both the bottom and the top of the chest. Since gravitational fields are multidimensional and have a specific *center*, the observer could also detect a slightly different intensity at the middle and the two edges of the chest at a certain height. Inertial accelerations are real due to tangible, material effects and can be modeled as resting gravitational fields *only within certain limits*. Therefore, in this case, this is indeed just an equivalence in the mathematical sense. Nonetheless, at a lower level, it has a real metaphysical basis.

Second, if there is real metaphysical identity between *gravitationally* accelerating systems and resting systems with gravitational fields, then it will mean that the Earth and similar resting systems with gravitational fields *are such systems at rest which, at the same time, are accelerating into every direction of their gravitational field*. It cannot be any exception in any direction; otherwise, the identity would not be real. More exactly, since the concept of the gravitational field is only a mathematical abstraction—and, in the case of chest A and similar, inertially-accelerating systems, on the basis of the equivalence principle, it is, in fact, used in this way—the real, existential meaning of this concept is the gravitational acceleration of those systems (e.g., the Earth that possess this property), not the gravitational acceleration of objects (which are, for instance, in the gravitational field of the Earth).

With Einstein's example: the physical state of the observer in the accelerating chest A is not just analogous in the mathematical sense to the physical state of another observer who is at the surface of the Earth "at rest" but also is identical in the philosophical (metaphysical) sense: both observers are *factually accelerating*. The only difference—which will also make a slight difference between the exact mathematical treatments—is that the observer in chest A accelerates upwards due to a tangible *material* effect, while the observer on the surface of the Earth is accelerating upwards due to the *gravitational* effect. With another famous example, the weightless physical state of a falling observer in an elevator is not just analogous to the also weightless physical state of another observer who is in space but also is entirely identical in the metaphysical sense. Both the falling observer and the other observer in space are *at perfect rest*. *The surface of the Earth* is accelerating toward the falling observer—not the falling observer toward the surface of the Earth—and this is the reason that he has no weight at all: there is no gravitational field at the place of the falling observer, only the acceleration of the Earth toward that point of space.

However, according to the mainstream physicalist metaphysics of positivism, this kind of understanding of the phenomenon is, of course, meaningless because it is self-evident that the Earth cannot accelerate in both directions of all three dimensions of space-time; or, more precisely, from the point of view of the Earth, if space-time was regarded to be the mathematical abstraction of a four-dimensional rigid material body, it is self-evident that space-time cannot accelerate toward the Earth from every direction: by definition, rigid, material bodies cannot go into two opposite directions at the same time. As we have seen, Einstein himself halted at this point in his thinking. But if we regard space-time *as real*, which has its *own nature*—and not just as the mathematical abstraction of a four-dimensional, rigid, material body—this will not only be possible but also really obvious. However, for this step, we have to change our view on the movements of Earth as much as Copernicus changed his own view when he left behind the traditional, Earth-centric view of the Middle Ages.

Galilei, expanding Copernicus's revelation, rejected the Aristotelian concept of the center of the universe. This is the main philosophical core (existential meaning) of the Galilean principle of relativity: there is no distinguished center in the universe in reference to which the movements of different objects can and have to be determined; rather, every object has its own center. Therefore, he concluded, which object is at rest and which object is moving is due to our chosen point of reference. The equivalence of rest and uniform motion, however, is not the straight consequence of the philosophical meaning of this principle but rather the consequence of a mathematical/practical abstraction: Galilei neglected gravitational effects and examined only closed type material entities among earthly conditions before one of a straight and rigid material background. Newton, following Galilei's method, on the one hand, abstracted an absolute background ("space-time") on the basis of an infinite, four-dimensional, rigid, material body, which became the new, absolute frame of reference of every motion instead of the Aristotelian center of the universe and, on the other, generalized Galilei's findings and defined the laws of motion and gravitation in this absolute and exact conceptual framework. Therefore, space and time lost their independent reality and became the lack of matter among material mass-points, and because of their supposed absolute nature, the Galilean principle of relativity does not apply to them.

However, later from the law of propagation of light, it seemed that the Galilean principle of relativity also does not apply to the real uniform motion of light. Einstein, on the one hand, introduced a new postulate about the constant speed of light from any inertial frame of reference and, on the other, created a new mathematical form for the principle of relativity to solve the problem. By this solution, he rejected the reality of Newtonian absolute space-time. Then, he generalized the Galilean principle of relativity based on the mathematical equivalence of acceleration and rest or uniform motion with gravitational field, and thus, the mathematical systems of Gauss coordinates became the new relative general frame of reference instead of Newtonian absolute space-time. This means, on the one hand, that Einstein's equivalence principle is, at least in the mathematical sense, an extension of the Galilean principle of relativity—which is already the extension of Copernicus's revelation—and, on the other, that now, at last, the last remnants of space-time are also under the validity of the principle of relativity.

Now, the question is: what could be said about the Galilean principle of relativity if (1) we do not neglect gravitational effects in the first place and (2) do not replace space-time with a mathematical abstraction of a rigid, multidimensional material body but (3) use the principle of relativity in the case of real space-time, too.

So, the main philosophical core of the Galilean principle of relativity is that there is no Aristotelian center of the universe which determines the movements of every object; rather, every object has its own center and determines its own movement according to its own nature. In this sense, they have their own natural movements until, of course, some external effect changes these movements. However, based on Alexander's theory of space and time as well as the empirical observations of light, the natural behavior of these centers—and, thus, the behavior of the objects that include these centers—are not the same in all cases, as Galilei supposed: there are not just closed type entities (or, with the Newtonian term, mass-points) but there is light, too—that is, open type entities which cannot be regarded as simple mass-points in a vacuum. Therefore, the existence and particular nature of these kinds of entities questioned the validity of the principle of relativity because it is not only due to the chosen frame of reference which objects are at rest and which objects are moving.

Suppose that, similar to my former example (6.4), there are two closed type entities, A and B, on axis X, and contrary to Galilei, do not neglect gravitational effects. In themselves, both A and B are at rest. But in itself, it is a nearly meaningless, tautological statement because there is no absolute center of the universe in reference to which this statement would have any meaningful content. So, the question is: they are at rest compared to what? In relation to B, A is accelerating toward B due to the gravitational effect between the two entities. However, it is true vice versa since, in relation to A, B is accelerating toward A due to the same gravitational effect. Therefore, it is only due to the chosen frame of reference which entity is at rest and which is accelerating. If we do not neglect gravitational effects and do not follow Galilei in the mathematical/practical abstraction of his own principle, then the philosophical (existential) meaning of the principle of relativity will not be that rest and uniform motion are physically the same states but rather it seems it will be *the equivalence of rest and acceleration*.

However, the situation is not so simple because, similarly to Einstein, we also have to face the fact that there is light and the law of propagation of it. Suppose that there is an open type entity, C on axis X, too. In reference to itself, it is also at rest—as are the open type entities of A and B—but this also is, of course, a nearly meaningless, tautological statement, as was our statement above. Thus, the real question is again the same: it is at rest compared to what? For the sake of clarity—and similarly to Einstein's theory of special relativity—let's neglect the gravitational effects for a moment. Then, in reference to A, C is uniformly moving at the constant speed of c; but in reference to C, A moves uniformly at the constant speed of c. It seems that it is only due to the arbitrarily chosen frame of reference which entity is at rest and which is in uniform motion.

However, we perfectly know that the behavior of light is *not* only due to the chosen frame of reference. Einstein's answer was an *absolute postulate*: light always propagates at the constant speed of c *in a vacuum*, regardless of the chosen frame of reference. This answer was based *on Galilei's and Newton's mathematical/practical abstraction* of the principle of relativity in the absolute framework of space-time—which, in turn, is the mathematical abstraction of a rigid, multidimensional, infinite, material body—due to their exact conceptual and explanatory framework neglecting our natural experiences (personal facts) of time and space, while our answer was based *on the main philosophical core* of the Galilean principle of relativity that there is no Aristotelian center of the universe which determines the movements of all objects but rather every object has its own center and determines its own movement according to its own nature in such a system of emergent space-time from which these centers emerge according to their own nature due to our conceptual and explanatory system based on our natural experiences (personal facts) of space and time. Consequently, closed type entities are *at rest in relation to space*, while open type entities, like light, are *uniformly moving in relation to space* and, as we have seen, this is the real natural reason behind the law of propagation of light, not an independent and abstract postulate.

Now, let's get back to the equivalence of rest and acceleration. What is the meaning that A is accelerating in reference to B (or vice versa)? Normally, it means that the speed of A *compared to B* is increasing in time (a $=\frac{v}{t}$) and thus, the distance between A and B is decreasing at an accelerating rate (vice versa, this is entirely true as well). However, notice that this is again a Galilean mathematical/practical definition, where both the concepts of space and time—in fact, measured distances by rods and mechanical clocks—are based on the abstraction of an infinite, four-dimensional, rigid, material body—that is, it is about *inertial* accelerations of material bodies before a distinct, quasi-material background (in an abstract and absolute conceptual framework). Now ask what is the meaning of gravitational acceleration—that is, acceleration without material effects—based on the main philosophical core of the Galilean principle of relativity and *in relation to real space-time*, which is also under the validity of the principle of relativity? And, more generally, what are the behaviors of closed and open type entities in relation to this kind of concept of space-time based on personal facts?

As we have seen in subchapter 6.2, an open (light) type entity is a comprehensive, material entity with a center that moves in its open dimension uniformly and has no physical time in this dimension. The former means that it moves in relation to space, while the latter means that it is at rest in relation to time in its open dimension; it has no persisting time in this dimension (or with Einstein's term: time stops at speed c).

A closed (electron) type entity is a comprehensive, material entity with a center that is at rest and has its own physical time. The former means that in itself it is at rest in relation to space—if there is no material effect (force) acting upon it, of course—while the latter means that it is moving in relation to time—that is, *it is continuously persisting in time*. The reason of this fact is that at the lower level, this comprehensive material entity is nothing else but the manifestation of time in three dimensions around the center of the entity; it has time which circles its center in three dimensions. This means that a closed type, comprehensive, material entity *as a material entity at the higher level of matter is at rest* in relation to the point of space-time of its center but at the same time *as time (that manifests itself in three dimensions) at the lower level of space-time is accelerating in both directions of all dimensions* in relation to the point of space-time of its center. My claim is that this is the real *metaphysical (existential) meaning* of Einstein's equivalence principle—based on Copernicus's revelation, on the philosophical core of the Galilean principle of relativity, and on Alexander's theory of space and time.

When Einstein claims that from the point of view of observer A, there is a gravitational field on the disc, he can claim this because of the following reasons: (1) he supposes that there is an external observer, B, who is at rest—although Einstein does not specify compared to whom this other observer is at rest because, compared to observer A, he is not at rest at all but rather rapidly accelerating, and there is no other possible frame of reference in the example—and from the point of view of this observer B, the disc is rotating (accelerating), thus there is an effect of inertia, a centrifugal force on the disc. (2) Then, according to the equivalence of acceleration and rest with a gravitational field present, from the point of view of A, he states that the disc is a resting system with a gravitational field present. The situation is also precisely the same in his earlier example of chest A and the resting observer of chest B—except for, of course, that in this earlier example, the acceleration is only one dimensional. And, as it was shown, the main problem with his argument is that he always has to change the point of view from which he speaks that, at least in a mathematical sense, he could identify acceleration with rest with a gravitational field present because, in reality, we perfectly know that neither chest A nor the disc is in a resting gravitational field. A material object as a material entity at the material level of reality *cannot be both a system at rest with a gravitational field present and a system in accelerating motion at the same time.*

However, if, according to the concept of emergence, a real difference can be made between the material level (frame of reference), where the comprehensive material entity is at rest, and the level of space-time (frame of reference), where the time (composite part) of the entity is in an accelerating motion, then there is no need for such problematic, external points of reference (like chest B and observer B, outside the disc) and the philosophical contradictions can be solved: the gravitating entity is at rest and in an accelerating motion at the same time. And, actually, this is the real metaphysical reason that Einstein's theory of general relativity works.

So, how does it work? How can a closed type entity be at rest and accelerating in space at the same time? The fact that a closed type entity is at rest in space is the consequence of its structure that due to its physical time, it has a *definite, comprehensive physical structure at the higher material level* in relation to the point of space-time of its center, and this relation does not change until the entity is persisting in time. However, *at the lower level of space-time*, it has no such definite structure but also, due to its physical time, *it is accelerating* from its center in every direction—that is, *toward every point of space-time*. Since, according to the Galilean principle of relativity, there is no absolute frame of reference (Aristotelian center of the universe), this latter statement is perfectly *equivalent* to the statement that at the level of space-time, *every point of space-time is accelerating toward the center of the closed type, material entity in question.* As a matter of fact, from the point of view of the material entity, this latter statement is, of course, the exact formulation of the acceleration. Naturally, in an absolute Newtonian concept of space-time or in Einstein's mathematical abstraction of Gauss coordinates, where space-time itself has no reality, this statement is meaningless. For the meaning of this statement, space-time has to be regarded, on the one hand, as real and, on the other, as a continuum, which is, similarly to other (material) aspects of reality, also under the validity of the main philosophical core of the Galilean principle of relativity.

How much will the acceleration of a given point of space-time toward the material entity be? Since space-time is an emergent continuum—and not a rigid, material body—(almost) every point of space-time will be accelerating at a different rate. According to the principle of relativity, the actual value of the acceleration of a given point of space-time is, of course, equivalent to the value by which the material entity accelerates toward the point of space-time in question. Thus, the actual value of the acceleration is the consequence of two factors: (1) the amount of time that manifests itself in the material entity—that is, the exact value of its moment of inertia, which, at the material level, is called *mass*; (2) the *distance* between the center of the material entity and the given point of space-time. We have seen three philosophical questions in the previous subchapter concerning Newton's formula ($a_g = G\frac{M}{r^2}$) for which we now have answers:

(1) Why is there no real medium in which the gravitational effect propagates? In other words, why are there no gravitons? Because there are no gravitational effects at all; there are no gravitational fields. The concept of gravitational effects or forces and the concept of gravitational fields are mathematical abstractions based on real material effects and forces. However, according to the real, existential meaning of the equivalence principle, at the level of space-time, there are no such material effects, just the gravitational acceleration of open type entities in space-time. *Material effects belong to the material level.*

(2) Why does the mass of accelerated (falling) objects not matter? Because the accelerated objects are *at rest* in space. Newton's well-known formula ($a = \frac{F}{m}$) refers only to material (inertial) accelerations, which take place at the material level due to material effects between mass-points in a vacuum or a material medium. Newton did not regard space-time as real according to its own nature and tried to model gravitational acceleration as a kind of strange material phenomenon. Gravitational acceleration,

however, takes place at the level of space-time, which means that the point of space-time is accelerating toward the accelerating object (e.g., Earth) at which the center of the accelerated object is at rest. It follows that inertial acceleration is the higher-level and gravitational acceleration is the lower-level case of acceleration, to which, according to the logic of emergence, *different principles* apply and *different laws* refer. This is the reason that it does not matter what the weight (or gravitational mass) of the falling object is. With Galilei's famous experiment, it does not matter that the material of the falling object is lead or wood, light or heavy, because gravitational accelerations take place at the level of space-time, between the center of the Earth and the points of space-time where the falling objects are at rest. The application of Newton's formula (F=ma) to gravitational accelerations—as, for example, Einstein puts it: "(Force) =(gravitational mass) X (intensity of the gravitational field)"—is false.[24] Weight is not the consequence of the fact that a gravitational field is pulling down an object on the surface of the Earth and a counterforce occurs; rather, from the point of view of the object, it is the consequence as the surface of the Earth is pushing the object up. The source of this interaction is, of course, the gravitational acceleration of Earth, but this interaction takes place *at the material level, between two material objects*. Therefore, at this level, from the point of view of the object, it is a simple, inertial acceleration due to the material effect between the surface of the Earth and the object, and thus the original Newtonian formula applies: F=ma. There is no gravitational mass, which is surprisingly the same in every case with inertial mass. There is only inertial mass, and, according to the equivalence principle, the gravitational acceleration of Earth. This is the reason that the situation of Einstein's chest A and the surface of the Earth are slightly different. In chest A, according to the inertial acceleration of chest A, at the material level, the acceleration is homogenous; the floor of the chest is accelerating toward the points of space of the chest of the same rate. On the surface of the Earth, however, according to the gravitational acceleration of Earth at the level of space-time, it is not homogenous; the surface of the Earth is accelerating toward the different points of space-time at a slightly different rate.

(3) Why is the decrease of gravitational acceleration proportional to the squares of the distance of the centers of the objects—why not only, for example, to the distance? Because from the point of view of an accelerated object (or, more exactly, from the point of view of the point of space-time of its center), it is a two-dimensional perspective on the physical time of the accelerating object—that is, the acceleration takes place in two dimensions.

24. Einstein, *Relativity*, 65.

The accelerating object itself is, of course, three dimensional, and its acceleration is the proportional consequence of the amount of time that manifests in it in three dimensions. But from the point of view of the accelerated object, this manifestation only appears in the two perpendicular dimensions: in the third, straight dimension, the physical time of the accelerating object is just a point—that is, it does not change and does not matter.

However, Newton's simple formula ($a_g = G\frac{M}{r^2}$) is not entirely accurate since space-time is not the abstraction of a four-dimensional, infinite, rigid, material body but rather an emergent continuum that behaves according to the Galilean principle of relativity; with Einstein's concept, gravitation spreads through in a "curved space-time" and changes the world-line of mass-points. As we have seen, in Einstein's understanding, every point of "space-time" can be exactly defined by a Gaussian four-dimensional system of coordinates—which, in fact, is also a mathematical abstraction of an infinite, four-dimensional, rigid, material body (only it is not "straight" but instead "curved"). However, contrary to Newton's absolute space-time, it cannot be regarded as real in any sense, only the "encounters" of mass-points in these infinite, four-dimensional systems of coordinates. Here, the philosophical (metaphysical) question is: in which medium material processes (or the famous gravitational waves) take place if on the basis of this theory, space-time itself cannot be regarded as real but solely mass-points have certain exact x_1, x_2, x_3, and x_4 properties? This is a serious metaphysical problem; however, from a positivist approach, it can be neglected.

Nonetheless, by this mathematical treatment, Einstein is able to very precisely describe, on the one hand, the gravitational accelerations of material objects and, on the other, the relativistic changes in distances of "space-time" due to resting gravitational fields present. According to this treatment, material objects (e.g., falling balls) are not at rest in space during gravitational acceleration but rather move in "curved" space as gravitational acceleration would be the consequence of a material effect. However, if space-time is real and emergent—that is, under the validity of the Galilean principle of relativity—the equivalence principle will not only be the mathematical generalization of the Galilean principle of relativity to accelerating systems but also the *consistent application of the principle, both to gravitational accelerations and to space-time.*

It follows that the new, general "body of reference" is not just the mathematical abstraction of systems of Gaussian coordinates without any reality but rather real space-time—more exactly, the point-instants of space-time from which every material object emerges—both which are at rest at the material level and, in the meantime, at the level of space-time, accelerate in relation to space-time and which are at rest in time and the meantime uniformly moves in space in relation to space-time.

It also follows that gravitational accelerations and relativistic changes in distances of space-time are the consequences of the always moving, real continuum of space-time. Space-time is movement itself. And one of its manifestations is the gravitational acceleration of material objects due to their physical times. From the point of view of a material object (e.g., the Earth), the other object (e.g., a falling ball) does not accelerate in space but rather space-time itself flows toward the material object and carries the other object with itself, while that object is, in fact, at rest in relation to the accelerating space-time. The relativistic changes in the three-dimensional fabric of space-time are, in turn, the consequence of the fact that the physical time of a material entity, according to the Galilean principle of relativity, has different relations to (almost) every adjacent point of space-time; therefore, the distances in space-time will change among the adjacent points and instances of space-time. These gravitational accelerations of material objects and space-time and the relativistic changes in the fabric of space-time can be perfectly modeled with an abstract system of Gaussian coordinates—which, contrary to Cartesian coordinates, can describe these movements as the "curvatures" of the four-dimensional system of coordinates from a chosen static frame of reference. From a positivist point of view, it will be perfect, and even the "most beautiful of all existing physical theories" but simply does not give answers to our most fundamental philosophical questions and personal experiences concerning the different aspects of reality—for example, what is time.

6.7 Conclusion

According to Lee Smolin, the big trouble with modern physics is that it denies the reality of time. However, time, in fact, is our "best clue to fundamental reality." According to Samuel Alexander's emergentist theory of space and time, time is fundamental reality itself: even matter itself is the emergent manifestation of time. My primary claim in this chapter was that the emergent reality of time complies with the coherent application of the main philosophical core of the Galilean principle of relativity to every aspect of reality—and thus real space-time, too: every aspect of reality has its own center and behaves due to the nature of its own center and every relation among these centers is relative.

It is important to see that these are philosophical (metaphysical) claims. Galilei's principle of relativity was also a philosophical claim against the Aristotelian philosophical claim that there is an absolute center of the universe. Moreover, Galilei could recognize the importance of his principle in spite of the fact that the Earth was still under his feet and it definitely seemed that everything moves around it. These claims are not against physics or science; on the contrary, they are for physics and for science. Galilei's claim was against the Aristotelian understanding of science, while Smolin's, Alexander's, and my own are against the positivist (physicalist) philosophical understanding of science. Only Aristotelian philosophers said the opposite.

The ruling positivist understanding of physics and science came to power with the birth of modern physics as we could see in Einstein's philosophical understanding of his own theory. The strength of the positivist understanding in the short term is exactly the same as its weakness in the long run: it ignores the always problematic philosophical (metaphysical) questions and personal facts and puts the exact, practical/mathematical solutions in the foreground. However, as every independent philosophy, it has its own metaphysics—called physicalism—which denies the reality of time. In this spirit, Einstein formulated the equations of special relativity and the mathematical equivalence of accelerating systems and resting or uniformly moving systems with gravitational fields.

Nonetheless, as Smolin noted, he was a real genius—not because of his complex mathematical solutions but rather because he recognized that the Earth not just orbits and rotates—as Copernicus and Galilei found out—but also there is no such gravitational force which pulls us down, on the contrary, we feel as the surface of the Earth prevents us from falling. However, to take one more step and claim that the Earth not just orbits, rotates, and prevents us from falling but also pushes us up in the literal sense because it accelerates toward us in exactly the same way as an accelerating spaceship would do, that cannot be done with the positivist spirit of our era. To make this one more important step, we have to recognize the emergent reality of space-time based on personal facts as the relative general frame of reference of every real movement.

Expanding Copernicus's revelation, Galilei rejected the Aristotelian notion of the center of the universe. This is a definite philosophical claim that has positive existential meaning: every aspect of reality has its own center and behaves due to the nature of its own center; there is no absolute/objective point of reference. But, at the same time, with his mathematical and practical solutions, he created a scientific tradition that at first led to the Newtonian abstraction of absolute space-time, then to the Laplacian ideal of objective knowledge, and finally, to the positivist concept of science, which "fixed" these mistakes by denying their ontological consequences and thus created even more exact and abstract mathematical solutions to "answer" our questions. Einstein's mathematical concept of "curved" systems of Gauss coordinates was only the first step toward this direction. Now we have arrived at string theories and theories of multiverses: time is dead, and the Laplacian beast happily lives on.

However, if we do not lose sight of the real existential meaning of the Galilean principle of relativity, then even Einstein's theory of relativity can be understood and regarded as the sign of a hidden reality: the sign of the reality of time behind the material surface. The concept of personal knowledge that every person sees the world from his own personal center, anchored in his own body in a particular space and time, in fact, entirely complies with the real existential meaning of the Galilean principle of relativity: every aspect of reality has its own center and behaves due to the nature of its own center. There is no absolute/objective point of reference, and both concepts are based on the reality of time. Without real time, there is no evolution and there are no real persons, emerged from matter, who see the world from their own personal center, anchored in their own body in a particular space and time; without real time, there are no real material centers, emerged from space-time, which behave due to the nature of their own centers; rather, only exact, mathematical abstractions of mass-points, Gauss coordinates, strings, etc.

Contrary to his master, Aristotle was right when he recognized that there are different levels of reality, starting with primary matter (space)—which does not exist in itself but rather is only the possibility-condition of the manifestations of higher levels. But he was wrong when he thought that the source of the higher-level aspects of reality is the manifestation of eternal forms and that there is an absolute center and a prime-mover in the universe which determines every movement. In fact, every higher-level aspect of reality, starting with a dimension of space-time, is the manifestation of time in points of space; there is no absolute center, and there is no prime-mover or God. Therefore, every manifestation of time has to be regarded as its own center, which, due to its own center, has its own nature and a relative relationship to every other manifestation of time. Time is neither eternal nor absolute; time is emergent.

7

The Theory of Boundary Conditions

7.1 Preface

In Part One, we spoke about the emergence of life. Contrary to the positivist concept of neo-Darwinism, life is not just a complex, material system but rather a genuinely new, comprehensive, orderly aspect of reality compared to the lower-level, random material processes due to its higher-level ordering principles—especially the ordering principles of life and evolution. In Part Two, we have so far seen that the claim of neo-Darwinism means that life is emergent in the epistemological sense, whereas our claim is that life is emergent in the ontological sense. In the last chapter, we have also seen that at the fundamental level, even matter itself is emergent (in the ontological sense, of course) and that it emerges from pure space-time due to the different kinds of manifestation of time in points of space. Therefore, the ordering principles of different kinds of matter are the different kinds of manifestations of time in space, and the general ordering principle of matter is but time itself. The emergence of the higher-level aspects of reality starts with the manifestations of time.

It follows that if life is emergent at the higher level, too, then the core of its emergence will *also* be the manifestation of time in the higher-level spaces of complex material systems; this is the reason that life can only be reduced in a diachronic way. However, there are such kinds of higher-level material complexes (in chemistry, geology, cosmology, etc.) that are merely the consequences of lower-level, material processes and principles—that is, they are just specific higher-level, material structures in space; they are emergent only in the epistemological sense, and, in consequence, they can be reduced in a synchronic way.

So, reality, in its original sense/aspect, is space-time, and the first kind of genuinely new manifestation of reality compared to space-time is matter. In a literal sense, the basis (or rather the framework) of any higher-level aspect of reality is, therefore, space-time, and *the most general ordering principle of any higher-level aspect of reality is time.* However, since, on the one hand, space-time itself has no focused structure determined by a center but rather three rapidly-expanding dimensions, surrounding all higher levels as well as time itself manifests itself at every higher level as the most general ordering principle of any higher-level aspect of reality and, on the other hand, matter is the most general and fundamental emergent manifestation of reality, the material basis of every higher-level aspect of reality, I will still call it the fundamental material level.

The question is this: what are the differences between epistemologically emergent levels of material complexes and ontologically emergent, comprehensive, orderly wholes? And how can these differences be conceptualized? The goal of the theory of boundary conditions was exactly this, to conceptually establish the point of these differences.

7.2 The Concept of Boundary Conditions

In the second half of the twentieth century, the concept of boundary conditions emerged from physics into the territories of cybernetics, life sciences, and philosophy. Several authors applied the concept to solve problems concerning some specific comprehensive features of life compared to simple material complexes.[1] Moreover, one of them, Polanyi explicitly stated that life was nothing but a specific comprehensive hierarchy of boundary conditions.[2] I think the fact that an application of boundary conditions proliferated from that time on is not accidental. The questions are why they use boundary conditions and what a boundary condition is. Nevertheless, I believe that these questions cannot be answered with only a detailed analysis of the works of the authors or by comparing them to each other; rather, I will focus on the historical and philosophical background of the concept itself.

Of course, it was not an accident that I mentioned Polanyi distinctively. I believe others had similar aims, at least tacitly, but he is the only one who uses the concept of boundary conditions in the framework of a genuinely new emergentist philosophy; he is the only one who, in a sense, really tries to find a path back to the times before Galilean and Newtonian physics and its influence on philosophy, not just use the concept in practice

---

1. See, for example, Ashby, *Introduction to Cybernetics*; Polanyi, "Life's Irreducible Structure"; Pattee, "Physical Basis"; Rothstein, "Generalize Entropy"; Rosen, *Life Itself*; Salthe, *Evolving Hierarchical Systems*; Korn, "Emergence Principle in Biological Hierarchies."

2. Polanyi, "Life's Irreducible Structure."

to describe the strange qualities and behaviors of living beings compared to pure, material complexes.

The concept of boundary conditions stems from physics; there are several types of them (e.g., fixed boundary conditions, linear boundary conditions, symmetric boundary conditions, time-varying boundary conditions, special boundary conditions, etc.). The differences between them are not relevant for the present purposes, only the two philosophically important, *main types* of them (from which follows the general concept of boundary conditions) and, more specifically, the reason why physicists apply boundary conditions in their works. Hopefully, the origin of boundary conditions in physics will shed light on the historical background and philosophical significance of the concept.

As mentioned above, in the second half of the twentieth century, several authors took over the concept of boundary conditions from physics. Nevertheless, some of them did not apply the term boundary condition but rather called it *constraint* (e.g., Ashby and Pattee). Let's compare, for example, Pattee's structural and control constraints to Polanyi's test-tube and machine type boundary conditions.

Pattee differentiates between two types of constraints.[3] The first type is called *structural* constraint. Structural constraints are *passive*; they do not control or govern the lower-level (at the end, physical) processes. Pattee's example of a structural constraint is a structure of a crystal or a balloon which is expanding due to the ascending temperature of the gas inside. Here, higher-level constraints are simple, passive *consequences of lower-level processes*—that is, the balloon's expansion is a consequence of the ascending temperature (faster moving of the particles) of a gas. The second type is called *control* constraints. These constraints are *active*, they control and govern the lower-level (at the end, physical) processes. Pattee's typical examples of control constraints are the specific structures of living beings (e.g., how an organism controls the functioning of its organs). However, the fact that control constrains control and govern the lower-level processes does not mean and cannot mean the breaking of the laws of the lower-level (e.g., physical processes) since these lower-level processes and their laws are exactly *the fundaments on which the higher level is built*—that is, the higher level cannot break the nature and laws of the lower-level processes because that would mean that it *breaks down its own fundaments* and would *destroy itself* in a short amount of time (as, actually, it happens when such a system loses control over its own lower-level processes and the machine breaks down or a living being dies).

3. Pattee, "Physical Basis."

In accordance with Pattee—but also independently of him—Polanyi states that we can distinguish two different types of boundary conditions. One of them is the *test-tube* type, which *does not influence* the elementary processes taking place within, and the other, the *machine* type boundary condition, has the function of *controlling* and *harnessing* the elementary physical and chemical processes for the sake of some *purpose*.[4] The test-tube in which different chemical processes are observed has no significant effect on the processes. There cannot be such influence because the whole function of a test-tube is making these processes *observable* by isolating them from their natural environment; it is purposeful only in this (epistemological) sense. In contrast, the structure of a machine has not got the function of making the elementary physical and chemical processes observable—these processes will be interesting only in the case if the machine fails—but it utilizes these elementary processes for some kind of work. Accordingly, Polanyi emphasizes that "living mechanisms are classed with machines"[5] because living beings have the function of *controlling* and *harnessing* the elementary processes for the sake of different purposes, too. This similarity does not imply that living beings are machines. Living beings only form another, natural *subclass* of machine type boundary conditions besides the subclass of artificial, machine type boundary conditions.

The main difference between test-tube and machine type boundary conditions is as follows. The structure of a crystal is merely a *consequence of the lower-level physical-chemical processes* of the crystal—as the balloon's expansion is that of the ascending temperature—due to the lower-level physical and chemical principles.[6] In contrast, the structure of a machine is not a consequence of the physical-chemical processes of that machine but rather is shaped *by humans* in accordance with higher-level principles of *engineering*.[7]

It follows that structural constraints and test-tube type boundary conditions have close and essential similarities just as control constraints and machine type boundary conditions. But there are also several differences in the details. As shown above, Polanyi's test-tube type boundary conditions have only one purpose: making some specific experimental processes *observable*. Its role as a test-tube is entirely *epistemological*. Similarly to a test-tube, the structure of a crystal has an important and necessary *epistemological role* in observing and analyzing the lower-level physical-chemical

---

4. Polanyi, "Life's Irreducible Structure."
5. Polanyi, "Life's Irreducible Structure," 226.
6. Polanyi, "Life Transcends," 286.
7. Polanyi, "Life Transcends," 287.

processes of any crystallogenesis because without a comprehensive structure, simply no one can observe and analyze these lower-level processes as processes of a crystallogenesis. Furthermore, like a test-tube does not control and harness the lower-level processes taking place within the test-tube, the crystal also does not control and govern its physical-chemical processes and principles; on the contrary, the structure of the crystal is entirely the consequence of these lower-level processes. The most important difference between test-tube tube type boundary conditions and structural constraints is that the formers are *artificial* devices.

The strong similarities between machine type boundary conditions and control constraints are more obvious. *Both* of them are controlling, harnessing, and governing their lower-level processes for some kind of *purpose*. In Polanyi's point of view, this means that as comprehensive structures, they have *existential meaning* and *ontological nature*—that is, they are not the consequence of their lower-level physical-chemical processes. The most important difference is that in Polanyi's concept, there are artificial machine type boundary conditions, too—that is, machines (and not just natural living beings) compose this category of boundary conditions.

There are two main types of boundary conditions: *epistemological* and *ontological*. Pattee's control constraints and Polanyi's machine type boundary conditions are equivalent: these are ontological control boundary conditions. (The main difference is that in Polanyi's system, there are two important subtypes of them.) However, the structural constraints and test-tube type boundary conditions are not equivalent but rather the two main *subtypes* of epistemological boundary conditions: *natural* and *artificial*.

Epistemological		Ontological	
structural (natural)	test-tube (artificial)	control	
	machines (artificial)		living beings (natural)

Table 6: The main types of boundary conditions, following Pattee and Polanyi.

In the following, I will use the centaur terms *structural* and *control boundary conditions* because I believe that these express the essence of the concept about which I like to speak the best. As I have mentioned, there are more of them than these two, but these two are the main types of boundary conditions which will lead us beyond physics to chemistry and similar territories as well as to biology and similar scientific fields; the others are only subtypes of these two, so there is no need to deal with them here.

7.3 Boundary Conditions from Physics

The concept of boundary conditions stems from physics or, more precisely, from Galilean and Newtonian mechanics. Take a simple, physical experiment—for example, from Galilei—in which lead and wooden balls are rolling down on a slope. The aim of the investigation was to establish the physical laws of acceleration, or, as it was understood at the time of Galilei, to settle what the correlation was between weight and acceleration. Galilei chose a slope for the experiment because on the slope, it was much easier to measure the acceleration of the balls than from the top of the Leaning Tower of Pisa. He supposed that there would be no connection between the angle of the slope and the interdependence of balls' weight and acceleration, so the angle of the slope was *not* derived from the laws of mechanics but was chosen *arbitrarily (randomly)*—or, more exactly, in accordance with the features of the experiments' instruments, the method of the measurement, etc. rather than the principles of physics. If he had had to derive the angle of the slope from the laws of mechanics, then he would not have been able to put forward the hypothesis that there was no connection between the angle of the slope and the interdependence of weight and acceleration. Contrary to this, Galilei chose the angle of the slope based on the principle of making the experiment as exact as possible. The angle could not be too big because then he would not have been able to measure the speeds of the balls precisley at different points of distance, but it also could not be too little because, in turn, the experiment would have become distorted by the phenomenon of friction. In consequence, the perfect angle for the experiment could not been determined by any exact calculation; it had been, in fact, chosen based on Galilei's tacit experiences of experiments. Nonetheless, my conclusion is that the angle of the slope was a random *boundary condition*, and although it had an essential role in the experiment, in the end, from the aspect of the mechanical laws in question, it was not given any importance. As a determining factor, it simply *fell out* from the equations.

Boundary conditions in physics are crucial because they can help us find out the physical laws of nature (e.g., the correlation between weight and acceleration). However, these boundary conditions, at least in physics, are never the focus of interest. Galilei was also not interested in the angle of the slope (it had only a subsidiary role, as Polanyi would say). The focus is on the physical *laws,* the material *substance,* and its *properties* hiding behind them. There is no strict correlation between the boundary conditions and the laws of physics. Boundary conditions are the random conditions of an experiment or a natural process. Therefore, in physics, boundary conditions are only *conceptual* and *instrumental tools* in our hands to reveal the deeper physical reality of nature.

In a physical universe—more precisely, in the universe conceived by the notion of physicalism—existentially, there are only physical laws, material substance, and the properties of this substance. Thus, the question is what the source of boundary conditions will be if (existentially) there is nothing but material substance and physical laws. Let's accept now that in this kind of (only) material universe, physicists (and thus persons or minds) do exist, applying the conceptual tools of boundary conditions in their work as Galilei did. Why do they have to use these tools?

First of all, because they have no ideal, objective knowledge—like Laplace's demon, who, *per definition*, knows every physical law and can observe the whole material substance of the universe (2.2). Secondly, it follows that a human physicist who does not know every physical law and does not "see" the entire realm of matter can conclude these laws, the actual material substance of things, and its properties *only by* relying on his previous knowledge of the boundary conditions that make material structures, properties, and the principles of things *observable* for him.

For example, with the help of a test-tube or a Petri dish as a test-tube type boundary condition, they *can observe* the material processes taking place within which, otherwise, as it is the case in nature, cannot be separated from other material processes. Or, with the help of the knowledge of the specific shape of a crystal as a structural boundary condition, they *can conclude* the exact material processes shaping the structure of that type of crystal inside. This principle stands behind Galilei's experiment, too; the slope, with its perfect angle as a test-tube type boundary condition, helps to determine a physical law. Before Galilei's experiment, nobody could establish that lead and wooden balls fall with the same acceleration. Without the higher-level, comprehensive knowledge, we could identify *neither* the specific type of crystal *nor* those particular material processes which were shaping it; as a matter of fact, we cannot establish that the thing in our hands is a crystal at all. The destructive analysis concerning the material parts always comes after the recognition (and usually after the categorization) of the comprehensive, orderly whole (3.3)—which, in this case, is an epistemological (test-tube type or structural) boundary condition.

Nevertheless, in physics, we are *only* interested in the physical laws and properties of material substance which determine the crystallogenesis and not the actual processes or the angle of the slope. So, it can be concluded that epistemological boundary conditions are such necessary *conceptual* and *instrumental tools* which, based on previous tacit and personal knowledge concerning different comprehensive, orderly wholes, allow us the examination and explanation of lower-level, material parts/processes to formulate their exact laws and properties.

However, the central question is what the *source* of epistemological boundary conditions is. As shown in the previous subchapter, there are such Polanyian test-tube type, artificial, epistemological boundary conditions, (e.g., the test-tube, a Petri dish, a slope, etc.) which are human-made tools and machines. Thus, test-tube type boundary conditions are such tools and machines which in themselves have to be regarded as machine-type control boundary conditions; however, *in science*, the role of these kinds of tools and machines are not to control and harness lower-level, material processes for the sake of some sort of work (as the function of a tool or machine is in everyday life) but rather only to observe/discover certain material processes/principles in a specific experimental environment. This, by the way, entirely corresponds to the situation where a machine goes wrong and thus does not function as a proper machine or a machine type boundary condition but rather as a test-tube type boundary condition as we try to find the lower-level reason of the failure: its structure becomes the specific "test-tube" or "Petri dish" of an observation process. So, if test-tube type boundary conditions are used due to their purpose, they will have to be regarded as epistemological boundary conditions, but since they are human tools and machines in themselves, their origin can be found in the territory of control boundary conditions.

However, the well-separated, initial compound in a Petri dish is, of course, not a human-made machine but rather a carefully chosen and observed structure of a kind of material. Accordingly, in the case of a crystallogenesis, the specific shape of the crystal as a natural, epistemological boundary condition is the consequence of the material processes taking place within. These processes are the consequences of the physical laws and properties of material substance. However, it is true of *every* crystallogenesis and every other physical process that they are determined by the physical laws and properties of material substance, and still, there are various crystals and various boundary conditions. Then what is the real difference between different crystallogenesises?

The answer is that although the physical laws and material substance are the same in each case, there are differences between the *initial* conditions. In two different Petri dishes, the physical laws and the material substance are necessarily *the same*—there are no other laws and substance in the universe according to our knowledge—but there can be differences in the number, type, arrangement, size, etc., of material particles. This means that as the laws of physics do not and cannot determine the angle of the slope in Galilei's experiment but rather he himself has to decide it (based on his tacit experiences), the laws of physics also cannot determine the choice of the chemist concerning the exact initial compounds of material elements in different Petri dishes and these initial differences in his experiments—that is, the *random, lower-level, spatial order of matter* in a Petri dish leads to different crystallogenesises and thus to different crystals as specific kinds of structural boundary conditions. Therefore, the answer is that the source of various structural boundary conditions is the different initial conditions of material substance. In a material universe, existentially, there is only physical laws and material substance—with its primary properties—but there *can be* differences in the initial conditions of material substance. So, it can be concluded that any formation of structural boundary conditions is the consequence of three random factors:

1. Physical laws.
2. Material substance and its properties.
3. Initial conditions.

In our universe, according to the traditional concepts, the first two factors are given; there can only be differences in the third factor. In principle, the first two factors could also be entirely different or changing due to the different manifestations of time (as we have seen in the previous chapter.) Nonetheless, now the point is that these factors are random to each other—that is, their relations to each other are emergent (4.5).

At this point, one can say that initial conditions are also boundary conditions; there is no important difference between the two. A reason for this may be that although our crystallogenesis example is very illustrative, it is also a little bit misleading. In the case of different Petri dishes, there are no *real* initial conditions due to some original manifestation of reality; in fact, in this example, the two Petri dishes are the initial *epistemological* boundary conditions, which determine the different crystallogenesises. It is the arbitrary choice of the chemist—like the angle of the slope was for Galilei—what determines the exact contents of the dishes, which forms a sharp boundary between the inside and outside processes. More exactly, the choice is determined by the actual *interest* of the chemist. For example, he intends to create the compound of a specific chemical. This choice is not determined by the physical laws of a chemical process—it is simply not part of the process, and thus, at the end, it can be left out of the results.

However, in the case of the *whole physical universe*, there are *real* initial conditions due to their own nature. They are *not* determined by the laws of physics *either*. Ultimately, every now-existing boundary condition is the *consequence* of these real initial conditions in the same way as the shape of the crystal as a boundary condition is the consequence of the former "initial" conditions of material substance in the Petri dish. This means that *every boundary condition can be reduced to these first and real initial conditions* plus physical laws and material substance and its properties. The primary goal of Galilean, Newtonian, and also modern physics is to find out the exact physical laws of nature and the exact properties of material substance. To do so, real—and, in this relational sense, random—initial conditions can *also* be left out from scientific inquiry as the angle of the slope in Galilei's experiment. It is *cosmology* and not physics itself that is interested in the real initial conditions. In theory, if initial conditions were different, physics would be the same, but not cosmology.

According to ideal mechanical knowledge, the knowledge concerning the initial conditions and boundary conditions are not parts of the knowledge of Laplace's demon. As a matter of fact, according to this ideal, there are no real initial conditions at all because time (more precisely, as we have seen in subchapters 4.6 and 6.2, the fourth dimension of space) is eternal (absolute and entirely independent from matter). For Laplace's demon, as we have seen in detail in chapter 2, there is only the actual state of material substance and the knowledge of physical laws—that is, only the first two factors of structural boundary conditions. For it, initial conditions (if there is any) and boundary conditions are not relevant. What is even more critical, the demon *does not need* any boundary conditions to conclude physical processes. It "sees" the exact physical state of the crystal in the Petri dish and it can conclude the exact physical processes of the crystallogenesis. For the demon, contrary to us, *neither* the final shape of the crystal *nor* the initial boundary conditions of the Petri dish chosen by the chemist are necessary for doing so. Moreover, it "sees" the physical processes of the body of the Petri dish *in the same way* as the processes inside of it. The demon is not a human being or a person. For it, *there is no difference* between the crystal and the body of the Petri dish or, as a matter of fact, between the crystal and the living body of the chemist. All it "sees" is the same structure and physical process of quarks and electrons, etc. The knowledge of initial conditions and boundary conditions is simply *not part* of its ideal physical knowledge as they are not part of (ideal) physics. This fact is the main reason why initial conditions and boundary conditions are random and can be left out of fundamental physical investigations. The final (but inaccessible) goal is having that kind of ideal physics and the final and perfect "theory of everything" (4.6). *The boundary conditions as conceptual and instrumental tools are necessary only for the human physicist*; however, they are not and cannot be part of ideal physics.

It is worth emphasizing once more that physicalism—instead of real human physics—leans on the ideal of physics because, as we have seen in the previous chapter, based on the results and theories of twentieth-century physics, it can be questioned firmly that time is eternal—that is, there are no real initial conditions—and that the real initial conditions of the universe, as well as the laws of physics, could be separated as an independent factor from the nature and properties of matter at the time of the Big Bang. In reality, the ideal of physics—pursuing the theory of everything, the final goal of this ideal—is a set of operational principles which can be used very successfully among certain conditions but can*not* answer fundamental questions about the real history and general nature of the whole universe (factor 1), about the emergence of matter (factor 2), and about the real initial conditions of the world (factor 3). Cosmology is not physics. Or, as Smolin puts it: physics is just a practically very successful "doing physics in a box"[8] as primarily Galilei established it, but not the real science of the whole universe itself. If time is real, then perhaps in certain conditions (e.g., in earthly conditions), physical laws, material substance, and its properties can and, in fact, are worth being regarded—as we will also do—as real, independent, and constant factors compared to boundary conditions. But *in the case of the whole universe, both physical laws and material substance will emerge and change by time*—compared to the real initial conditions of our universe. Randomness and independent random relations among different factors always *mean emergence* and *change* over time and not absolute and constant factors (4.5, 4.6).

7.4 Boundary Conditions in Physical Sciences

It has been shown in the previous subchapter that the concept of boundary conditions stems from physics, but boundary conditions are only conceptual tools in the hands of human physicists to help to find out the physical laws and fundamental properties of material substance. Boundary conditions can be reduced to initial conditions, physical laws, and material substance and they can be and must be left out at the end of the investigations. Boundary conditions are simply not part of ideal fundamental physics. To make such a clear statement, however, we have to sharply differentiate between fundamental physics, which tries to follow the Laplacian ideal of objective

8. Smolin, *Time Reborn*, 37–45.

knowledge to reach perfectly exact knowledge, and other sciences, which focus on higher-level boundary conditions and give up on achieving perfectly exact knowledge—although to a very different degree. Now, the question is: what happens when one focuses on boundary conditions?

There are two fundamentally different possibilities. The first and simpler one is the case of the physical sciences, and we have already seen examples of it in the case of crystallogenesis and different questions of cosmology in the previous subchapter. The second and more complicated one is, in turn, the case of life sciences and engineering, which will be discussed in the next subchapter. (I will not speak about social sciences in this chapter yet, but they, of course, are parts of the latter category.)

Contrary to physics, cosmology is not interested in physical laws and the properties of material substance but rather supernovas, comets, nebulas, extrasolar planets, etc. It merely accepts and uses the achievements of physics for its own purposes *to define and explain cosmological, comprehensive, orderly phenomena*. Similarly, chemistry is interested in *chemical* processes, reactions, connections, forces, properties, etc., at a higher level—that is, when a chemist sets an experiment concerning crystallogenesis in a Petri dish, he is interested *only* in the chemical processes (e.g., the relations between initial conditions and the structures of the evolving crystals) and not in the physical laws and properties of material substance. Moreover, the chemist applies the knowledge of physical properties *at the level of chemical elements* and he is not at all interested in the equations of quantum mechanics or string theory. So, both the chemist and the cosmologist intend to study and explain a *higher-level* comprehensive phenomenon in contrast to the substantial matter of physics. Since these disciplines are interested in higher-level phenomena, in these disciplines, scientific knowledge consists of higher-level principles, laws, forces, properties, etc., *concerning higher-level boundary conditions*.

We have seen in chapter 5 that the description of a higher-level comprehensive order (boundary condition) and the fundamental topography of it at the lower level are never equal because they use different concepts, laws, and principles; however, this in itself does not lead to an ontological gap between the two levels since the higher-level description can be reduced to the lower-level one in the synchronic sense (5.4, 5.6). This means that the *ordering principles* which determine the process of crystallogenesis and create the structural boundary conditions of the crystal are *intrinsic* in nature (4.4) and can be found *exclusively in the physical laws and material conditions of the crystal*. Therefore, in this case, it is meaningless to speak about two different levels of reality: a crystal is a material entity which has several comprehensive emergent properties in the epistemological sense.

At the same time, it is important to emphasize that although the laws and concepts of chemistry can be reduced into the laws and concepts of quantum mechanics (at least in theory), quantum mechanics cannot replace chemistry—not even in theory—because chemistry asks its questions concerning the *actual* higher-level orderly structures of chemistry (structural boundary conditions) based on the personal experiences, tacit, intellectual skills, and particular interests of chemists, while fundamental physics, due to the Laplacian ideal of objective knowledge, has to ask its questions concerning the fundamental material processes in *any* given conditions. For example, oil research is one of the most important branches of chemistry, but quantum mechanics has nothing to say about it. In the words of the chemist Polanyi:

> Consider the chemical aspects of matter. They are fully determined by atomic physics, yet no Laplacean Mind schooled in quantum mechanics could replace the science of chemistry. For chemistry answers questions regarding the interaction of more or less stable chemical substances, and these questions cannot be raised without experience of these substances and of the practical conditions in which they are to be handled. A Laplacian knowledge which merely predicts what will happen under any given conditions cannot tell us what conditions should be given; these conditions are determined by the technical skill and peculiar interests of chemists and hence cannot be worked out on paper. Therefore, while quantum mechanics can explain in principle all chemical reactions, it cannot replace, even in principle, our knowledge of chemistry.[9]

Contrary to fundamental physics, physical sciences examine such comprehensive, orderly phenomena of matter which, according to the theory of boundary conditions, are epistemological, structural boundary conditions. The main difference between fundamental physics and the physical sciences is that due to the Galilean spirit, fundamental physics focuses on physical laws and material substance itself and uses the knowledge of other sciences concerning higher-level boundary conditions only in a subsidiary way, while the physical sciences—vice versa—focus on higher-level boundary conditions and use the knowledge of fundamental physics merely in a subsidiary way (3.3). Therefore, if we do not identify physics exclusively with fundamental physics—which we do not normally do—then physics, as we have seen in subchapter 5.3, will perfectly comply with comprehensive, emergent

---

9. Polanyi, *Personal Knowledge*, 394.

phenomena; moreover, *the whole aim of physical sciences is to explore the realm of comprehensive, emergent phenomena of matter.*

However, it is important to note that the relation of the two levels, due to the logic of emergence, is not symmetric. This means that for fundamental physics, the higher-level boundary conditions are only instrumental tools which have no role in the final results, but for physical sciences, the basic principles, laws, and results of fundamental physics are fundamental; this is the reason, actually, we call it *fundamental* physics. Ontologically speaking: *the laws of fundamental physics and the fundamental properties of matter determine the conditions among which any higher-level boundary condition can emerge.* However, as Galilei rightly observed, these fundamental conditions are usually constant (e.g., on Earth), and for physical sciences, the third factor—that is, the actual initial conditions—become the most important one to explain the origin of different higher-level, comprehensive phenomena called structural boundary conditions.

7.5 Boundary Conditions in Life Sciences and Engineering

The exploration of boundary conditions becomes more fascinating when we arrive at the territories of engineering and the life sciences. As we have seen in subchapter 7.2, the structures of living beings control and harness the lower-level processes in the same way as the structures of machines—in both cases, we are speaking of control boundary conditions. The two main differences are that the structures of living beings are determined by the principles of biology, life, and evolution—and not by that of engineering—and the aims of the former are not determined by man but rather by nature. The two main goals of living beings are *self-preservation* and *reproduction* because this is the way that living beings preserve their unique structures and can persist in time (9.5). Contrary to this, the aims of machines are entirely subordinate to man, and they cannot preserve their unique structures in themselves (8.5). Nonetheless, now, the point is that both of their structures are control boundary conditions.

Similarly to chemistry and cosmology, biology is also not interested in fundamental physical laws or properties of material substance (some biologists have perhaps not even heard about up and down quarks, not to mention multidimensional, small strings) but rather in species, organs, and such biological processes as digestion, regeneration, reproduction, etc. In the same way, as seen above, when it is possible or necessary, biology also accepts and applies the achievements of physics to define and explain biological phenomena, but normally not at the fundamental quantum mechanical level. Similarly, engineering is interested in nothing besides higher-level mechanical processes, correlations, structures, and properties, and it typically uses classical mechanics, thermodynamics, or electrodynamics to help its work on the higher level—not fundamental physics. So, as in the case of cosmology and chemistry, a biologist or an engineer also study and explain *higher-level comprehensive, orderly phenomena*. Thus these kinds of scientific knowledge also consist of higher-level principles, laws, forces, properties, etc., concerning higher-level boundary conditions.

As we have seen in subchapter 7.2, two main types of boundary conditions can be distinguished as Polanyi or Pattee did. Test-tube type boundary conditions or structural constraints can be identified in chemistry or cosmology and machine type boundary conditions or control constraints in biology or engineering. Now, the question is what the exact difference between the two is and whether it is a well-established differentiation. The fundamental difference between boundary conditions in biology and chemistry is intuitive; compare, for example, a crystal with a frog. The former is a lifeless, inert thing, while the latter is an active living being. But between chemistry and engineering, the difference is less noticeable. Moreover, it might be even counter-intuitive that boundary conditions in engineering are in the same category as biological boundary conditions since machines as crystals are not living beings at all.

As seen, both Polanyi and Pattee state that the fundamental difference between structural and control boundary conditions is that the latter *controls* and *harnesses* the lower-level processes taking place within, while the former does not. Think about, for example, a piston—as the example we used in subchapter 5.8—that transforms the chemical energy of exploding petrol into rotary motion or a water mill that does the same with the kinetic energy of flowing water. In these cases, the lower-level processes do *not go freely*, according to their lower-level principles alone; rather, the *specific structure* of the piston (or the water mill), according to their higher-level engineering principles, govern (control) and harness these lower-level and, at the end, physical processes in several distinct steps (in order to move a car, grind wheat, etc.):

> Engineering and physics are two different sciences. Engineering includes the operational principles of machines and some knowledge of physics bearing on these principles. Physics and chemistry, on the other hand, include no knowledge of the operational principles of machines. Hence a complete physical and chemical topography of an object would not tell us whether it is a machine, and if so, how it works, and for what purpose. Physical and chemical investigations of a machine are meaningless

unless undertaken with a bearing on the previously established operational principles of the machine.[10]

The fundamental difference between the two main types of boundary conditions is that structural boundary conditions are merely the consequences of the *lower-level physical processes and intrinsic material principles*—and, as we have seen, the actual lower-level processes are the consequences of definite initial conditions—while control boundary conditions are the consequences of *higher-level processes and emergent principles*. In the case of a machine, this means, of course, the *expertise* of the engineer, based on his personal experiences and tacit skills, by which he can plan and create this particular machine or, at the explicit level, the *patent* in which it is defined precisely what this machine is. These processes and principles are *extrinsic* compared to the machine and compose a set of *higher-level* knowledge compared to physical knowledge. In other words: these processes and principles are *random* compared to the material conditions of the machine. This is the reason that these processes and principles can create such independent structures in the body of the machine that can control and harness the lower-level material and chemical processes.

The situation is entirely parallel with the first case of our Wales example (in chapter 4), where there is a recognizable, comprehensive pattern of order in the pebbles arranged intentionally by the stationmaster: the meaningful pattern is the consequence of an extrinsic process based on the higher-level principle of the English language and the intention of the stationmaster. A lower-level, purely material process (like a tornado) cannot create such a real, meaningful pattern—or, by chance, at most an illusory one (4.3). It follows that *control boundary conditions*, contrary to structure boundary conditions, *are random in relation to their own material possibility-conditions*.

In the language of cybernetics, the essential difference between the structural and control boundary conditions as systems is that the latter is closed to control and information[11]—but *not* to energy flow or other simple physical parameters which also exist in the case of structural boundary conditions. If the electric kettle is not under power, it will simply not work. So, in the case of machines, this closed state means that although energy (the petrol in the piston) or the material on which the machine works go through the system, the controlling structure—that is, the machine type boundary condition—is fixed.

---

10. Polanyi, *Tacit Dimension*, 39.
11. Ashby, *Introduction to Cybernetics*.

Contrary to this, objects with structural boundary conditions are closed neither to control and information nor to energy flow or any lower-level flow of material parts; these objects are merely the consequences of these processes. This means that *the information describing the order of their structures is entirely determined by their actual material structures.* By the classic cybernetic formula: I=~E, that is, the information of the given structure equals the negation of its entropy. However, since these orders are determined by lower-level (random) material processes, their information has no genuinely new content compared to their material structures—that is, it has no any existential meaning but rather *only denotative one*, which, in fact, refers to the actual lower-level, material structure (5.4).

The situation is entirely parallel with the third case of our Wales example in chapter 4, where there is a recognizable, comprehensive pattern of order in the pebbles—a Wales scheme—that is not the consequence of some intentional human activity but rather the material processes in the garden (e.g., of a hurricane)—that is, it has no real meaning; in this sense, it is only an illusion. Later, I will call (and establish in detail) this kind of information, entirely determined by material structures, *parametric information*, after Vilmos Csányi (9.4).[12] According to the random nature of lower-level, material parts, this kind of information—and thus the structures described by it—is always destroyed by the necessary increase of entropy (I=~E) over time if there are no other external or higher-level processes which return the process (4.5); or, more exactly, if the given structure is not part of a higher-level, comprehensive system with higher-level ordering principles as, for example, any living being is necessarily the part of the higher-level, evolutionary system of the Earth and are determined by the principles of life and evolution (9.3; 9.7).

However, control boundary conditions are random to their lower-level parts and created by extrinsic processes of a higher-level, comprehensive system, according to its higher-level principles, which means that the information describing the order of their structures does not comply with the parametric information of the parts (only partially). *The structure of the machine contains such information due to which it can control and harness the lower-level processes* described merely by parametric information; actually, it is its exact purpose or *function*. Later, I will call (and explain the origin of) this specific kind of information *contained* but *not determined* by material structures *functional information*—also after Csányi. Since the control structures of machines described by functional information have genuinely new content compared to their material parts, this genuinely new content

---

12. Csányi, *Az evolúció általános elmélete*, 34.

has a real existential meaning which, of course, refers to the higher-level control functions of the machine.

It follows that, contrary to structural boundary conditions, control boundary conditions have to be regarded as emergent in the ontological sense. In the case of natural control boundary conditions (living beings) we have already argued in detail for their emergent reality (5.5), and I will return to this topic of the emergent reality of machines in the next chapter (8.2, 8.4). Machines are basically the extensions of the emergent human body based on the operational principles of the human body—that is, they are tangible external tools (3.3), and the reason that this fact is not so evident (as it is in the case of such simple tools as a hammer) is that they are capable of independent operations among certain limits. It is entirely true that machines and the human body are similar objects; nonetheless, the human body is not a machine but rather the original and natural "prototype" of artificial machines: they are the two main types of control boundary conditions.

In the case of such specific machines which are in an active relationship with their environment—called automats by Norbert Wiener[13]—the situation becomes more complicated. The typical cybernetic examples of automats are the photocell, the thermostat, and such different life processes which can be described as cybernetic regulations (e.g., one of Ashby's favorite example is the regulation of the pH value of blood). Automats not only have fixed control boundary conditions but also such *sensors, regulation-center(s)*, and *feedback mechanisms*, which allows them to react to the changes in their environment and material conditions during work. For example, a thermostat detects any change in the temperature of the room and is able to translate this material process into a sign that starts a feedback mechanism, which, in turn, switches on the heater, a simple machine. Therefore, an automat, contrary to a simple machine, is in an active, informational relationship with its environment: it not only has parametric and functional information shaped into its body but also a kind of *specific, focused knowledge* concerning its environment, coded in its center, which can govern its feedback mechanisms (see in detail in 8.4).

In the case of living beings as natural, control boundary conditions, this active relationship with their environment becomes more and more obvious as we reach higher animals. At the end, this process leads to a situation where the observation of living beings will become nearly meaningless if they are separated from their natural environment. Therefore, boundary conditions in chemistry (and cosmology, geology, meteorology,

---

13. Wiener, *Cybernetics*.

or other, similar disciplines) are much easier to study and explain with the help of physics than boundary conditions in biology (or similar disciplines like psychology, sociology, economics, history, etc.). Since the boundary conditions of chemistry are simple, physical systems, without control, and determined by lower-level processes/principles, one can set simple physical parameters on the boundaries for the sake of exact measurement and examinations—for example, in a Petri dish—but one can hardly do the same in biology because a Japanese macaque, for example, is in an active, informational relationship with its environment and thus captivity in a laboratory changes its behavior entirely. The whole evolutionary system simply cannot be brought into the laboratory (5.5).

So, the structure of a machine is not the consequence of the elementary physical processes of the machine but rather higher-level, external processes and principles. This fact, at the same time, might suggest that when an engineer plans and creates a machine, he violates the fundamental physical laws and principles of nature. Moreover, the fact that the purpose of a machine as an ontologically higher-level boundary condition is to control and harness the lower-level physical-chemical processes could also strengthen this impression.

However, as we have seen briefly in subchapter 5.8, a machine can *only* control and harness the lower-level processes *via its material parts* in full accordance with the fundamental laws and principles of physics. The fixed walls of a piston, while controlling and harnessing the flow and explosions of petrol, do nothing against the fundamental laws and principles of physics. Higher-level, *emergent* boundary conditions are not independent/distinct vital forces or Cartesian substances. Higher-level, *emergent* boundary conditions do not work on their own—that is, against their own material conditions—but on the contrary, according to the logic of emergence, they lean on them and work by them in full accordance with the lower-level principles of physics. A piston is an artificial control boundary condition shaped into its material fundaments. Its function can be defined by the functional information shaped into its material conditions creating those fixed walls and other structures which actually control and harness the lower-level processes *by their shaped material conditions*. Therefore, the interaction between the piston as a higher-level boundary condition and the controlled and harnessed lower-level physical-chemical processes inside the piston *can only be understood at the lower level*. Accordingly, the engineer who plans and creates the piston also shapes the piston via his material conditions and the material fundaments of his body, as the piston does with the petrol, and not by some mysterious mental force or magic trick. So, contrary to first impressions (which are exclusively based on materialist convictions), neither the engineer nor the higher-level, emergent structures violate the fundamental physical laws and principles of nature.

Among other reasons, the claim that the ordering principles of control boundary conditions in the case of living beings are also extrinsic and higher-level could seem very problematic as well, since these principles are, at least partially, coded in the DNA—especially, if, according to the neo-Darwinian approach, we are inclined to identify genes with DNA sequences. Then it would follow that natural control boundary conditions and genes should be regarded as structural boundary conditions, determined by the lower-level, material processes and principles of a chemical molecule. Polanyi's argument against this neo-Darwinian interpretation is the following:

> Whatever may be the origin of a DNA configuration, it can function as a code only if its order is not due the forces of potential energy. It must be as physically indeterminate as the sequence of words is on a printed page. As the arrangement of a printed page is extraneous to the chemistry of the printed page, so is the base sequence in a DNA molecule extraneous to the chemical forces at work in the DNA molecule. It is this physical indeterminacy of the sequence that produces the improbability of occurrence of any particular sequence and thereby enables it to have meaning.[14]

If the chemistry of the printed page—or, more exactly, the chemical laws and the chemical properties of the given material—determined the order of the words that could be printed on that page, then the words could not have independent meaning; we could not print different texts on the same page. In the same way, if the laws of chemistry and the chemical properties of the DNA determined the configuration of sequences in a given DNA, then that given DNA could not code any independent information and could not be the source of the higher level, boundary conditions harnessing the elementary processes. However, both in the case of the printed page and in the case of the DNA, the laws of chemistry and the chemical properties of the given material *left open the possibility* of what the actual order of ink on the page or the actual order of the DNA sequences can be—that is, what can be written or coded in the actual material. This means that in different cases, the same page (and ink) or the same DNA—due to another, independent pattern or sequence on the page or in the DNA—can code entirely different information. The material properties of the pebbles in the garden and the physical laws of the various lower-level processes present do not determine what message can be coded in the pebbles by the stationmaster. This material

14. Polanyi, "Life's Irreducible Structure," 229.

page does not determine what you can write on it either. The relation of the coded information and the material level is random.

But if we still identify the lower-level material conditions (that is, the DNA) with the comprehensive system of genes, that means that the DNA, in fact, *does not code any real information. The code has no existential meaning at all*, the same way that the W-shape of Cassiopeia does not code any real information—it is just a random, illusory constellation due to the lower-level material conditions (movements) of stars (4.5). In this case, the information content of the DNA would be entirely identical with the parametric information describing the state of the lower-level parts.

It is even evident for neo-Darwinians, however, that the DNA can code real information (which can control and harness the lower-level processes of the cell) and create the higher-level structures of the body during ontogeny (which, in turn, can control and harness such lower-level—albeit necessary—processes like metabolism). The *only* reason and (theoretical) situation in which biologists would question these obvious personal facts is when they try to meet the dogmas of the ruling positivist and physicalist philosophy in sciences—which, in biology, is represented by neo-Darwinism. However, in reality, even convinced neo-Darwinians do not think that the information content of the W-shape of Cassiopeia (parametric information) perfectly complies with the information content of DNA (functional information) in its type, and the latter does not code any real (genuinely new) information to create the body of living organisms; they identify the coded information of the DNA with parametric information due to critically correct manner of speech because parametric information can be exactly defined, measured, and formalized due to the Laplacian ideal of objective knowledge. However, this identification can only be made if one substitutes the place of parametric information with the real functions of the genes concerning the structure and behavior of the living being in question; these latter functions can be understood as functional information, but, as we can see, this information is not so exact that the parametric one because both the higher-level structure and behavior of living beings are real, comprehensive orders, the deepness of which can only be determined based on the personal experiences and tacit skills of biologists (4.4, 9.6). Biology is not physics.

So although the place of the DNA and its code is in the cell which, in turn, is in the body of living organisms, it still functions as a higher-level, emergent ordering principle which creates the complex, multileveled structure of living beings during ontogeny. According to this:

[A living being's] structure is that of a boundary condition harnessing the physical chemical substances within the organism in the service of physiological functions. Thus, in generating an organism, DNA initiates and controls the growth of a mechanism that will work as a boundary condition.[15]

Therefore, in the understanding of Bernd-Olaf Kuppers, the DNA has to be regarded as a *primary* boundary condition that creates the hierarchy of normal control boundary conditions of the living body.[16] It follows that the (meaningful) order of a given DNA is also not the consequence of random material processes of the lower-level (e.g., random mutations in the DNA due to copy errors or radiation) but rather the result of interactions with the whole evolutionary system of the higher level due to the principles of evolution and emergence via the lower-level mechanism of natural selection (9.3, 9.7). It also follows that the (existential) meaning of the code in the DNA can only be understood in this whole evolutionary context of higher levels (9.2) just as the meaning of the Wales lettering can only be understood in the higher-level context of the English language:

> Thus a boundary condition which harnesses the principles of a lower level in the service of a new, higher level, establishes a semantic relation between the two levels. The higher comprehends the workings of the lower and thus forms the meaning of the lower.[17]

The order of the pebbles in the garden of the railway station is utterly meaningless in itself. It only gains meaning due to the higher-level ordering principles of the English language. As a matter of fact, the meaningful Wales lettering can only be born in the context of these higher-level principles— that is, if these principles are used by the stationmaster, according to his intentions. Most of the possible orders of the pebbles—which are, indeed, the consequence of lower-level, random processes and have nothing to do with the higher-level ordering principles of English language—have no meaning at all (4.3). Similarly, the order of a DNA is utterly meaningless in itself; it only gains meaning due to the higher-level principles of the whole evolutionary system. Most of the possible orders of the DNA—and there is almost an infinite number of such possible orders—have no meaning at all either; however, those that do are the consequence of the comprehensive evolutionary processes of Earth due to the principles of life and evolution. A

15. Polanyi, "Life's Irreducible Structure," 229–30.
16. Kuppers, "Understanding Complexity."
17. Polanyi, "Life's Irreducible Structure," 236.

random order of DNA in a Petri dish would probably not have any meaning, but in a living cell in the oceans of Earth, it certainly would.

These life processes, as we will see in detail in Part Three: Evolution, take place according to the same principles of emergence that we have seen in the case of machines—that is, emergent life processes also do not break the laws of physics. Although the structure of a living being or an order of a DNA is not the consequence of lower-level, random processes due to intrinsic, material principles but rather higher-level process due to extrinsic, emergent principles at the level of the chemical/material parts of the living being or the DNA, the effects of these higher-level processes and principles can only be understood as material/chemical processes that take place entirely due to the laws of physics and chemistry. Higher-level, emergent processes and principles, as we have already seen several times so far, do not work on their own; rather, they lean on their material conditions and work by them. However, in the case of the higher-level principles of life and evolution, these material conditions cover the material level of the whole evolutionary system—not just some compound in a Petri dish.

So, according to the logic of boundary conditions, the relation between a boundary condition (the complex, comprehensive structure of a system) and the material parts (the lower-level possibility-conditions of that system) is either *random* or *determined*. If the relation between the two levels is determined, we will speak of structural boundary conditions, which have no existential meaning (only parametric information)—that is, they are emergent in the epistemological sense and can be reduced synchronically. However, if the relation between the two levels is random, we will speak of (natural or artificial) control boundary conditions which have real existential meaning (functional information) and control and harness the lower-level processes of the given system for some purpose. These boundary conditions are emergent in the ontological sense and can be reduced only diachronically.

7.6 Boundary Conditions in the Light of Philosophy

We have seen that the concept of boundary conditions stems from physics, but boundary conditions in physics are only conceptual/instrumental tools in the hands of physicists and are not part of ideal (fundamental) physics. They are neither material substance and its (primary) properties nor physical laws (principles). At the same time, in physical sciences or the life sciences, the boundary conditions are not only conceptual tools but also the essential goals of scientific inquiry. Moreover, in life sciences and engineering, we have to regard these boundary conditions as real, meaningful (functional information), emergent structures of living beings and machines. Boundary conditions are not part of ideal physics, but the concept still spread to the territory of life sciences from physics—the question is, why?

We have seen that boundary conditions are in close connection with the structures and shapes of things and the shaping processes of things as well as with different boundaries between things, processes, and systems. Even though boundary conditions stem from physics, the philosophical understanding of structures, boundaries, shapes, and shaping processes of things is much older.

In Aristotelian philosophy and science, the shapes and structures of things are the consequence of *substantial forms* and the shaping processes are the consequences of *potential forms*; for example, the cause of the shaping process of a goat is the potential goat form in the zygote. Therefore, there are two inseparable, substantial parts of a thing: *matter* and *form*. Every terrestrial thing consists of these two parts, and every higher-level thing can be reduced to these two substantial parts (i.e., matter and form). However, in the Aristotelian philosophy, there are not just two levels—the level of fundamental substances and the level of comprehensive, orderly objects—but several *hierarchical* levels where higher-level forms *determine* (control) the lower-level processes (e.g., as a multileveled, living being develops from a zygote, organizing all four kinds of element into its body due to its potential form). The difference between a crystal and a frog is that the crystal is a *homogenous* higher-level entity, while the frog is a *heterogeneous* one; different types of forms determine the two during the processes of ontogeny and crystalogenesis. There are the same elements (fire, air, water, earth) at the first material level and there is a controlling, active form in *both* cases.

In Aristotelian philosophy, the forms determine the boundaries, shapes, structures, etc. of a thing. It follows that in Aristotelian philosophy, there is no question concerning what a boundary condition or an initial condition is. There is *no need* for boundary conditions—the notion of forms plays their role—and there is no need for real, initial conditions because both the world and the forms are eternal.

Aristotelian philosophy and science ruled the world of medieval universities, but at the beginning of the modern era, everything was changed. Mainly in accordance with René Descartes's (and later with Newton's) mechanical worldview, it was supposed that every higher-level (or secondary) property (thus, the shapes, shaping processes, boundaries, etc. of things) is the consequence of *mechanical (physical) processes* of material substance—i.e., in Descartes philosophy, the *res extensa*. We have seen in subchapter 7.3 that this means that every higher-level property of objects can be reduced to (1) physical (mechanical) laws, (2) material substance and its (primary) properties, and (3) the initial conditions of the evolving processes of that given object. There are no hierarchical levels, only two: the fundamental level of matter and the comprehensive level of objects. *There is no significant difference* between a crystal and a frog; both of them are purely material things without any independent, active behavior. In consequence, in this modern mechanical worldview, there is a place for both the concepts of initial conditions and boundary conditions. The world is not eternal (only a few thousands of years old), and every secondary property and structure of the objects can be understood as a kind of boundary condition. However, since there is no significant difference between material objects and living beings, both are the consequence of the same mechanical processes; there are *only* structural boundary conditions.

Nonetheless, it is important to note that the concept of matter is significantly changed compared to the Aristotelian notion. According to Aristotle, matter itself is entirely passive (inert), and even the four elements of matter are the consequence of the manifestations of primary forms in primary matter—that is, in space. Therefore, matter is just a passive possibility-condition of the higher-level manifestations of reality: no order or structure can be explained by it alone—that is, there are no intrinsic material ordering principles; every kind of order (structure, property, etc.) is the consequence of the active manifestation of forms. However, the modern concept of matter includes particles with definite (exact) primary properties (shapes, sizes, and weights) and later, such active phenomena as momentum, different forces, and energy as well as the concept of mechanical (physical) laws—which are often regarded as parts of the material universe. In consequence, there are now intrinsic material ordering principles, too, which will start to work if certain initial conditions are given. The modern concept of matter is useful for the explanation of certain higher-level, orderly phenomena *only due to these changes*. However, this kind of explanation became successful *only in the territory of physical sciences*, while in life sciences, Aristotelian biology was present much longer. Then, in the eighteenth century, vitalism emerged, defining modern biology and the concept of evolution long before Darwin—not to mention neo-Darwinism (9.2).

Nonetheless, in Cartesian critical philosophy—based on Platonic and Christian traditions—there are substantial *res cogitans*, too. That is, human beings (and solely them) are not only mechanical, material things but also specific beings with *mind* or soul. This is the traditional modern, dualist position, defined by Descartes. It implies that the higher-level properties of a human being (thinking, consciousness, etc.) cannot be reduced to material substance, its primary properties, the laws of physics, and the initial conditions of the evolving processes of that certain human being alone. Similarly to Aristotelian philosophy, in this specific case, the higher-level properties of things can only be reduced to the *two* substances (i.e., matter and mind) and the initial conditions because the latter still cannot be left out from the mechanical evolving processes of material substance to conclude boundaries and shapes of things (in this case, the structures of human bodies). It is clear from this that there is neither identity nor close connection between the shapes and structures of things and the minds or souls of human beings as there is between the forms and structures of things in Aristotelian philosophy, where the human soul is also a (specific sort of higher-level) form which controls and harnesses the lower-level processes in the same way as lower-level forms do (e.g., the form of a crystal). The Cartesian mind *only recognizes* the shapes and structures (secondary properties) of things and remembers them (denotative information in the mind), but he himself is not a shape, a form, or a boundary condition (as a matter of fact, due to the consistent critical thinking of Descartes, the *res cogitans* has no extension at all). The Cartesian mind is, in fact, the existing physicist himself, who uses boundary conditions as *conceptual* and *instrumental tools* to conclude mechanical (physical) laws and material substance and its primary geometrical properties. Without substantial minds, there are *neither* physicists (or other human beings) *nor* boundary conditions but rather only fundamental processes of material substances—that is, particles and their primary properties.

This is the physicalist position of the modern era, which left out Cartesian minds (and Christian souls) from the mechanical (physical) worldview. This means that, according to this worldview, there are, in fact, neither higher-level shapes and structures nor any kinds of boundary conditions in the universe. And yes, indeed, the ideal physics of Laplace's demon does not need any conceptual/instrumental tools such as boundary conditions; rather, only exact data of material substance and the knowledge of mechanical laws. Now, the question is: who will recognize the shape and structure of things as boundary conditions and who will use boundary conditions as conceptual/instrumental tools if there are neither forms nor minds or souls (5.7)? As we have seen, there is no significant difference between a crystal and a frog in modern critical thinking, both of them being higher-level, structural boundary conditions—that is, conceptual tools and not existentially real things—and now, there is no significant difference between a frog and a *man*; as higher-level structural boundary conditions, both of them are *only conceptual tools* and not existentially real things. *Conceptual tools cannot recognize each other*, and neither words nor fundamental material particles (e.g., quarks and electrons) can recognize each other. As Laplace's demon cannot recognize any higher-level, boundary conditions by his ideal physical knowledge either (2.3). The physicalist position of the modern era is based on the Laplacian ideal of objective knowledge and, as we have seen, it is not a positive (in a sense, real) ontological conviction because it is only the expansion of the critical thought on the concept of spiritual substance—that is, it is, in fact, *only the negation of* the fundamental beliefs of the Cartesian (modern dualism) and Christian (classical dualism) traditions and does not give us any real philosophical answers to our most important questions: in this case, who recognizes the higher-level shapes and structures of things? Who are these living, natural boundary conditions at all, and where have they come from?

Then, at the end of the modern era, in Polanyi's emergentist philosophy—which, in a sense, tries to find a path back to the hierarchical worldview of Aristotelian philosophy—a close connection has been established once again between the structures and shapes of things and human minds or souls in order to answer the question of who uses boundary conditions as conceptual and instrumental tools if there are no Cartesian minds or Christian souls. There is a close connection—not because human souls or the shapes of things are substantial forms but rather because *both of them are boundary conditions*. A crystal is a structural boundary condition, which is the consequence of its material conditions, thus a crystal is existentially identifiable with its material substance, while a frog or a man, who is the achievements of evolution, is (hierarchies of) control boundary conditions, not existentially identifiable with his material conditions. The essential difference between a frog and a man is that humans are not only biological but *also cultural* beings (the consequence of the second main stage of evolution—that is, cultural evolution). However, both frogs and human beings consist only of *material substance* and a specific *hierarchy of boundary conditions*. In an emergentist philosophy, there is only *one substance*: the *material*; every real thing of higher levels is *real* not because it is substantive but rather because it is *emergent*. In the Polanyian universe, in contrast to Aristotle and Descartes, there are no necessary, infinite, higher-level substantial things—such as forms and minds or souls—there are only evolving, emergent boundary conditions, which can be reduced to material substances, physical laws, and initial conditions. The only question is how: synchronically or diachronically, in space or in time.

Perhaps it is now clear why in the second half of the twentieth century, the concept of boundary conditions emerged from physics into the territories of cybernetics, life sciences, and philosophy when boundary conditions are, in fact, not part of ideal physics. Ideal physics is not a real thing and it never was. After the Copernican revolution, real physicists—like Galilei and Newton—always used boundary conditions and initial conditions during their work. Aristotle was wrong when he thought that forms controlled the lower-level processes during a crystalogenesis. There are only structural boundary conditions in the material world due to the intrinsic ordering principles of matter. However, in life sciences, this kind of explanation—based on modern mechanical physics—was never really successful. The Aristotelian tradition held its position much longer than in the territory of lifeless phenomena, and then, a new, dualistic tradition emerged swiftly (vitalism). Although positivism and materialism won the major battles of the first half of the twentieth century, several philosophical questions had to go into hiding, but the explanation of living phenomena—along with the explanation of the new kind of complex machines (automats)—was still not satisfying. *In a sense, the concept of boundary conditions replaced the Aristotelian concept of forms*, but it comes from mechanical physics—that is, it is a "metaphysically innocent" concept which, at least originally, perfectly complies with the ruling positivist and physicalist philosophy. However, if we start to use and consistently explain this concept on living phenomena, it will swiftly become obvious that it is pushing the boundaries of positivism and physicalism.

The same is true—as we have seen in the case of DNA—for the concept of information. Even the term information comes from the Aristotelian concept of form: information—that is, a *coded* form *in* a thing (for example, the memory of a vase in the mind of a person). In the philosophical sense, the only main difference between the Aristotelian and the neo-Darwinian explanations of ontogeny is that Aristotle claimed that the *form* in the zygote governs the process—that is, the form determines that a zygote becomes a goat or a sheep—while neo-Darwinians claim that the *information* coded in the DNA of the zygote does the same. It is clear what an Aristotelian form is—an independent, eternal substance compared to matter—but neo-Darwinians cannot tell what information really is. Due to the ruling positivist and physicalis dogma, they identify it with matter (parametric information)—that is, they try to reduce it (in the synchronic sense) to matter, but we have seen that this reduction, in fact, cannot be done. I will return to the question of information in subchapter 9.2 because it is a crucial concept for understanding what evolution really is, but for now, let's focus on the question of reduction. Why does synchronic reduction not work in the case of living phenomena?

7.7 The Reality of Time

As we have seen in the previous chapter, according to Samuel Alexander, matter is the most general, focused manifestation of time in points of space around/due to a specific center. Contrary to Aristotle's eternal (timeless) and theoretical primary forms—the manifestation of which creates the four material elements: fire, air, water, and earth, the primary order of which is determined by the (resting) absolute center of the universe—time is emergent and thus every material entity, photon, electron, quark, etc. has its own center and actively behaves according to its own nature, determined by this center. This is the reason that matter has it own definite, primary properties (mass, spin, size, etc.), active interactions (preservation of momentum, gravitation, electromagnetic force, etc.), and there are initial conditions due to its emergence from space-time—that is, different intrinsic, material ordering principles work in material complexes. There is no need for the Aristotelian concept of forms to explain the process of crystalogenesis in the world of physical sciences.

At the same time, in normal earthly conditions (and, if one chooses such a practical approach to the physical aspects of the universe as we have seen from Galilei and Newton), matter—more exactly, the different kinds of elementary particles of matter—can be regarded as indivisible (atomic) elements of an eternal (timeless) substance with definite (exact) primary properties, the behaviors of which are also determined by eternal (unchanging) laws. During normal crystalogenesis, both the material elements in the process and the physical laws can be regarded as utterly stable. This means, on the one hand, that the result of the process is essentially the consequence of the third factor—that is, the initial conditions, the only factor which can change—and, on the other, that the process perfectly complies with the Laplacian ideal of objective knowledge. There are exact laws and there are exact data of the initial positions of matter from which the accurate and unambiguous results can be deduced. Of course, every crystalogenesis or any other higher-level structure formation of matter happens over time, but this time *is neither time itself* nor a genuinely new manifestation of time *but rather only the fourth dimension of the ideal Laplacian*—or, more precisely, Newtonian—*absolute space-time*, in which the process can be modeled due to the exact, mechanical measurements of this abstract fourth dimension.

Synchronic reduction reflects the point of these kinds of structure formations in material complexes when there is no manifestation of time in the given space—that is, (1) there is no genuinely new behavior or quality in the system, (2) the interactions among the material parts are all mechanical, and (3) *it can be modeled in an exact, four-dimensional matrix* called space-"time." Structure boundary conditions, which can be reduced synchronically, are comprehensive, orderly structures *only in space*, determined by their lower-level, material parts and intrinsic ordering principles. *Only their material parts persist in time* due to their own physical times which are indeed the genuinely new manifestations of time at this level of the parts compared to pure space-time. This is the reason why I claimed earlier (5.9) that synchronic reduction complies with the nature of space: *it reduces only (four-dimensional) spatial relations* in different material complexes. The real, physical times of the stable, material parts of the process are *constant*; therefore, their behavior and structure formation can be modeled in a four-dimensional, definite matrix. As a matter of fact, according to this, the most straightforward case of synchronic reduction is the relation between two and one plus one (or, of course, other similar mathematic relations).

Contrarily, diachronic reduction reflects the point of such structure formations when time manifests itself in the given space and genuinely new behaviors and qualities emerge in the system. We have seen in the previous chapter (6.2), that in the case of matter, this means the different kinds of two- and three-dimensional manifestations of time in certain space-time-continuums as systems; for example, when time manifests itself as physical time, the mass and gravitational behavior of matter emerges. In the same way, control boundary conditions, which can only be reduced diachronically, are comprehensive, orderly structures *both in space and time*, determined by both higher-level, ordering principles and lower-level, random material conditions—that is, they persist in time due to the genuinely new manifestation of time at their level. Now, the question is: how does time manifest itself at higher levels, how does time manifest itself in the higher-level spaces of different material complexes, and how do genuinely new behaviors and qualities emerge in the given systems? In short: what is the meaning of *biological time*?

To show this, I will use the simplest conceivable living being: Tibor Gánti's so-called "chemoton"—which, of course, never existed (and never will) but is perfect for my actual goal.[18] According to Gánti, as the simplest conceivable living being, the chemoton has to possess three sub-systems to be regarded as a living being.

1. *Membrane*, which is, in fact, a boundary that separates the chemoton from its environment, thus it does not directly depend on environmental conditions (e.g., like a single RNA). The chemoton can therefore be regarded as a *closed, independent space-time-continuum*.

18. Gánti, *Az élet princípiuma*, 116–23. In English, see Maynard Smith and Szathmáry, *Major Transitions*, 20–24.

2. *Autocatalytic metabolism*, which provides the necessary materials and energy for the chemoton for its self-preservation and replication.

3. *Controlling/transmitting structure*, which regulates the workings of the other two sub-systems and copies (replicate/duplicates) itself. This is the *center* of the chemoton, which determines and sustains the whole system.

In the case of physical time, by the new kind of manifestation of time, a closed, independent space-time-continuum emerges—a particle—which has genuinely new behavior and qualities compared to space-time (mass, gravitation, etc.) and a center that determines its behavior and qualities and sustains the whole system from its emergence until its dissolution. The situation in the case of biological time is perfectly parallel—actually, nothing surprising happens, we only have to recognize and acknowledge it—by the new kind of manifestation of time, a closed, independent space-time-continuum emerges—a compartment or a cell—which has genuinely new behavior and qualities compared to matter (autocatalytic metabolism, regenerating membrane, coded functional information, etc.) and *has a center* that determines its behavior and qualities and sustains the whole system from its birth until its death. In the case of higher-level biological beings, this means (1) the *self-preservation* of the entity by regulating the entire system like a cybernetic automat, which preserves the system from the perspective of the given system and (2) the *replication/reproduction* of the system, which could preserve the existence of the system from the perspective of the whole evolutionary system (9.5). Higher-level biological beings are not so stable as several lower-level, material entities are (e.g., elements) because they are integrated parts of the whole higher-level, comprehensive, evolutionary system due to the principles of life and evolution; nonetheless, they have their own methods to preserve their existence and persist in time. Biological beings behave according to their past interactions coded in their controlling structure and according to their future goals to replicate themselves and preserve the existence of their kind. This means that a biological being is *not just a comprehensive, orderly whole of the present* but also, in a sense, *identical with all of his ancestors of the past and his descendants of the future*: evolution is a long, one-way challenge (process) by time.

Diachronic reduction, as we have seen from another perspective in subchapter 5.5, has to face these facts: (1) there are several genuinely new behaviors and qualities in the evolutionary system (just compare Earth to Mars); (2) the interactions among the parts are functional and informational (e.g., as we will see in subchapter 9.5 in detail, replication itself is not a material process at all); (3) it cannot be modeled in a four-dimensional matrix because time manifests itself, again and again, in higher and higher-level material complexes, and new kinds of biological beings emerge. Diachronic reduction has to deal with these time relations of the evolutionary system.

I will, of course, discuss this whole topic in detail in Part Three: Evolution, but I dare to hope that my point is clear: due to the new kinds of manifestation of time, living beings are such emergent, orderly wholes that have their own centers and actively behave according to their goals: the driving force of evolution is nothing else but the *personal achievements* of these active living centers (9.7).

If someone forgets for a moment the ruling dogmas of positivism and physicalism and the false dichotomies of our thinking, the meaning of biological time of living beings will become one of the most trivial personal facts of the world: we are also living beings. In consequence, we experience our own biological time at all moments of our personal life, from our birth until our death. And it has nothing to do with the precisely measured time of our mechanical clocks that are, in fact, measuring the Earth's orbit (that is, the extension of a specific geometrical object called ellipsis) around the Sun.

> Time will turn out to be the only aspect of our everyday experience that is fundamental. The fact that it is always some moment in our perception, and that we experience that moment as one of a flow of moments, is not an illusion. It is the best clue we have to fundamental reality.[19]

7.8 Conclusion

I started this Part Two with the claim that the point of personal knowledge is that there is no objective point of reference—that is, everything should be understood in a relational way, from our personal perspectives, which are rooted in our centers of a specific point-instant of space-time—and that this claim is true even for the smallest parts of matter. Perhaps at that point, it was a strange, bold claim. However, if we are not just piles of meaningless, random motions of quarks and electrons in a four-dimensional, abstract matrix or created in the image of an eternal God over and above of space-time, but rather, in fact, the achievements of evolutionary emergence in this three dimensional space-time, then reality should have a single spine—from the deepest bottoms of reality up until its highest level achievements.

It is clear that every human person sees the universe from his personal point of view, from his center in space-time. We have seen in chapter 6 that

---

19. Smolin, *Time Reborn*, xxxi.

the smallest parts of matter are determined by their centers which are the consequences of the manifestations of time in a specific space-time-continuum. The personal point of view of a human person is determined by his personal past and his future goals: he has his own psychological way of seeing. The link between the two levels is life and the biological times of living beings. The chemoton is between the atom and the human person.

However, as we will see in detail in Part Three: Evolution, the evolutionary emergence of living beings is not a straight path: the emergence of multicellular life, the emergence of individuality, and the emergence of sexuality all determine the personal life of human beings in different ways and we have not yet talked about the second major step of evolution—that is, about the evolution of cultures, the profoundly various aspects of which, of course, also actively determine the personality of human beings. But first, we have to examine, in detail, the logic of achievement—both in the cases of natural and artificial control boundary conditions—by which we can understand the real driving force of evolution and what evolutionary emergence really is.

In this Part Two, I have argued against positivism and physicalism. The basis of these views is Aristotle's mistake of the teleological nature of the purely material phenomena, Descartes's mistake of the substantial nature of the human mind, Galilei's mistake to neglect the real meaning of his principle of relativity for practical reasons, and Christianity's mistake of the eternal God over and above space-time. However, positivism and physicalism are not real and honest ontological convictions based on the facts of time, evolution, living beings, and human persons but rather only the deceptive negations of these previous convictions. They do not give us real philosophical answers to our most important questions about science, life, or culture; rather, they only try to dissuade us from asking these questions because they are "unscientific" and "obscure." But, as we have seen in this Part Two, if we start to see the facts of science and life from another angle, which has a real and honest philosophical basis and does not make the same mistakes of Aristotle, Descartes, Galilei, and Christianity, then the house of cards of positivism and physicalism will quickly collapse.

One might ask at this point: if there is no objective point of reference and, in a sense, this is the point of reality, so everybody sees the world from his own personal center as, for example, materialists and emergentists see the world so differently, then there will be no truth and everything is relative (that is, as relativism understands the term and not Einstein)? No, the objective versus subjective dichotomy is false. The personal is not the contrary of the objective; that is the subjective. There is, indeed, truth. But truth—as everything else—is rooted in the emergence of time: in the evolutionary emergence of living beings and human persons. So, before we start to deal with the materialist relativism of our era and its primary predecessor—dialectical materialism—in Part Four: Personal Reality, we first have to understand how universal norms, values, and truth are not rooted in the false ideal of objective knowledge but rather in our personal evolutionary heritage. We are not created in the image of the Laplacian demon but are instead the children of evolution.

Bibliography

Alexander, Samuel. *Space, Time, and Deity*. London: MacMillan, 1920.
Ashby, W. Ross. *An Introduction to Cybernetics*. London: Chapman and Hall, 1957.
Bedau, Mark A. "Downward Causation and Autonomy in Weak Emergence." In *Emergence: Contemporary Readings in Philosophy and Science*, edited by Mark A. Bedau and Paul Humpreys, 155–88. London: Bradford, 2008.
———. "Is Weak Emergence Just in the Mind?" *Minds and Machines* 18 (2008) 443–59.
———. "Weak Emergence." *Philosopical Perspectives* 11 (1997) 375–79.
Broad, C. D. *The Mind and its Place in Nature*. New York: Routledge, 1925.
Csányi, Vilmos. *Az evolúció általános elmélete*. Budapest: Akadémiai, 1979.
Darwin, Charles. *The Origin of Species by Means of Natural Selection, or the Preservation of Favoured Races in the Struggle for Life*. London: John Murray, 1872.
Dawkins, Richard. *The God Delusion*. Boston: Mariner, 2008.
Donald, Merlin. *Origins of the Modern Mind: Three Stages in the Evolution of Culture and Cognition*. Boston: Harvard University Press, 1991.
Einstein, Albert. *Relativity. The Special and the General Theory. A Popular Exposition*. London: Methuen, 1920.
Gánti, Tibor. *Az élet princípiuma*. Budapest: OMIKK, 1983.
Gulick, Walter B. "On the Adequacy of Neo-Darwinism: A Reply to Daniel Paksi." *Tradition and Discovery* 38.2 (2012) 56–60.
Hawking, Stephen W. *A Brief History of Time: From the Big Bang to Black Holes*. New York: Bantam, 1988.
Kim, Jaegwon. "'Downward Causation' in Emergentism and Nonreductive Physicalism." In *Emergence or Reduction? Essays on the Prospects of Nonreductive Physicalism*, edited by Ansgar Beckermann, et al., 119–38. Berlin: de Gruyter, 1992.
———. "Making Sense of Emergence." *Philosophical Studies* 95 (1999) 3–36.
———. "Mental Causation and Consciousness: The Two Mind-Body Problem for the Physicalist." In *Physicalism and its Discontents*, edited by Carl Gillet and Barry Loewer, 271–83. Cambridge: Cambridge University Press, 2001.
———. *Mind in a Physical World: An Essay on the Mind-Body Problem and Mental Causation*. Cambridge, MA: MIT Press, 1998.
———. *Physicalism, or Something Near Enough*. Princeton: Princeton University Press, 2005.
Korn, Robert W. "The Emergence Principle in Biological Hierarchies." *Biology and Philosophy* 20.1 (2005) 137–51.

Laplace, Pierre-Simon. *A Philosophical Essay on Probabilities*. New York: J. Wiley and Sons, 1902.

Laughlin, Robert B. *A Different Universe: Reinventing Physics from the Bottom Down*. New York: Basic, 2005.

Lewes, George Henry. *Problems of Life and Mind. First Series. The Foundations of a Creed*. Vol. 2. Boston: James S. Osgood, 1975.

Margulis, Lynn. *Origin of Eukaryotic Cells*. London: Yale University Press, 1970.

Maynard Smith, John, and Eörs Szathmáry. *The Major Transitions in Evolution*. Oxford: Oxford University Press, 1995.

Mayr, Ernst. *One Long Argument. Charles Darwin and the Genesis of Modern Evolutionary Thought*. Cambridge, MA: Harvard University Press, 1991.

———. *What Evolution Is?* New York: Basic, 2001.

McLaughlin, Brian P. "The Rise and Fall of British Emergentism." In *Emergence or Reduction? Essays on the Prospects of Nonreductive Physicalism*, edited by Ansgar Beckermann, et al., 49–93. Berlin: de Gruyter, 1992.

Montero, Barbara Gail, and Davis Papineau. "Naturalism and Physicalism." In *The Blackwell Companion to Naturalism*, edited by Kelly James Clark, 182–95. Malden, MA: Wiley-Blackwell, 2016.

Morgan, C. Lloyd. *Emergent Evolution*. London: Williams and Norgate, 1923.

Nagel, Ernest. *The Structure of Science: Problems in the Logic of Scientific Explanation*. London: Routledge and Kegan Paul, 1961.

Needham, Paul. "Reduction and Emergence: A Critique of Kim." *Philosophical Studies* 146.1 (2009) 93–116.

O'Connor, Timothy. "Emergent Properties." *American Philosophical Quarterly* 31 (1994) 91–104.

Oppenheim, Paul, and Hilary Putnam. "Unity of Science as a Working Hypothesis." In *Concepts, Theories, and the Mind-Body Problem*, edited by Herbert Feigl, et al., 3–36. Minnesota Studies in the Philosophy of Science 2. Minneapolis: University of Minnesota Press, 1958.

Pattee, Howard H. "The Physical Basis and Origin of Hierarchical Control." In *Hierarchy Theory. The Challenge of Complex Systems*, edited by Howard H. Pattee, 71–108. New York: George Braziller, 1973.

Polanyi, Michael. "Life Transcends Physics and Chemistry." In *Michael Polanyi: Society, Economics, Philosophy. Selected Papers*, edited by Richard T. Allen, 283–97. New Brunswick: Transaction, 1997.

———. "Life's Irreducible Structure." In *Michael Polanyi: Knowing and Being: Essays*, edited by Marjorie Grene, 225–39. New Brunswick: Transaction, 1969.

———. "Logic and Psychology." *American Psychologist* 23 (1968) 27–43.

———. *Personal Knowledge*. London: Routledge and Kegan Paul, 1962.

———. *The Study of Man*. London: Routledge and Kegan Paul, 1959.

———. *The Tacit Dimension*. London: Routledge and Kegan Paul, 1967.

Reid, Robert G. B. *Biological Emergences: Evolution by Natural Experiment*. Vienna Series in Theoretical Biology. Cambridge, MA: MIT Press, 2009.

———. *Evolutionary Theory: The Unfinished Synthesis*. New York: Cornell University Press, 1985.

Rosen, Robert. *Life Itself: A Comprehensive Inquiry into the Nature, Origin, and Fabrication of Life*. New York: Columbia University Press, 1991.

Rothstein, Jerome. "Generalize Entropy, Boundary Conditions, and Biology." In *The Maximum Entropy Formalism*, edited by Raphael D. Levine and Myron Tribus, 423–68. Cambridge, MA: MIT Press, 1979.

Rueger, Alexander, and Paul McGivern. "Hierarchies and Levels of Reality." *Synthese* 176.3 (2010) 379–97.

Salthe, Stanley N. *Evolving Hierarchical Systems: Their Structure and Representation*. Cambridge, MA: MIT Press, 1985.

Sanderson, Stephen K. *Social Evolutionism. A Critical History*. Cambridge: Blackwell, 1990.

Smolin, Lee. *Time Reborn. From the Crisis in Physics to the Future of the Universe*. Boston: Mariner Books, 2013.

———. *The Trouble With Physics: The Rise of String Theory, the Fall of a Science, and What Comes Next*. Boston: Houghton Mifflin, 2006.

Turnbull, H. W., ed. *1688–1694*. Vol. 3 of *The Correspondence of Isaac Newton*. Cambridge: Cambridge University Press, 1961.

Wiener, Norbert. *Cybernetics or Control and Communication in the Animal and the Machine*. Cambridge, MA: MIT Press, 1965.